Against Eurocentrism

Against Eurocentrism: A Transcendent Critique of Modernist Science, Society, and Morals

A Discursus on Human Emancipation
[Purporting to be a Speculative Critique and Resolution of the Malaise of Modernism]

Rajani Kannepalli Kanth

palgrave
macmillan

AGAINST EUROCENTRISM

First published in 2005 by
PALGRAVE MACMILLAN™
175 Fifth Avenue, New York, N.Y. 10010 and
Houndmills, Basingstoke, Hampshire, England RG21 6XS
Companies and representatives throughout the world.

PALGRAVE MACMILLAN is the global academic imprint of the Palgrave Macmillan division of St. Martin's Press, LLC and of Palgrave Macmillan Ltd. Macmillan® is a registered trademark in the United States, United Kingdom and other countries. Palgrave is a registered trademark in the European Union and other countries.

ISBN 1–4039–6737–7

Library of Congress Cataloging-in-Publication Data

Rajani Kannepalli Kanth.

Against eurocentrism : a transcendent critique of modernist science, society, and morals : a discursus on human emancipation : purporting to be a speculative critique and resolution of the malaise of modernism / by Rajani Kannepalli Kanth.

p. cm.

Includes bibliographical references and index.

ISBN 1–4039–6737–7

1. Postmodernism—Social aspects. 2. Eurocentrism. 3. Libery. 4. Social history. 5. Economic history. I. Title.

HM449.R35 2004
300′.1—dc22 2004049757

A catalogue record for this book is available from the British Library.

Design by Newgen Imaging Systems (P) Ltd. Chennai, India.

First edition: February 2005

10 9 8 7 6 5 4 3 2 1

Printed in the United States of America.

We will grieve not, rather find
Strength in what remains behind;
In the primal sympathy
Which having been, must ever be …

William Wordsworth, *Intimations of Immortality*

For Cory, Malini, Anjana, Antara, Indrina, Shikha, and Kesavan Kesari:
who have given me, in incontinent largesse, that which is ineffable

Contents

Acknowledgments

This, though the most complete docket of my *oeuvre* by far, has been the hardest to write of all my works.

Neither fate, nor friends, nor family, conspired with me in the writing of it.

As such, few works, part dream, part delirium, in the darkest night of my life, could have been conceived in such radical and complete isolation: and written in such a profound sense of total abandonment by the universe.

No matter: *d'une maniere ou d'une autre*, it still got done, with the added *bonum* of keeping my debt to society low and affordable.

For daily inspiration, and I mean that quite literally, I must thank my two little girls, Malini and Anjana, only 2 and 5 when I began the book and just 8 and 11 when I finished it, who kept me marginally self-possessed through the years-long odyssey, albeit from afar; they were the sole trustees of my psychic well-being. They remain, apart from my (now *ex*) wife Cory, and my older daughters, Antara and Indrina, my reasons for writing.

At another remove, in the more inhospitable nonfamilial domain—though some named here have been my effective family—where affections enter, apparently, only at peril, Noam Chomsky (who stands alone in all scales), Paul Feyerabend, Evan Jones, Tony Lawson, James Galbraith, Janeen Costa, Steve Fleetwood, Robert Heilbroner, Immanuel Wallerstein, Roy Bhaskar, James Ryan, David Roche, Wolfram Elsner, Satyanarayana Raju, Peter Bell, Geoffrey Harcourt, Peter Skott, Paul Sweezy, Murray Kemp, Steve Marglin, Roger Owen, Gayatri Spivak, J.M. Blaut, Paul Sweezy, Harry Magdoff, Ivan Illich, David Gordon, Chris Terry, John Lodewijks, Bill Brugger, Phil O'Hara, Kamal and Anu Chenoy, Tobin Brown, Jonathan Joseph, Carolyn Currie, Alex Pritchard, Angana Chatterjee, Samuel Dunn, Wolfram and Angie Elsner, Jennifer Socey, Nancy Kelly, Tracy Lee, Maureen Silos, Vandana Shiva, Alex Pritchard, Mark Lutz, Mark Blaug, George Gheverghese Joseph, Vikram Kannepalli, Basil Davidson, Shaun Lovejoy, Paul Hanson, Chng Meng Kng, Lim Boon Tiong, Ali Shamsavari, Mat Forstater, Neil De Marchi, Sudipta and Nilanjana Kaviraj, Kathy Hawkins, Kho Tung-yi, Tom Nechyba,

Kho Kwang-po, Uday Chatterjee, Connie Ng, Madhu Batheja, Kamna Batra, Jean-Marie Pincemin, Janet Darley, Kathleen Hawking, Beatrice Quasnak, Shikha Dalal, Tony Donovan, Nitasha Kaul, Nilima Bhalla, Sharon Jasper, Uma Grover, P.C. Joshi, C.P. Bhambhri, K. Seshadri, Ahmet Tonak, Robert Pollin, Sanjay Bharadwaj, Tim Wonderly, Amit Basole, Jennifer Socey, John and Linda Stout, Tony Hum, Tian Shian Chian, Milton Wee, Janaka Biyanwila, Solomon Namala, and Mahan Vir Tulli, provided various qualities of support, howsoever unknowingly,—in word, spirit, or deed—at various times, that were, across this lonesome traverse, vastly welcome and much needed. To their contributions, I owe much that can all too easily be said, but not altogether fully acknowledged.

At the critical publishing end of matters, enormous gratitude is owed as much to the very forward and unflinching vision of Anthony Wahl, Senior editor at Palgrave as to his stoic patience, in gently steering this project through the contract stage—and beyond; and to Ms. Veena Krishnan whose generosity in the delicate copy-editing of the irrepressible prose of this title stands in itself sentinel tribute to the scheme of values celebrated in the work. Inordinate gratitude is also owed the indexer, Ms. Rebecca DuBey, who pulled off a tight little coup of an index, concise and yet complete, in a impossibly short time frame.

This *excursus*, simultaneously both a personal, *de profundis*, and representational *cri de couer discourse of the Other* matured over a period of fragmented, and frazzled years while in forlorn transit across three continents, beginning in Sydney, Australia, continuing fitfully in New York and Singapore and cobbled finally in Salt Lake City and Durham, N.C.

If the flavor, or fervor, of the passages is at all uneven, it could well be the reflection of the radically altering environs.

Preamble

This is an uncompromising work that renders an uncompromising verdict on the scourge of our millennium: *modernism*, itself the artefact of certain Late *Eurocentric* propensities. In this profound lack of "balance" the work falls prey, it must be granted, to the very masculinist, epistemic orientation that it lays at the feet of what it opposes; in this there is no paradox—after Godel, if not otherwise, we must know that logical completeness is a chimera and the hobgoblin of the hegemonic ideologue. But, more seriously, this confession is honest; and if this characteristically masculinist, but quite solitary, error (*exceptio probat regulam*) is recognized, possibly little else in the work may be held to serious fault.

It is not that modernism has no virtues or benignities; it is that they are purchased at too high a cost, indeed a cost that neither the species nor the planet can, on any scale, find affordable: in brief, modernism imperils the existence of all species and the mother of all hospitalities, the planet itself. Given the imminence and the gravity of this threat, no other posture would have been at all, in the highest sense, ecologically responsible. We must, stated simply, break with the manifold paradigms of the European Enlightenment or find ourselves, soon enough, as mutant beings in an alien habitat.

However, be that as it may, this work is not, primarily, in the first instance, a call to *action* but rather an invitation to reflect, *feel,* and ponder the meaning of the life we see constructed around us as the Global impulse of European expansionism runs amok, wreaking havoc on societies, ecologies and, worst of all, on human and nonhuman lives: *feelings are the crucibles of human* endeavor, much as the passions are the instigators of the human will.

Change is not, *in the first instance*, a practical action or activity; it is as simple as the construction within the human psyche of an *Idea*, itself expressive of something even more powerful: the *Will*—which then, almost all on its own, fulfils itself. This is indeed how modernism was established; and it is how it can/will be transcended.

The ideas in this work are not new, nor are they entirely original: they are, and have been for a while, "in the air," hovering above our somewhat atrophied sense of responsibility. The solutions to human problems are always thus found amply supplied, awaiting only our ever laggard notice; it is, in that regard, a solicitous universe and considerate of our many, desultory delinquencies. As such, for all the dire and dismal *apercus* that litter this work, there needs prevail, in our minds, the supernal confidence that, to all of *Man*'s (gender as intended) iniquities, there is, providentially, a "natural," if not always humanly palatable, answer. The universe, to wax anthropic a bit, was not, perhaps, created in vain—nor will it, possibly, succumb to Man's incorrigible vanities (*dum spiro, spero*): the only lingering fear, though, is whether this irresistible, and irrevocable, cosmic answer will be inclusive of the human species' presumable desire to continue to exist. *Absit Omen.*

I. The Modernist Revolutions: The Ascent of Europe

1. The Modernist Problematic: The Crossing of the Rubicon

(1)

How it all originated, how could we possibly know, other than taking stealthy recourse to the old standbys of conjecture, inference, and attribution? Interpreting history, that is, delineating a coherent rationale for its momentum and trajectory, in some senses, is anyone's problematic, parlor-room game of *post-factum* sapience (and, in that sense, the bold historian reveals usually just as much about herself, and her driving motivations, as any actual revealments of historical pattern). The problem is the perennial one of *existential transitivity*—or epistemic interference—in the wilful production of human knowledge about humans. Since there is no ideal, ontic resolution of this difficulty (the *ontic* circle may not be *epistemically* squared), despite the conceits of traditional *positivism*, and the *nouvelle* ambitions of *critical realism* (as inspired by the work(s) of Roy Bhaskar), this discourse will simply note that as a disclaimer before proceeding to discern, decipher, and allocate, albeit in speculative fashion, a distinctive *logos* (if not a *telos*) to the advent of *modernism* in its founding (and confounding) European guise.

At any rate, the chronic, and inevitable, uncertainty of what cannot be directly perceived—as is the case in all "*histories*"—is much mitigated when we examine *present* consequences, which appear far easier to identify, expose and situate. In this regard, it is reasonable enough to suppose that effects that are extant today must owe their currency to some form of evolutionary inception so long as the process is not reduced to the terrain of direct, flat, and *linear* inference—beloved to some tendencies in social speculation—wherein every previous step is merely an inlaid stepping stone to some, conveniently predefined, preordained end.

The cultivated, late European passion for *linear*, graduated sketches of history and social evolution, so distinctive a hallmark of the so-called

"*Enlightenment*"—the fateful crucible within which the metaphysical mores of modernism were invented—itself an indirect expression of the portentous *Colonial Encounter* (which both preceded and proceeded alongside the former) reflected only a generously self validating perspective where the elite European, in the *male* voice (it was a securely *andro-centred* viewpoint), placed himself majestically on a silver step ladder leading (only) his elevated kind to high power and even greater glory. Hegelian and Marxian visions of "*history*," much as Smith's and the Scottish Historical School's accounts of putative "*stages of societal development*" are cut of the same vainglorious, if irregular cloth; and, taken together with Durkheimian and Comte's similar projections, on the continent, only outline the gleeful Enlightenment vision of the unique, triumphal destiny of Europe.

Be that as it may, for the critical scholar (a vanishing species in the modernist wasteland) interested in unlocking the secrets of modernist history (and there are yet a few to be revealed), but without the burden of received opinion, the problems are quite formidable. If she sticks with tawdry, univocal, and monovalent, *Euro-versions* of history (*his* story, that is: there are *her*-stories, and *their*-stories as well) the truth is paltered with, to put it mildly; if she bypasses those unedifying scenarios, the genus of substitutes, to be discovered at all, have need of a "*rational reconstruction*," oddly perhaps extrapolating the past from the present.

It is not that such luminous "*counter-intuitions*" are lacking; it is that they are, in general, remote and inaccessible, even ghost-like, given the implicitly systematic project of devaluation of non-European ideograms inaugurated by the Enlightenment: in the *vernacular*, for one thing, and embedded in oral traditions distal from the great ideological enterprise of the modernist *university—the flagship factory and grand centrepiece of all its ideological superproductions*. When and where available, such alternate traditions, all but inchoate and amorphous to the modernist eye, present the further problem of requiring an healthy, epistemic dose of *prior* validation made necessary by their long subjugation by Europeans, and their cronies, lest they sound, and appear to be, archaic, anile, and moribund—"*nativist*" to use the ultimate modernist insult!—given their feckless location in myth, song and legend, all debased by the modernists as lower, inferior, and degenerate forms of knowing. As such, modernist revisions have succeeded in devaluing—and not fortuitously—the very instruments that offer a stinging critique of their intrusions into everyday life; in that exsanguinary effort, not only was the realm of the *knowable* constricted to a few—privileged—domains: even the card-carrying castes of the *knowers* were to be radically reduced to a select circle prepared to accept the stunting covenants of modernist practices.

Not only then does any such enterprise of *counter knowledge* have to necessarily start *from below* and from afar—*sotto voce, de novo*, and impuissant—so to speak, in the company of pariah and parochial forms of information, banished to the gloom in the far hinterland of traditional (almost forgotten) and less structured ways, it also needs to be, importantly, validated *in advance*, a difficult proposition for the sobrietous, scientifically minded, scholar raised under the proper and pressing delusion that science in itself offers the chastity of a sacralized heuristic and a legitimized (and legitimizing) fount of acceptable knowledge (other than a secure and steady form of resources and employ).

In other words, quite apart from a simpler initial *arriere pensee* disquiet *vis à vis* received knowledge, something approaching a sort of *faith* in the inherent integrity of the non-European (i.e., the non-*Modernist*) world, its manners, moods, and mores, *prior* to European intrusion needs be a radical *a priori*—to many an impossibly heroic step—before commencement of the arduous, indeed heroic, task of demonstrating its effective truths in more conventional ways, ultimately employing perhaps the eminently sensible device of "*competitive plausibility*" as recently suggested by Martin Bernal. Yet, faith is the one article that is not merely in severely short supply, but also one subject to ritual radical debasement, and debauchery, in the tawdry bazaar of modernist discourse.

The elevation of such forms of elemental faith *in the primal genius of the anthropic experience*, as the *ethno-equivalent* of the Western investment in the dry, instrumentalist, abstract cosmology of (putatively) pure reason can, at least initially, be only an act of an obdurate and unyielding *will*, of which only a few may be likely to be possessed; but it is a vital *sine qua non* without which the enterprise of reinterpreting the world of ideas, concurrent with the inevitably "*masculinist*" project of changing it (on which more in later sections) simply cannot be undertaken.

The fact that such an epistemically "weak" position is forced upon the *critic* of modernism is only a reflection of the iniquity of history, and the place and position of both victor and victim within the European scheme of oppression by *select omission* (the greatest act of historical vandalism lies less in the torching of *contra* evidence as in the quiet, supercilious *disregard* of it; non-European achievements have been disparaged largely by this species of wanton *neglect*). However, lest the wrong deduction be drawn, at a more sophisticated remove, it can, and will, be shown quite easily that some such quality of *aprioristic*, and all-encompassing, *self-referential "faith"* also underlies the various accoutrements and *ex cathedra* pronouncements of European rationalism, too, in more than equivalent measure.

Even faith at its purest, needs a bulwark of support in the conviction of the inherent truth of some larger, more encompassing belief: in this case, the vital anthropic principle that European chauvinism openly derided, throughout its modernist devolution, is the *real pre-cognition of the equal capacity of human societies, as anthropically equivalent species, to solve such problems as they encounter in the vicissitudes of living, if but within the preset limits of their cultural imaginations.* In effect, all surviving societal entities have cracked the codes of their environmental constraints, leastways to their own satisfaction. This is by far the strongest *realist* argument for *Cultural Relativism—the only sustainable philosophy for peaceful coexistence available to humankind*—that Europeans had to disdain almost axiomatically in order to assert their innate superiority in all spheres. Progress and regress, the *alpha* and *omega* of Eurocentric discourse, are but chimeras in cultural affairs; worse, ideologies and practices based upon such notions have been the patent pretexts for the imposition of unilateral designs on weaker entities, being both self-congratulatory and imperial in outlook and orientation. The moral cannot be drawn more sharply: *Cultures may not be judged from the outside* (of course they may be so "judged": but to what avail?) except in critical, last-ditch, survivalist, *pis aller* acts of (planetary) *self-defense*, as with the ideas proffered here rejecting modernism.

The great, even overriding, advantage of the European world view today is that it is overwhelmingly "supported," that is, buttressed, by the simple material fact(s) of European domination of the world's "*major*" activities—the *adjectival* definition itself a reflection of singularly *modernist* priorities—in the present period. This does appear to advance an inhospitably "vulgar" materialist thesis of the legitimacy of extant power; but some plain truths in the world of domination have, inescapably, precisely that uninspired character, although the overall compendium of facts, as will be seen, is somewhat more nuanced. World domination in the material arena did not *automatically* (as against *eventually*) give European *ideas* the hegemony they enjoy today (throughout their unwelcome sojourn in India, for instance, it is doubtful that any segment of India's society, other than the crassest apologists, were ever bowled over by any sense of the obvious *superiority* of English ways, outside the grim technologies of cannon and chicanery); equally was it a spectacular failure of the moral *will* of non-European peoples (today in various stages and forms of slow reconstruction) who capitulated, astonishingly, in areas where Europeans were not even familiar with the alphabet, a resignation forced upon the majority of the non-European peoples as much by the conciliatory acquiescence of their suitably sybaritic ruling orders, past and present, *as by the inexpressible largesse of their own pacific indulgence toward the conquering armies of ignorance.*

However, ruling orders, even at their most repressive, rule only by virtue of the implicit consent of the ruled, no matter how perfunctory; and, as with the recent case of insurrectionary Iran, once that delicate accord is lost, or forfeited, they can still, swiftly, crash, and crumble with all the dignity of ninepins: it is this fate that lies securely in store for the vast majority of European dependencies in the non-European world. Stated somewhat differently, the *living cultures* of the oppressed in the periphery of the European world, in contradistinction to the hopelessly tangled skein of their *material* relations, are relatively free of modernist contamination; and it is their, as yet still parsimonious, struggles for breathing space, outside of European domains, that will decisively define the social (cultural) politics of the twenty-first century.

The task of debunking is ever an unattractive one, and quite alien to the inherent human traits of consilience and *bien etre*, but it is an epistemic imperative today when European ideologies, in typical slash and burn vein, are sweeping the world and laying waste, willy-nilly, the inherent diversity of human existence in the name of the ever spurious project(s) of progress, development and amelioration. But those who, in the European style, reify the *modus* of science should find it quite their staple diet, because in their own history of science, and the social ideology that envelops it, there has really been no other way to proceed. To lay bare the spirit of an epoch, to discover its essence, is to wield the scalpel of criticism such that the great crusty rim of sage convenance, rationalization, and deceit, is pared away to reveal the residual trove of *truth*, almost indistinguishable and incomprehensible to the idle, arrant scientific driveller ever ensconced in a soporific state of *reverie* that protects conventional wisdom from its critics, buried deep within his/her ritually and routinely immunized world.

Oddly, then, this necessary effort to expose the sophisms of the late European scientific temper, and the social paradigm undergirding it, flirts uneasily, but only in part, with the specious methodological feints of that which it is itself trying to resist. The dilemma is an acute one and needs be met head on, and early on, without dissimulation; *suffice it to say that in a truly convivial world, not only would European or Modernist (for the first term, now, always implies the second) science not exist, there would also be no need for a critique such as this if it did.*

In effect, social argument need not be conducted in this inhospitable form of *critique*; far more effective, usually, to adopt the age old feint of ancient cultures of simply bypassing the infelicitous silently by eliding it in *practice*. There is much to be said in favor of such a *concrete criticism of silence*; however, we endure now in an enforced age of communications where the "*word*" is in control, no matter how apocryphal and corrupt the tales that are weaved from it, so to engage in the shallow and syncretic pedagogy of words seems, at some level, to be a minimally warranted, and unavoidable, *desideratum*.

There is also one other important *lacunae* that can simply not be remedied, at least by this author: *the contributions of the ancients to the wisdom and the welfare of this planet and its denizens is the one certainty of our knowledge of structure and process in the natural and social world*: however, the many resplendent sources of this knowledge are not evenly spread with respect to our modernist information about them. The resurgence of Asia today and, to a lesser extent, Africa, has made possible construction of bases of indigenous social productions, *sites* if you will, that have significantly demystified modernist propaganda; but access to other, collateral wisdoms—of the Mayas, Incas, Aztecs, Sumerians, Babylonians, Native Americans, Australian Aboriginals, to name but a few—where available at all, is still mediated by modernist preconceptions. As such, the fuller task of placing *alleged* modernist discoveries in the corrected perspective of the genius of these civilizations is far from even begun.

If European claims to originality (priority) are belittled by simple reference to only *some* of the works of ancient India, China, and the Arabs, one can estimate the likely loss of credibility when the full measure of human achievement is taken into consideration. A trivial, but useful, example would be to evaluate how many medicines in use today by the contemporary, profit-driven pharmaceutical industry, that have any real healing value (as opposed to being harmful palliatives whose so-called side effects, relegated to small print, are generally more dangerous than the malady being treated) aside from the debilitating drugs that are its staple originated, in lineage, paternity, and inspiration, *outside* of modernist laboratories. Indeed most of modernist medicinal therapies, effective or not, are merely the necessary countervailing checks to the many novel maladies of its own invention (as with the abominable sanitary conditions created by the enforced massing of near pauperized working peoples in the industrial litter-bin townships of industrial revolution England, for example). If to this theory of the *epidemiology* of modernism is added the fact that even prophylactics such as the small-pox vaccine probably infected and/or killed as many as the disease it was supposed to protect against (to say nothing of the probable sources in the contemporary era of the large scale incidence of autism, allergies, multiple sclerosis, AIDS, and the so-called "*sudden infant death syndrome*"), one gets a perspectival sense of the *real* picture of modernist achievement in such fields.

To state the crux of the matter: the rejection of *Eurocentrism*, as offered here, is not intended to supplant it with an equally strident *Asia-centrism* (*though the content gain, admittedly, is quite obvious*) but with the larger, and more accurate, vision of the *collective*, if *unevenly* distributed, wisdom of the human race, within which latter-day European knowledge occupies a distinct, if not always a *primary*, space. The fact is that it is the monopolistic, appropriative, mindset of modernism that necessitates such a *reactive*, historical, even *revolutionary*, correction to its wanton, and wayward, liberties with the truth (and truth, regrettably is always a species of *Deus Minorum Gentium*); but the task, though required, and important, is far from being either pleasant or enviable.

It is a signal index of the largesse of non-modernist wisdom that it accommodatingly let the European conquerors persist in their illusions of superiority without finding it necessary to assert priority. Indeed, it is the modernist that has compelled, by dint of force, fraud and chicanery, these quiescent ancient cultures to turn, quite uncharacteristically, and as a latter-day transmutation, *assertive. Quieta non movere* was emphatically *not* the code of these gallant conquistadors: indeed, letting sleeping dogs lie has never been a modernist trait—and if some disturbed dogs often take on, as in current times, the guise of hounds from hell, the efficient cause(s) can hardly be in doubt.

At any rate, to return to the argument: some importunate constellation of forces, inspirited Europeans to finally and forcefully reject the subventions of their own patrimony, after which desecration of that of others was mere child's play. What were these forces? What gave them their specific potency? And how was this internal strife related to the eventual conflict with the "*other*" worlds that lay (once upon a time) far beyond their reach?

(2)

Modernist self-explorations of such phenomena—that is, accounts that describe the rise of *modernism*—fall, by and large, under the traditional either/or of *institutional* and *ideological* alternatives in explanation, the so-called *Liberal-Whiggian-Marxian* view of history supporting one, and the more nuanced *Weberian* and *neo-Kantian* epistemes bolstering the other. Indeed, it is far too easy to succumb to the raw allure of drawing a *simpliste* divide between apparently "*idealist*" and "*materialist*" criteria, as generations of scholars actually did. But in truth, this classical contradistinction between the two (putatively opposed) views is false in relation to the very hiatus it tries to establish. Human practice, of necessity, is necessarily involute with respect to these factors; *practice is impossible without ideas and vice versa*—any prioritization of one over the other being just so much vapid, and ignorance-based, logomachy. Marxian material causes, and Weberian ideational constructs, are two sides of the same (Janus faced) historical coin: the task here will be to fathom how, when, and where, such coin was minted, and why it gained as much currency as it did.

However, otiose whilst the debate may be, for expositional reasons it is still useful to examine these false antinomies, if but briefly. Indeed, heuristic logistics leaves no other choice: *it is in the process of critical interrogation of existing and preexisting knowledge, in relation to its correspondence with the known world, that content gain, where at all possible, occurs* (so-called "*hermeneutics*," in the long and weary tradition of French rationalism takes *step one*—interrogation of texts—but baulks at *step two*, viz., *relating it to the experienced world*). *At any rate, the Euro-Marxian logos*, materialist in inspiration and eristic in consecution (the "determinism" running from consequent to antecedents now viewed as "necessary" in a form of *reverse teleology* of hindsight) goes roughly like this: developments within "*late feudalism*" produced a crisis in the fourteenth century that presaged the eventual demise of its dominant institutions. The expansion of trade within feudalism, concomitant with increases in agrarian productivity, had led to various forms of economic growth that the shortage of specie in Europe, not to mention the traditional heirarchies within feudalism, could not sustain; efforts to break up the Arab control over trade routes, though successful, brought with it the unexpected vengeance of the Black Death that depopulated the peasantry such that their class position was strengthened further, leading to more favorable contracts, commutation of feudal exactions, and a general easing of traditional restraints, often forced by peasant revolts now made more feasible by the economic and political presence of a merchant class, based in autonomous chartered towns, that could play peasants off against the nobility, and *vice versa*, as and when it suited its interests. The necessity of suppressing peasant revolts leads to the formation of *absolutist* feudal states which standardize the new-fangled "nations" and national markets that they now rule over; however, the continued growth of productivity soon undermines the stability of absolutism itself leading to new challenges from a commercialized peasantry and its industrial and intellectual allies.

Colonial wars are now fought to protect international trade routes and supplies (a process that leads to permanent occupations of overseas colonies). Eventually, the mercantile oligarchs and their royal allies are defeated by a combination of peasant and industrial classes that take over state power and establish the parameters of the *capitalist* revolution as we know it today, the great moments of which are the Dutch, English, and the

French Revolutions, and the great American War of Independence. Although brutal to the underclasses, the capitalist revolution builds the productive forces, laying the foundation for international markets, commodification and trade, ushering in the Age of Modernism and hence civilization (!) across western Europe first—then by slow extension to the peripheral world. All that remains, in this "*progressivist*" narrative is, to take the next step in a Marxian discourse, for the working classes to unite, overthrow capital and build a rational, socialist society on the immediate basis of *ability mediated by need*: end of fairy tale. And the liberal tale runs neck to neck with Marx up until the bourgeois revolution before abruptly, and expediently, dropping out of the race.

The Weberian version does not directly challenge the "*material*" causes listed above, but intentionally: Weber's project being to show that credible alternatives to social explanation necessarily exist (*epistemic relativism*) since everything is a matter of the vantage point being adopted (Weber, curiously, considered such fundamental assumptions/standpoints to be "*arbitrary*"). Here, it is the Protestant Reformation that is the great mover of the European *juggernaut* in its particularly compelling forms of the Lutheran and Calvinist sects (but particularly the latter, for its transparently *accumulationist* orientations) that transform values and social behaviors in more "*capitalist*" directions by their insistence on parsimony, thrift, and productive labor—but not *prodigal consumption*—as the new cardinal virtues to establish true Christian worth on earth, if still in the eyes of an extraterrestrial god. As such, it is "*reformed*" Christianity—*in effect, a Europeanized and modernized Christianity*—that helps inculcate the standard mores of capitalist *rationality* as the dominant ideal in an entire people, this in itself being the great European innovation in history.

Contra Europe, the non-European world is "revealed" (by the customary recourse to ignorant conjecture) to be in various stages of primitive, *subrational* conduct in the economic life, despite (or because of!) their achievements in other aspects of *culture*. Thereby Hinduism, Confucianism, and the like, are portrayed as inefficient conductors of the *capitalist spirit*, at least relative to Christianity. Weber was not particularly enamored of this acquisitive *geist*, being a traditional conservative at heart, but fully appreciative nonetheless of the superiority that it conferred on Europeans (being, also, a conventional *racist* at heart) *vis à vis* the heathen, or pagan, world.

At any rate, only the European exhibited the *Triumph of Reason* immanently inscribing it deep in his capitalist heart first, and then as a social norm applicable to all domains afterwards; and yet, paradoxically, the "*iron cage*" of capitalism (i.e., *bureaucratized* society) was the net, unwelcome, result of that singular prepossession. The only possible challenge to this order could come, if at all, from a *Great Charismatic Interruption* (from Carlyle to Nietzche, the romantic hope of a "superman/hero" to spark up the *ennui* of modernism has been a perennial *cross current* in modernist history: ironically, and tragically, in Weber's own Germany, in the mid-twentieth century, such an "*interruption*" was to be actualized, but with no easing of the onerous burden of *Organization*, which lived up far more reliably to the speculations of Michelsian "*iron laws" of oligarchy*); but more on that later.

Given Weber's clear statement of the *limited* nature of all perspectives, including, presumably, his own, it remains a tribute to the sectarian propensities of modernism that subsequent debates were to counterpose Weber to Marx, and both heroically, as the very embodiments of *ideal* versus *material* choices in social theory. For someone not enamored of schoolboy struggles in the domain of casuistry, these views are quite happily *complementary* and make up, for the serious student, a thematically tight story—but only a *story*, nonetheless—of the onset of the modernist epoch, if taken *together* and read *conjuncturally*. In the one case, of course, the emphasis rests on the *schemata* of a material revolution—in the other of an ideological one. Matters are then, of course, satisfactorily set to satisfy the vulgar penchant of contrasting ignorantly antipodal positions, so as to engage forever in the futile task of asserting the primacy of one over the other, illustrating only the sterility of *intra-modernist* discourse.

(3)

The point of this disquisition is not to debate the rival merits of whether ideas or practices are the "driving forces" of history, it being a useful measure of the ignorant exiliity of modernist discourse that it could, for so long, actually see these interlinked correlates of social life as independent options to be taken apart, and counterposed, as paradigmatic necessity dictated. Rather, it is to arrive at the real, exigent causation that separated Europeans, happily from their point of view, from their anthropic cousins elsewhere, escaping from the desultory vacuity of the Marx-Weber debate. Suffice to note that, on that topic, idealists and materialists are both convinced of the factuality of "progress" and the superiority of European formations (as "advanced") over others. The agenda, presumed by this discourse, *au contraire,* is a mite more ambitious: to determine why Europe felt impelled to distinguish itself as apart from the general run of world history, when this moment actually occurred, and the implications of this Great Divide for the subsequent history of the planet.

If capitalism is seen as the great, epideictic watershed—*as the prized sophism of Western historians holds*—that marked the critical parturition, then the question is begged as to why capitalism took that special form (given its ubiquity, if "wage-labor" is all it takes to define it, in history) that we know today as the *Great European Way*. Almost *en passant*, then, we have to evaluate the merits of institutional arrangements, including ideational ones, in accomodating certain paths and closing off others (both inside and outside of Europe).

One amongst the many theses forwarded in this work may now be very provisionally, and somewhat incompletely, stated: the demarcation between east and west (or *north* and *south* in today's politically correct parlance) was fundamentally based on the adoption in western Europe of a *radically reformulated Christian ideology*—this might be termed the *modernist Europeanization* of Christianity—that would empower certain pragmatic urges that traditional religions, including more orthodox catholic Christianity, might have abhorred as a gross violation of moral law (in licensing usury, marketization, and monetization of this and that). *The consequent sanctification of private right, and the corresponding devolution of public claim, in early modern Europe, has no real parallel in the history of the world.*

Capitalism (or even industrialism in general) might well have subsisted without any *absolutism* in the domain of *private right*, as say in the case of the independent evolution of the Japanese economy before World War I, and its variant in India both before and during British conquest, but it could not possibly have assumed that predatory, uncompromising, form—celebrated today as the very *acme* of the process of "mature" capitalism—that it took in the largely *Protestant* Northern segment of Europe without some truly exceptional factors at work (as will be seen, this approach extends Weberian insights in many respects).

This idea privileges the Reforming (in truth, these are better termed *De*forming) sects within Christianity, of course, but one must not casually absolve even classical Christianity from its signal service to the birth of an ideology that succored European capital so very faithfully: *anthropocentrism*, or the idea that all of creation was merely an adjunct to the service of *Man* (there were, as must be, honorable dissenters from this tenet such as St. Francis who proclaimed the equality of all species only to be excommunicated for that and other heresies) *thereby counterposing a materialized nature against a humanized Man*. To that extent, in combination with specific codes of material conduct to be discussed, and given that signal, and strong, prepossession, Christianity was to become the *classical locus* of the specific *Eurocapitalist* impulse of limitless, exploitative domination and extirpation that put traditional tyrannies of world conquest at the level of child's play—be they the exploits (fabled or real) of an Attila or an Alexander. Super-rational, calculating, economic gain-seeking, that saw the universe as its oyster, was the *leitmotiv* of the European advance into the noncapitalist *periphery*, first within itself, and then in its captive colonies in the new world, Asia and Africa, and now perhaps, ready to range illimitably into the realm of *outer* space.

Only granted this fundamental *ideational* project—and humans are driven by little else other than ideas, right or wrong, for better or for worse—does the subsequent dialectic of capitalist *greed*, and *resistance* to it on the part of the peasantry, workers, women, and indigenous peoples, suffice to explain the twists and turns of the actual dynamic of the capitalist revolution in western Europe. In human societies, it is ideas and beliefs, regardless of their *validity*, that drive, and legitimate, social practices.

On the face of it, it was a rather curious amalgam of propensities that had come together: *rational-reductionist calculation, material greed, anthropocentric vanity, theological justification*: easy to see how European historians, even putatively progressive ones at that, have no difficulty admitting, nay celebrating, the *first two* attributes (though the glaring "*reductionism*" of the "rationality" they celebrate usually escapes them), since they see nothing fundamentally "*wrong*" about that, but baulking at conceding, or even being aware of, the last two. All the more curious, given that these latter attributes were probably the more decisive features of their conjoint evolution. Now, lest we give too much credit to Christianity, we must note the essential *continuity* of vision that this latter faith embodies with its great predecessor: *Judaism* (interestingly: of the great monotheistic *desert faiths*, Judaism and Islam were *not* to be swept away by any great climactic "reformation" thereby remaining, leastways in ideology, "true" to their original inspiration; the modernist corruption of Judaism was a *practical*, not a theological matter, assisted by the absence of a Jewish "State" to enforce Talmudic prohibitions throughout medieval and early modernist times in European history). Small wonder, scholars like Sombart readily attributed capitalism to a creation of the Jews, much like Weber easily assigned it to an invention of Luther and Calvin.

At any rate, by means of many meanderings, the conjoint predilections of the *Judaeo-Christian* faith apparently found their capitalist apotheosis in Calvinism (and Lutheranism), and the mood of the "Reformation" generally. Even smaller wonder that the non-European world saw, in some bewilderment, its colonizers flying the tri-colors of trade, flag, and the cross simultaneously. European capital was baptized *Christian* (*religion is, perhaps not accidentally, singularly of non-European provenance*; Europeans succumbed, so to speak, to the lure of a West Asian, desert faith, prior to remolding it carefully on modernist lines) albeit of the "reformed" that is, *corrupted* mode; and therein its decisive difference from the non-European world. Stated boldly, *Reformulated* Christianity was, in its *geist,—anthropocentric, accumulative, reductionist, and god-serving—the founding metaphysical spirit of capitalism.* In that special sense capitalist colonialism was yet another self-ennobling and lustrating crusade, driven by the inexorable force of its own intrinsic faith.

In many regards, anthropocentrism has remained a powerful driver of European ideology, reaching its apotheosis in the rationalist *telos* of Levi-Straussian anthropology where *culture* is triumphantly transposed against *nature* to the latter's detriment symbolizing a sort of a "victory" of "man" over "nature" (the highly mechanistic *nature-nurture* debate in social ideology that endures is profoundly connected to this antiquarian, and *andro-centric* view of creation). *Emotions*, wrote Levi-Strauss proudly, explain nothing; they that must be explained. In effect, *reason* being putatively the sole propensity gifted to "*man*" (quite literally), and "*man*" *being the centre of the universe, emotions had to be part of the "lesser" animalistic traits shared by women, workers, and "savages*" (the simple *reason/emotion* binary far from exhausts the paraphernalia of tools that sustain our *anthropic* understanding of the universe: we are, as hominids, given many other faculties which are less understood for being less pliantly serviceable to the modernist project: *instinct, intuition, and, ultimately "revelation*"—all of which play a vital part in our day-to-day perceptions).

Of course such precepts are the very founding, metaphysical underpinnings of what passes for "*social science*" today and are specious in the extreme. In truth, much of the *social* is "intentionally" a *sublimation* of various natural *instincts*, as Freud well understood (*it is important to note that all of Freud's insightful commentary on "human" sexuality is fatally flawed by its purely, and quite unselfconsciously, masculinist voice: any satisfactory narrative of "human" sexuality needs to go beyond the errant fantasies of men in this highly charged domain*) but much of it is also a simple *extension* of basic, innate, "*natural*," drives vested in our *species-being* by virtue simply of *humans being part of the extended family of hominids*. "*Human* aggression," an ideological euphemism for *male violence*, may take on all manner of social modifications and mystifications, but it is at base just that and no more.

So, *contra* the European penchant of counterposing binary oppositions—so characteristic a feature of Enlightenment based ideologies, *such as nature–culture, male–female, orient–occident*, and so on—only to assert the dominance of the one over the *Other*, it is time we understood the inexorably *dualistic* heritage of humankind if in quite another sense: *human* behavior is only a cultivated, acculturated form of *mammalian/hominid* behavior *en generale*, with the added dimension of pre-calculation and planning. *Further, as clarified in later sections, it is an egregious error to use the term "human" as a unifying monolith—because men and women neither share, nor exhibit, the same set of traits, instincts, behaviors and, drives: in effect, the paradigm of masculinity and the paradigm of femininity dwell apart. In all cultures, men and women occupy neither the same ontic, nor epistemic, space.*

At any rate, the European, convinced of his own civilizational accomplishments, thought blandly to be *sui generis*, could not bring himself to acknowledge that he was, for all the high refinement of red wine and classical music, only an *animal* underneath it all (of course he was far from disinclined to view *non-European* species as just a bunch of coarse lower life forms—as a cursory review of the *Tarzan* tales will illustrate—whenever so prompted). Nature had to be, perforce, "left behind."

(4)

Anthropocentrism, rational-reductionist calculation, material greed, and a materialistically warped "god-given" *mission*, were the stellar ingredients in the great *European Ascent* (or *descent*, rather, into a radically different metaphysic), but the picture is still far from complete; another, defining, indeed *over-determining*, complement was *Patriarchy*—or institutionalized *misogyny*—as handed down, in ideological discourse, from the canonical patriarchs of the same Judaeo-Christian tradition. At least in this regard, the European heritage was not unique, since *Patriarchy is, as far as we can know, an anthropic universal*; however, the inherent sexism of its private and public morality was acutely sharpened by the adjunct addition of *rationalism (again in its modernist, reductionist form)*, calculated greed, and naked androcentrism. Placed in that feckless crucible, women were to face a fate that they, but partially, escaped in *other* cultural forms of patriarchy: that is, *commodification*. This latter was, like other things, a *process*; only completed and completable with the victory of both Reformation ideology and capitalist practice, culminating in the revivalist reformulation of antiquarian Roman legal codes that embodied the Renaissance equivalent of far older canons of *patria potestas*.

The lie all this gives to the ever gaily caparisoned, self-congratulatory, *progressivist* histories of capitalism is singularly telling: even as late as 1981, responsible Swiss males were still deliberating the merits of granting women the right to vote; and yet this did not prevent Swiss democracy from being held up as the very acme, indeed the text book case, of Western republicanism and democracy (indeed the struggles of workers, women, and minorities merely to get *effective* suffrage—which is far from sufficient to have a say in *governance*—is even now, at the threshold of a new millenium, an ongoing trial; and the great surge of corporatist neo*liberalist* hegemony today can only spell more travails for that ilk). The simple charade of European modernist commitments to civilized values (in the empirical light of erstwhile Italian, Spanish, German and, Greek, Portuguese, and South African versions of outright *fascism* and/or dictatorship, and the not so friendly *techno-fascism* of daily life for minorities in the United States, that have characterized the experience of the twentieth century, to say nothing of their combined savagery *vis à vis* the non-European world) could not have been more cynical, as they sedulously conquered non-Europeans under the guise of the grave carriage of the *white man's burden*, even while trampling on worker's, women's, and minority rights at home. The fact that the many newfangled *neo-capitalist* clones in the far east (the so-called Asian *Tigers*) closest to the prevalent norms of *Euro-modernism*, exhibit similar authoritarian traits today (aside from being well known international *loci* for the most exploitative forms of sex-tourism) is possibly not entirely fortuitous.

At any rate, Shakespeare's revelatory *Taming of the Shrew* could, in this vein, well be read as a vivid metaphor for the *domestication* of women under way in Shakespearean England, and one can hardly forget hoary biblical sanction for the notion of the ineffable evil that supposedly lurked in the sinful natures of women as given in the fable of Eden and the equally perverse semiotics of the notion of an *Eve*-inspired "*fall*" from grace. European patriarchy was not merely a practical, material, arrangement for gender oppression devised by powerful capitalist males—it had primordial sanction from their *extraterrestrial* faith itself; indeed from a faith that venerates, if paradoxically, the ideal of the Madonna with such lyrical passion in art and architecture. The service to *sexism* paid by canonical biblical ideology in its pedagogy of the "Fall" of "Man" is quite striking, although it can hardly be denied that the *woman-as-designing-temptress* (as against the virtuously resisting, "noble," male), or as a weak dupe of temptation (consider Shakespeare's "Frailty, thy name is woman" trope), theme abounds in many cultures from the sirens of Greek mythology to the astral nymph who tries to seduce the young Buddha out of his deep, meditational trance *en route* to his enlightenment in Buddhist lore (indeed, as an aside, it is worthwhile, in another frame of reference, to contrast the meaning of "*enlightenment*" to the Buddha in relation to its usage in the history of modernism: the seamlessly cosmic nature of the one and the entirely mundane nature of the other is illustrative of the great cultural divide between Europe and the "*Other*").

At another remove, a generation of *feminist* scholarship has made obvious—and that in itself should debunk the myth of the *unbiased* nature of modernist science, and reveal just *one* of the many ideological blinkers donned by its parochial tribalism—, if to a still largely disbelieving world, the rabid *misogyny* involved in the notorious *witch-hunts that* martyred many women (as symbolic warning to millions of others), divesting them of property, skills, accomplishments, liberty, and even ofttimes life, of which the *genre* of Joan of Arc would represent only the best known. It would bc grossly simple-minded to think that the path has, today, been cleared for women to freely fulfill their personal/social ambitions in the modernist wasteland of today. They remain, like workers, and ethnic and religious minorities, *structural victims* of late modernist patriarchy, not so much in their *exclusion* any more but in their increasingly *enforced integration* into the inclement mores of *masculinity* (being sent into war now to gleefully maim and kill like their male counterparts standing at the apex of that regressive brand of perverse "equality").

Given such cross-historically invariant and invidious *gender defamation*, witnessed in the lore and literature of a myriad cultures, it can only be a sterling tribute to the inherent *philanthropy* of women to still participate, however distastefully, in the rabid society of their oppressors. At any rate, *androcentric* sexism of the *rational-reductionist* kind (as opposed to its *gynocentric* equivalents in precapitalist societies), geared to securely and sytematically reaping the reward of unpaid labors and gratifications at home, was a vital auxiliary of *Euro-modernism*.

Granted such unedifying prepossessions, it would seem a grotesque paradox, to the outsider, that the very peoples who gave the largely unsoliciting world two Great Conflagrations—and prepared actively to blow the globe apart in a deliberately planned, and even greater, *third* one for decades after World War II—could yet solemnly swear fealty, on all sides of the conflict, throughout the carnage, as pathetically expressed in the wretched bunkers of the First War, to the humble, exiguous vision of the gentle lamb of Nazareth. It must seem a sacrilege, leastways to any brand of true believer, to witness the putative "word of god" being so desperately solicited to sanctify the recurrently wretched misdeeds of men. In that frame, the "*last Christian*" may indeed have died—as legend will have it—on the cross.

(5)

However, the composite picture of the arrival of modernism is still far from complete. Completing the litany of *sexism* was the liturgy of *racism*, the other great, even obsessive, European passion. If the domestic life of the capitalist could not be complete without the oppression of women, the external domain for capital could not be secured without the subjugation of "*Other*" cultures, and other peoples, of this world. As such, *Racism* was the other powerful "rationalizing" instrument of world domination, as eternally epitomized in the poetical tropes of vulgar *Kiplingese* (Kipling was, lest we forget, but a mild racist; there were scores more potently rabid than he) version of the *White Man's Burden*. Shakespeare's *Othello* straddles the cusp of the great transition in the European view of *Other* (even today, in the twenty-first century, and even in a medium as permissive as Hollywood to show romance between a white woman and a black man is pure anathema); beyond that, alongside routine colonial quests, was the gradual construction of *classical white racism* whose sway, far from being eroded on the eve of the new Millenium, two centuries after putatively "*universal*" declarations of the canons of classical liberalism, is all the more secure today as the dominant, unwritten, cultural code of European hegemony.

Few that operate even in intellectual history realize the depth and extent of the racist passions that were unleashed upon a prostrate world as the Europeans ran through non-European realms like the biblical horsemen of the apocalypse. The Columbian genocidal tragedy visited upon the hapless Caribs, the grim litany of the African slave trade, echoing not in some suitably distal primeval past, but barely a century or so ago, and in the very teeth of the celebration of "human rights" and the advent of Napoleonic and American codes of liberty, life, and property, that is, the ideals of the *Great Bourgeois Revolution*, as duly consecrated even in Marxian fantasies of a rather fancifully conceived *Euro-history*, must rank high in the docket of the *Great Anomalies* of modernism, gainsaying all its progressivist pretensions dispositively.

As European capital and state, in conjoint alliance, wreaked their racial obsessions, satyr-like, and without mercy, in the colonization of the so-called *New World* (from Columbine massacres in the Caribbean to the grotesque atrocities of the Belgians in the Congo, Europeans revealed their unmistakable genocidal passions—whenever the opportunity presented itself—not much abated even today, as the pirate-plunderers of yesteryear now don the modernist halo of benign, neoliberalist *statesmanship*), their intellectual apologists were busy refining doctrines of *polygenesis* that preserved the purity and *separateness* of the white race as an isolated evolutionary event far apart from the lower forms of life that populated the warmer and darker continents.

Darwin's ideas on evolution were, as such, not merely resisted for challenging biblical versions of creation, but also for suddenly pulling the rug, inadvertently, from under white delusions of *exclusivist ethnic purity* (*Copernicus*, *Darwin*, and *Freud*: the *amour propre* of the European was to creditably survive all of these abrupt and anomalous challenges to the hegemony of the capitalist, European male). The fact that, to this day even responsible modernist scholarship continues to routinely hail the *Columbian* "discovery" of the Americas, in the stark face of the ancient occupation of those pristine continents by native—but *non-European*—peoples, is a telling and instructive index of the calm continuity of prototypically racist ideas even amongst the allegedly "*liberal*" intelligentsia. Not that long ago the proud progeny of Newton proclaimed "eugenics" a science—and yet still affect to scorn voodoo in Haiti as the ideology of primitives.

As such, the facade of *political correctness* that is paraded today, specially in the permanently hypocritical *Disneyworld* of the United States, is only a tactical concession to a carefully considered political pragmatism, not at all allowed to retroactively correct tendentious, misanthropic, misreadings of "histories." Indeed the exclusivist paradigm of white peoples went so far as to even treat *one part of a continuous landmass—Eurasia, if you will—as a separate "continent": that is, so-called "Europe" itself*; separatist ideology apparently required a measure of *physical distance*, even if it involved the diverting invention of wholly mythical boundaries by purely ideological cartographers.

Viewed in these uncompromising terms, it must be recognized, with some sense of shock, that *Hesperian*, white, racism is a unique concoction far apart from the normal chauvinisms and petty *ethnocentrisms* of *other* peoples, which are real enough; in its stark denial of the very *humanity* of all non-white peoples, Europeans, in the very modern era of *Newton, Adam Smith and Darwin* (and not in some preliterate, uncivilized, or barbaric past) stand alone and apart from the rest of humanity, crowned in the rank infamy of their pet perversion, all the more grotesque when weighed against the ringing declamations of universal human rights that, paradoxically, emanated from them as characterized both the French and American Revolutions. It is one thing to believe, in all *naïveté* that, one's tribe is the center of the world (and even this conjectural prepossession is *not* as universal as is usually imagined): another to give that stance, in all "scholarly" seriousness, both a high "scientific" and theological justification.

As such, as an aside, all the liberally funded, rationally allocated, and pompously paraded, "*social science*" studies of "race and racism," as routinely, piously, and self-righteously, spun out by the liberal-modernist university (a tactical concession to the rising numerical importance of American minorities in the U.S. polity) committed to examine and study such putative *deviations* from the liberal norm, intelligently to the limits of the public purse, traduce reality and stand history on its head: *racism was not an aberration within capitalist modernism, but was, and still is, an integrally structural part of it.*

The modern era, proudly invented by Europe (it is for this reason that the terms *European* and *Modern* are used virtually interchangeably in this text) rested on rabidly pernicious ideological stilts; bizarre, therefore, to accept at face value the extraordinary claim, *à la Kipling*, of a "*civilizing*" mission to be performed in other climes—the shoe, one would think, would have to be *on the other foot* (*materialist, amoral, asocial, and anti-cultural, techno-fascist* barbarism was the great "gift" of the European world, for which the world's people and the planet are still paying dearly, and at an ever escalating cost). The *rationality* of European capital, to say nothing of its civility, sad to say, was not even skin-deep. To accept the idea of a Euro-capitalist "*rationality*" as is, let alone to venerate it like Weber (and Marx, albeit in a different frame), and the mainstream economics tradition generally, as some high-flighted, high-minded, *optimizing* norm, is to wantonly ignore its near incredible generic, even apodictic propensity to piracy, plunder, and rapine. Between the high ideology and the low *praxis*, one could, as it were, drive several chariots.

The correction to the Marx/Weber narratives must now appear obvious: *Marx quite ignored anthropocentrism, since he too was under the spell of the self-same Judaeo-Christian prepossession, and his robust "materialism" would not weigh the newly innovated Protestant notion of the "white man's burden" with any degree of seriousness as a mover of history. In the case of Weber, paradoxically (given his putatively "idealist" notions) far closer to reality than Marx, the error lay, first, in the acceptance, at face value, of the idea of a Protestant "Reformation" failing thereby to see the wholesale Deformation of the ethics of classical Christianity it really involves; and second in being blind to the incredible "reductionism" to vulgar material gain that the notion of modernist "rationality" really involved.* By assimilating a rank materialism to the likes of the newfangled paradigm of "rationality" Weber was making a simple, if common, species of a rather serious philosophical error: to state matters simply, *there is nothing remotely "rational" about wanting more.* Rationalism and materialism are two very distinct philosophies that suffer arbitrary fusion, by sleight of hand no less, in the grey amalgam of Euro-capitalism.

(6)

Freewheeling pirates and plunderers set out, *ex animo*, to pillage the world: such was the grim reality of the European, civilizational "mission"; from the Norsemen to Drake and Pizarro, down to Cecil Rhodes (and the neoliberal hucksters of our own times), the lineage was the same—or so it would seem. But why? How did such a "*calling*" arise? Far too easy to answer at one level of *materialist* explanation, provided one is ready to pay the requisite metaphysical dues to materialism: they who had nothing and wanted all, could only act in that way in line with the idea of *necessitas non habet legem*. That is to say, the very *relative paucity* in critical resources (but only so when judged in a uniquely "*modernist*" frame) of early European pioneer countries, England specially, meant that greed—much as need—had to look far and beyond for easy acquisition and accumulation: to the east, mainly, for the fabled wealth of the Indies and China.

Or, perhaps, one could point to the hostile climactic environment of Europe where long winters necessitated the fairly humble means of preservations of foods not easily available locally that is, *spices*; again, the direction of need would point to the spice sanctuaries of Asia. Finally, one could refer to the limited availability of *specie* in Europe as commerce expanded in the late Middle Ages: again, Asia beckoned, as might a fat rabbit attract a pack of hounds. Indeed some version of such a charter of "causes" dominates materialist explanations of the fateful trajectory of European colonialism whose net historical consummation was that, in effect, but two relatively sub-numerous European tribes ended up occupying nearly three entire continents, while threatening, materially and ideologically, the economic and social space of all others.

Greed and need: a fateful conspiracy! How much of world history might safely be attributed to these very "human" traits! And yet, in point of exoteric fact, such *meta-theories* are altogether too *simpliste* and/or explain too much, and perhaps too quickly. Humans are mere brutes, in such accounts, driven willy-nilly, by subhuman drives. A touch of the venal now makes all the world kin; yet it is not, indeed cannot, be the whole story for the simple reason that other societies have *not* acted that way despite the ease with which one can construct and foist imaginative scenarios of greed and need. The Chinese made successful voyages to Africa but neither colonized nor enslaved entire peoples, for the extraction of wealth on a continuing basis, as a matter of course; indeed a purely "*economic*" motive for the voyages was conspicuous by its absence. Similarly, the Mogul empire (though there are empires, *exceptis excipiendis*, not of this mould) lived largely, if fitfully, within its borders, and so on: of course, Attila and Genghis ranged across continents but with little will to supplant, with any degree of seriousness, what they found: their *adventurism* was apparently just that, and went no further. Of course, they were not "*capitalist*," and perhaps thereby had no such putatively systemic "drives"; but that only raises the important issue of what capitalism is, especially as evolved in its generically *European* provenance.

I will be arguing that *Euro-capitalism* was quite a different breed than its cousinages (as with its recent transplants in the Pacific Rim that were, strictly speaking, artificial *policy* creations of the cold war) in Asia and elsewhere, despite many formal similarities. European capitalism was defined, as such, by the *adjective* not the noun. Curiously, the European was not merely dreaming up his now permanent, overriding *idee fixe—his much vaunted radical difference with the human family*—as a matter of simple racial chauvinism; he had become—and it was a process of *becoming*—*ex voto*, vitally different in some rather important respects. It is this singular, self-absorbed, *autism* of the late modernist European that was to have such earth shaking consequences for the rest of the planet.

(7)

Definitions of *capitalism*, as they abound in the literature, are a matter largely of taste and orthodoxy; given its multiple forms, stages, locations, and so on, there is no warrant for believing that an occlusion is possible, or even necessary, on its semantics. Marxists assimilate it usually to "*wage-labor*" (partial or general) although left merely at that, such relations have probably existed through much of the world without occasioning any such earthshaking European outcomes. More refinement in that tradition would add continuous *reinvestment* of the product of wage labor as more satisfactory, alluding to the "*werewolf lust*" for accumulation that is putatively characteristic of putatively "advanced" capitalism.

Another kind of closure might be achieved, in a different frame, if we speak of the emergence of near-perfect *markets* in land, labor, and capital as characteristic of the "maturity" of this formation. But this does raise an issue; such a sufficient definition could hardly be applied to the sixteenth, seventeenth or even the eighteenth century, even in the putatively "advanced" segments of Europe without seriously affronting reality. In effect, such wholesale attributes are possibly more the *effects* of real capitalism as it matured in Europe than its *founding* elements which would have to be, therefore, discovered/located elsewhere. Capitalism is a real historical, conjunctural entity, not a heuristic or exemplar for deriving abstract generalities. *History may well have a logos, but it is not "logical."*

The exploitation of wage labor in some normal fashion is far from sufficient to explain the European explosion, since such attributes, in subsectors of the economy, were available even in Oriental Japan and India prior to British conquest without any such cataclysmic effects being felt (the wake up call to the Japanese modernizers was delivered by European and American expansionism; as such, much of subsequent Japanese evolution was aggressively *reactive*). *Indeed, it was a signal Marxian error to presuppose the virtually complete absence of private property in the non-European Periphery* (the breathtaking audacity of the "*Asiatic Mode of Production*" wherein Marx assimilated entire continents and cultures into one *simpliste* grid should rank as one of the outstanding exemplars of Euro-centric arrogance/ignorance), an error further compounded by Marx *in making no inquiry into why this was the case*, since the answer would have involved an impolitic recourse to reduction to "*nonmaterial*" causation foreign to his philosophy. Truth is that *affective modes of social existence preclude absolutist private appropriation for disabling the social tie*: that is, the inherent bonding, and sharing, that underlies the *nexus* of communal life defined by the anthropic compact of empathy. *In effect empathy foreclosed the road to a potential mimicry of Euro-capitalism, not idiocy* (or lack of means, mechanisms, and modalities).

At any rate, given the foregoing, some other ordering of phenomena becomes warranted to close the gap between the Capitalism of the west and the capitalisms of the east. One usual exit is to postulate the environs of an extraverted *capitalism plus colonies* in the west accounting for the earth-shaking metastasis of the so-called "*industrial revolution*" *(which really originated not in Europe, as usually imagined, but in European colonies overseas long prior)* whereas in the East it's a capitalism far more domesticated, introverted, localized, and regional (it is not enough to suggest that Eastern capitalism were *mercantile* and not "*industrial*," because colonies were sought just as eagerly by *mercantile* Europe in the *colonial* era as by "industrial" Europe in the "*imperial*" era; nor does it suffice to suggest that "empires" preclude capitalism, because there is nothing in historical capitalism that precludes coexistence with any form of political absolutism). However this only defers the problem: whence the difference? Which brings us back in a circle to the original problem, *viz. the distinctive peculiarity of the west.*

In this regard, due reflection might yield that it was not the inscrutable orient, *but the all-too transparent occident*, that has always lain in crying need of historical explanation. In fact, by setting itself up as the standard and *modus* of evaluation, the west successfully prevented examination of its own peculiarities, parochialisms, and idiosyncrasies, preferring to see the rest of the world—specially the notorious "*orient*"—as *anomalously* worthy of its special attentions. It is this historical *ethnocentrism*, that infects modernist discourse quite thoroughly, which this work decisively debunks and corrects.

As every Eurocentrically inclined Japanese schoolgirl is aware, it is quite commonplace to suggest that the capitalist revolution in Europe—described in roseate hues even in putatively *rejectionist* Marxian accounts—drew its historical specificity on account of the parcellization of sovereignty, the power vacuum at the apex, and the consequent decentralized polity that "permitted" (owing to its weakness) urban mercantile interests much as peasant struggles within the feudal epoch to consolidate and expand their sway without being swamped by the obstacular apparatus of empire, eventually leading, after an appropriate political revolution, to a relatively linear transit to the modern era. Here is a ruggedly materialist analysis that shuns the dispensable artefacts of *culture* and *ideology* while elevating the *economy and polity*—that which is to be explained—to the status of being both cause and effect of the Euro-capitalist endeavor. Curiously, liberal analysis (specially the so-called *Whig* view of history) adds little more than a sundry garnish to this *entree*, sharing the Marxian penchant for simple materialism in even measure. But facts, when placed in *situational* context (for only then, in a human society, are they assumptive of that title), are obdurate things—and quite recalcitrant *vis à vis* the demands of such—flatly apocryphal–interpretive latitudes.

Japan is, of course, a useful case in point. Many of the factors described as unique to Europe were available in reasonably approximate form in Japanese feudalism, and some species of the genus that we might very casually term capitalism—*though modern, organized industry is all we really mean* (the presence of industry cannot be assimilated into the fact of capitalism: Eurocentrism, however, excels in collating the two as synonymous)—did develop indigenously there, but with little of the former's catastrophic consequences. The more spectacular, *modernist*, character of Japanese industry developed only after it had become an involuntary suzerain of Western (U.S.) capital. The flesh was willing, so to speak, in the case of Japan, but the (*Euro-capitalist*) spirit was altogether weak. The United States, of course, at the point of mighty gun barrels, loaded with a misanthropic mission, as much as explosive power, never before witnessed on the face of this planet, was to remedy that deficiency quite fully. On the other hand, the more recent *entres* into the capitalist wonderland in East Asia were the contrived *policy creations* of the cold war marked by a pervasive *étatisme*, and an authoritarian blend of communitarianism, insulation, and social control, which make them a breed somewhat apart from the more characteristic asocial and antinomial *individualism* of their Western tutors.

Latter day neoclassical economic deductivist theorizing, and fundamentally chauvinist accounts of European supremacy generally, place their money on the development of "*efficient*" property rights as the *sine qua non* of European advance but this factitious argument fails, as alluded to earlier, for the simple reason that such "rights" developed well *after* and not *before* the capitalist revolution, as far as one can deduce, as *consequence* and not *cause* of the processes involved. *The neoclassical, like all ideologues (and this the hallmark of vulgar Marxism as well) does not seek, he finds*—but only what he himself has carefully planted surreptitiously the night before; best to leave such voyages of vacuous self-discovery, completely to one side.

(8)

Truth, whether the adage of *veritas vos liberabit* applies or not is, by its very nature *revolutionary and benumbing*, and as such outside the quiescent protocols of *normal* science (I doubt there are many scientists left who can even define the term, let alone comprehend its meaning: *indeed the search for truth transcendent, as opposed to knowledge, is virtually conspicuous by its absence in modernist philosophy*), and the motivated pleadings of *Eurocentric* scholarship out to celebrate the European achievement as a unique, *self-starting* feat of history. *It was, of course that* (and a conservative whose heart does not miss a beat when he contemplates the sheer *magnitude* of the achievement is not worth his salt) *and, also, paradoxically, not that*—as we shall see; but, at any rate, there is little really, from the standpoint of its *victims*, to celebrate in that torrid dance of the tarantula (not least of all for Europeans themselves) since the real rationale for that perverse singularity can only come as a revelatory shock to the naive and the uninitiated. What then did the European possess, outside of his seven league boots and his outsize guns that made him such a world ruler, tamer, and lawgiver? To answer this question is to unlock the riddle of the sphinx of modernist history and free an entire epoch of soporific delusions lovingly fostered by disingenuous Eurocentric scholarship fulsomely in love with itself.

Of course, the Europeans asked this question of themselves and entertained, indeed regaled, each other (and others, unfortunately) with lavish and temerarious tales of their special, and super-ordinary, endowments. Genetic exclusivity ("eugenics") and superiority ("polygenesis"), sexual continence, rationality, intelligence—even geography (latitudinal and longitudinal placements, nature of coastlines, etc.), demography, environment and climate, were all eagerly, if incontinently, appropriated as hereditary (and/or original) European advantages unavailable to the rest of the rabble constituting the human race scattered over less felicitous continents. It goes without saying that this classical, if quite factitious, segmentation of the human species into *noble* and *savage* (if there were such a scalar distinction, it is doubtful whether the European, after the European twentieth century of Hitler and Stalin, would be at the end of the divide he usually imagines himself to be), was capable of still further refinement *internally*, such that *northern* Europeans could also separate themselves from their lesser country cousins to the east and south, and so on.

The human is a *conceptual* animal, driven, sometimes passionately, by the nature, strength, and intensity of her beliefs. The fact that such orientations may be referred back to *context* (as in *materialist* theses) by way of a *post factum* "*explanation*" is, in itself, of little significance; in fact, to the extent that such *extrinsic* "explanation" often defies the more apparent *intentionality*, which is the grace of human action, it is not an explanation at all but a spectatorial, *third party rendition* of a set of formal, speculative propositions about actions undertaken by sentient beings who are, above *all moved* to do such things. As such, the more abstract and general the declamation of the social scientist—*and nothing modernist science worships more than abstractness and generality* (in line with its flair for *obscurum per obscurius*)—the more devoid of *meaning* it is. What matters, however, is that ideas when churned into sentiments, are moving forces, the efficient causes, now as ever in human history.

The roots of anthropic action must be sought thereby in the sphere of *ideas, but as refined in the high alembic of feelings*, that motivate the actors, despite the inherent contradictions in that not always consistent set of social forms. Consistency, or its absence, again is of no great moment—the populist world view, being more spontaneous, is not *schematized* like the *pseudo-scientific* one—so long as a certain discernible preponderance exists in favor of a certain direction at a given point of time. Human life, in its ordinary dimension, is not possessed of a great deal of care, consistency, or coherence—habit and custom rule as ratified by the norms of the prevailing convenance. It is this important, if subtile, fact that is missed by both rationalists and materialists who seek to impose highly parsimonious, iron grids for various *raisons d'états* quite impossible for humans to be contained by or in.

Stated differently, *determinism*, materialist or rationalist, fails of its own insubstantial weightlessness; and the argument adduced here for the governing role of ideas (and ideals) is not a *determinist* one, since the outcomes are left wide open (i.e. "open" system assumptions fare better in this regard than "closed" system dialectics) for the operative effects of conjuncture and context. By its very nature, such conjunctures, barring a fluke, are not repeatable. Thus, the specific circumstances governing the ascent of Europe are simply singular historical artefacts not open for emulation, suggestion, or enterprise. Easy to see the contrast with the various determinisms, liberal and radical, outlined above, where patterns are seen as transferable and repeatable—an error of Marxian and mainstream "*social science*," alike. *Stated succinctly capitalism was neither a necessary, desirable, consciously sought, "goal,"* nor even a vital feat of social evolution: it was a purely fortuitous development owing to a specific conjuncture of forces, events, and suitabilities, that has done little to enhance welfare when weighed against the costs it has extorted. The world was *not* predestined to arrive at that terminus: nor is the non-European world to be derided for nurturing no such indecorous ambition. As such, the thesis outlining the reality of this vein of European "advance" (if but in a certain misanthropic direction) is not a "*model*" or a heuristic; it is, if you like, a *just so story*—but carrying a useful pointer or two in the expositional process of the *parable-pedagogy* of oppression.

Of course, points of view are neither privileged nor privileging; as such, the ideas outlined here represent only one way of comprehending the myriad petty facts that litter the various trashcans of history favored by the interested *raconteur*. This is by no means to belittle the interpretation offered here; only to *contextualize* it. The episteme it presents, despite its intentional *one-sidedness*, is arguably "rational" (in its *nonreductionist* usage) and supported by historical trends of evolution comprehensible to those who take on the broadest possible canvas in their take on the making and unmaking of history. The elevated level, nonetheless, of a *concrete* generality vested in it is its own defense; no trivial, or singular set of *micro facts* can gainsay its irrefragable significance.

Stated differently, the medley of argument offered here needs to be accepted or rejected *in toto* by the critic—it may not be chipped away by the narrowly conceived chisels of the academic illiterates who mistake their abysmally sectoral hebetude and ignorance, for specialized knowledge. In social and historical explanation, it is only *organically* conceived *totalities* that encapsulate *meaning* at the deepest levels; anything less misses the proverbial forest for the trees by a farmer's mile. By atomizing the social, and mechanizing a highly presumptive *logos*, indeed a *telos*, to history, modernism achieved the end of fragmenting not only social life but also the very possibility of social *self*-knowledge. *The whole is neither greater nor lesser than the parts: it belongs, rather, to a different domain.*

It might well be supposed, much as in cosmic physics, that there is, in conjectural terms, an "*anthropic principle*" at work, even in human societies, which makes mutual comprehension possible in an epistemic sense, no matter how difficult this might be as an ontic proposition. Truth, in societal matters, is both knowable and realizable, if only because the human condition—in its anthropic ontology—for all the various orders of sublimations involved, is not entirely dissimilar. It is true that language and culture set barriers to mutual dialogue, but language can be learnt, and cultures decoded, as the travels of the ancients, from Marco Polo to Ibn Batuta easily reveal.

Social science, unlike the humbler missions of such travelers of yore, is invested with the drive principally to *police* the gates to such knowledge, set formal licensing procedures, and collect appropriate tolls, so only the duly consecrated can engage in the ancient, and congenial, art of *free observation*. The knowledge *business*, as consecrated within the modern university, is in effect, an *institutionalized means of separating the analyst from her means of research*, so as to assert *systemic* control over both the process of inquiry and its fruits. The level of misinformation, and outright *disinformation*, that exists in the United States about, say, for example, the Iraqi people, despite having the vast riches and the hypertrophic, epideictic, paraphernalia of media and university is a practically instructive index of the real social role of the production and dissemination of socially sanctioned, and politically approved, knowledge under modernism. Of course *Enlightenment and post-Enlightenment "social science"—works emanating from personages such as Comte, for example,—stemmed from a perceived desire not to repeat the trauma of the French Revolution*: "social science" was the organized means of burying the dangers of *philosophical* "free thinking" (a perception that is extant to this day).

Knowledge is today a simple adjunct of power, its willing servitor, sage and soothsayer. Even if the enterprise were to be less disingenuous, the attempt at "*self-measurement*" (difficult even in as impersonal a science as physics) might be construed, given anthropic passions and interests, to be problematic in the extreme. Of course, it might have taken the relatively benign form of a search for "*meaning*," as say with ancient *philosophy*; but that manner of undertaking, with us for millennia, would have little to do with any of the postures, policies, and protocols of modernist "science." Modernist science retired philosophy—for being too *open* a system—swiftly to the outhouse, fit demesne of derelicts and outcasts. *Truth, and the search for it, were never high priorities of the Enlightenment—ars gratia artis* is not a modernist precept—*unless it happened to be serviceable*.

(9)

What we need to reject, in the many twice-told tales of the secrets of European economic evolution, and advancement, is the fable of steadily increasing productivity as its *ultima ratio*. *Simpliste* economic histories (is there another kind?), therefore, that begin with the sallow banalities of either demographic change or the switch from the two-field to the three-field system, as drearily popularized in generations of introductory textbooks, as the great prime movers of economic advance need to be queried closely and critically—for such species of minor innovations in the material life are the part and parcel of the story of *all* human civilization, not merely the European segment of it. In the material life, the innovation requisite to sustaining a particular *cultural* definition of comfort and civility is usually, and quite easily, forthcoming; As such, the titanic forces that produced the industrial revolution did not, indeed could not follow merely as the accidental, evolutionary peak of primal processes set off by some such glibly post-designated and ingenuously simple prime mover(s); in themselves, they simply lacked the cumulative impetus ascribed to them by historians with imaginative, if ideologically weighted, agendas.

Nor could "class struggles," the *deus ex machina* of tired, hoary, Marxian argument, in of themselves lead to such elevated plateaus of misconceived achievement. If history is no more than merely a fable agreed upon, as Voltaire had it, either story would suffice; but at least some real consequents out there enshrine equally real causes and hence the need to suspend such obvious strains on credulity. In a memorable passage, which incidentally is quite a disclaimer of vulgar materialism, Marx once noted that humans first erect a building—as opposed to bees and ants, as he would have it—*in their minds* before constructing it on *terra firma*; what we need to look for, accordingly, is such operative constructions within the mind of the European that led to such momentous consequences for us all. The Deceivers who overran this world were not merely armed with Big Guns, as the colonized were to note grimly, and hopelessly, but with *Big Ideas* that proved even more irresistible—despite their vapid, hollow, and dissimulating misrepresentations. Marx did not understand that there are many other conflicts significant for society, as we shall see, that far override skirmishes over the material surplus.

To seek to produce, and be even normally (i.e., *normatively*) useful, in any "mode" of production, requires far more encouragement than the whip and the carrot can ordinarily provide; easy to see that such normative inducements were far from absent in the non-European world specially at the time of their conquest by Europe. *As such, the major European break with history lay in its will and ability to radically redefine the "meaning of life" itself, prior to placing the latter in (a very minor) context of the material life*: all its idiosyncrasies, perversions, and achievements make sense only in light of this *primary alienation*. In effect, a new worldview, a new vision of human life (more correctly an *anti-life*), a new philosophy of the concrete, was a consummated European achievement long before they smelted steel and perfected finance.

In succumbing to this *nouvelle* outlook, Europe placed itself radically distant from its own history, as much as from the histories of those it was to brutally trample without the slightest trace of remorse or compunction. *Metaphysics*, rather than physics, the nurturing mother of all modernist evolution; in keeping, the European revolution was a profoundly *ideological* one.

(10)

Values, at best, valorize—and, at the very least, delineate models of ideal behavior. Changes in human values are possibly the slowest of all social processes since so much of value systems is patient consensus building across time and space. And yet, despite the fact that, conceived as an evolutionary process, social time slows down, the initial rupture of values is nonetheless always a sudden and explosive one. *Nor are all values created equal*; instead, there is a discernible hierarchy where *the apex drives the base*; and at the very top of human values is the large question of *human placement in a nonhuman universe*, that is, the question of *religiosity* and *spirituality*. All other values take their inspiration, that is, *devolve*, from this higher epistemic matrix. Stated differently, the guide to *mundane* conduct is a corollary and a minor derivative of much higher order canons of *moral* behavior. What set Europe off on a distinct and lonely path—where it still has but few non-European companions—was some such radical epistemic and moral break with the old(er) matrix ordering of values that characterized its otherwise humble, adventitious, exoteric and quite pedestrian beginnings.

Interestingly, Max Weber (like so many "enlightened" German scholars) had both an interest in, and an understanding, however skewed, of such phenomena, both in the European and some (select) non-European contexts. On the other hand, his pervasive *Eurocentrism* (a euphemism for simple chauvinism in his case) prevented him from a fuller, richer understanding of the implications of his own research. Glancing but lightly, and inclemently, at certain Indian and Chinese philosophical systems, the colonial encounter having reaped a rich dividend in this regard, he arrived at the unduly hasty conclusion that these ancient *civilizations* (in the fullest sense of that grand term) lacked the rational spirit of dispassionate calculation that Europe was to excel in; of course, *it never occurred to him that this putative rejection of a "rational" Reductionism, within the "Other," might be a civilizational virtue* (i.e., a deliberate *choice*) to be commended!. Weber's *materialism* (a conservative materialism in his case) could only despise and disparage this radical dearth, in the "periphery," of what might loosely, but nonetheless properly, be called *moral debasement.*

And yet, paradoxically, conservative that he was, Weber would end up lamenting, often implicitly, the *overdevelopment*, within his own beloved Western culture, of that very "*Protestant Ethic*" that assured, in his own cosmology, the *superiority* of Europe, even if paradoxically located in the dry desert of *disenchantment*. Despite these radical, and conflicting, limitations, Weber was a great scholar who grasped the critical importance of the *explanatory value of civilizational genius* for what it was, before the sordid materialism of the newly constituted "*social sciences*"—purveyors of the chimerical gospels of modernism—eliminated such ideas, and the considerations they entail, entirely from their conceptual vocabulary.

The net consequence of Weber's speculations in this domain was to appropriate the holy grail of *reason* for Europeans, while leaving the rest of the world in various stages of a child-like, emotive state that is unable, to borrow tenuous Freudian terminology, to fully tame the *id* with the *ego*, let alone develop an autonomous *superego*. However, this did beg the question of whether capitalism was "*rational*" outside of its own internal *logos*; and it took a Marx to point out, in ringing declamations, the numerous societal *irrationalities* (and so-termed "*contradictions*") that, in his view, fatally beset that otherwise rationalist mode.

Furthermore, and this was never fully understood by Weber, rationality, in its own philosophical terms, could vouchsafe no substantive statements about the *ends* of social behavior without requiring an important auxiliary aid: a predominant *philosophy of greed*. To this day, one overarching variant of Euro-capitalist ideology—*mainstream economics*—repeats its vacuous banalities about "rational" behavior without realizing the hollow emptiness of that presumption stripped of the slew of prerequisites, and highly specific normative drives, that are themselves far outside the paradigm of rationality. As the much wiser Schopenhauer had it, *reason is merely the handmaid of the will*, a slave of specific human passions rather than their *ex cathedra*, efficient arbiter assumed to have the detachment of a solemn, chaste, chorus out of a classical Greek play.

In chaining the idea of *rationality* to a Protestant *ethic* Weber was indulging in a species of egregious error, an error that is extant to this day amongst conservative historians (and economists) extolling the virtues of capitalism: as will become apparent, rationality was merely the *qualifying adjective* to a much more powerful social ideology, far more important to the development of capitalism, that was to coil itself, python-like, firmly around the "advanced" centers of European industrial growth: *reductionist materialism. The great gift of the Protestant Reformation was, in truth, stark human debasement as never conceived of before in human history*. Rarely in human history have the evolutionary gifts of culture and *co-respective* social behavior been so readily sold out, and so very swiftly, in the name of righteousness no less, to the regular, if sordid, worship of Mammon.

Materialism as a requisite response to both the iniquities, and instilled properties, of nature and society (humans are inescapably "material" creatures, and require a variety of "material" resources to survive) is a readily comprehensible human reaction, but as a wholesale *bent*, it has always been confined to a limited, and limiting, domain. In effect, Europe no more invented human greed than human gregariousness, but what the Enlightenment succeeded in enshrining into the human lot as a permanent condition was the extension of ordinary, commonplace *greed—crass* materialism, if you will—as a generalized approach to, and a philosophy of, life itself. In this momentous metastasis, turning but a human frailty/necessity into an overriding, encompassing, even overwhelming preoccupation, Europe had broken with the established, and received, patterns of human and social history forever, in a default whose scars now indelibly tarnish the fair face of this hapless social and ecological universe that we now inhabit so very precariously.

The episteme of modern "*economics*," itself engendered within this critical time, which *prescribes*, rather than *describes, requisite* modernist behaviors, was to be run through with this affection, as such acquiring its modern role as the *flagship social discipline of the modernist temper*, now forever cut loose from its traditional incarceration within the inhibiting straitjacket of *ethics*. Worse, materialism was now deemed synonymous with *rationality* in human endeavors thereby elevating greed to the level of an *optimal* principle of social behavior. All the anile constructions—and there is little in mainstream economics that is not either facile and/or truistic once its charlatan axioms are presupposed—of economics rest on this *amoral, positivist* foundation.

It is a strikingly revelatory insight into the latter day *modus* of European civilization to note that many, at the inception of this *nouvelle* tradition (from Adam Smith to the Manchester free trader, Cobden, for example), were to actually see greed itself—in the European context—as a *civilizing* force. The preoccupation with the accumulation of wealth was seen, in all *naïveté*, as taming "other," even more vicious, drives, such as the lust for conquest and domination (even the otherwise prosaic Schumpeter was to find merit in such specious argument) which it was putatively, and thankfully, believed to be replacing. In effect, a Hobbesian view of "*human*" nature was being taken as primally given, only to be mercifully smoothed over, and overridden, by the fortuitous, *ex machina*, unleashment of the untender manifest of greed! Avarice and covetousness were to be the new, dependable, levers of "civilization": therein lay the much touted "civilizing" mission of capitalism (to be *civilized by greed* might yet be granted an odd, near-oxymoronic supposition).

The fallacy in the argument is so obvious as to defy credulity, failing in lapidary fashion, to see the *macro* implications of *micro* drives (i.e., Hegelian "unintended" consequences of simpler intentions). Individuals, pursuing only the putatively "peaceable" end of wealth, nonetheless, may clash with others similarly inclined, which *in the aggregate*, can generate (and indeed have produced) *world conflagrations* greater in scope than the Crusades, or the dynastic wars of medieval Europe. Of course, as another matter, to verily see one vice as more socially affordable than another, is a telling index of the underlying *matrix of morality* implicit in the latter-day European temper, underscoring its view of the social as a *balance of terror* and/or conflicting material "*interests.*" Having relinquished all concepts of *ethics*, it is only natural to take refuge in a conception of terrestrial life as a sort of a "contract" or settlement with, and a "rational" capitulation to, putatively lesser evil(s).

(11)

That science itself, as a process, could be considered the special, esoteric activity of a chosen few (by *self-selection*), as against the random and free exercise of the *creative intelligence of humankind* is itself an issue that must occasion questioning in minds that are intellectually open in the general area of social speculation. Its very existence—that is, in the "*organized*" public domain—provokes a different, but not unrelated, mode of questioning. *Who are we to study others? What gives us the right? What might the object be of such a study?* These are questions that the capitalist Enlightenment pushed quietly into the background, although viciously critical in itself of the pretensions of the Church whose hegemonic ideological intrusions into public life it opposed on not dissimilar grounds.

The modern scientific worker—a petty academic bureaucrat generally working as a rather minor cog in a great and powerful machine—rarely questions the *project* of science (if he/she is aware of it at all, which is doubtful), only currents within it that dissatisfy him/her; one does not, in all prudence, "question" the process that feeds one regularly, if not always handsomely. As such, such queries as have appeared and exist, have been posed either by *dissenters* from the *Great Scientific Project*—a randomly distributed group—or by the fast dwindling tribe of *free lance* philosophers (standing outside the box) whose freedom to raise such questions is the price of their complete irrelevance to the vast policy game of power and control in the arena of dissemination of information. The resulting ignorance, even amongst the elite intelligentsia, of the grim nature of the origins of European social science is little other than spectacular.

Few anthropologists today could be expected to know (let alone care and/or react in a *corrective* way to that history) the rabidly racist and colonialist nature of its not so ancient "*Royal Society*" beginnings. *The only thing, in effect, that science will not let one be scientific (i.e., critical) about is science itself*: legitimacy is achieved by the practised art of forgetfulness, that is to say where outright deception and lies (giving a new twist to the trope of the *"white lie"*) are not the routine, as with the case of well bred Europeans having us all believe, until quite recently, that Cleopatra was *white* (and the mythical invention, no less, by "scholars," of a light skinned race of crypto-European *Hamites*, speaking a fictitious "*Hamitic*" tongue, who arrive in Africa, presumably from some unspecified "European" hinterland, to build its great civilization), and that Black Africa had no civilized accomplishments to speak of. Very important to recall that such myths were not the creation of some marginal cranks on the fringes of civility, as is still the prevailing impression, but at the very epicenter of the claret sipping liberal "scientific" intelligentsia, that presumably read John Stuart Mill with their feet on the fender.

Modernism as a polity is based on subjugation of any and all alternates to its hegemony; and science is simply the necessary record keeping and surveying tool of the relevant subject population(s). Initially, the incumbent European elites studied their putative *inferiors* (workers, women, and "ethnics") domestically (much like Thomas Malthus "*studying*" the laboring classes and the Irish); then this classic gentleman's *military* hobby was extended to their non-European subjects, *en masse*. However, the issue is not merely the *political* objective of a social science; germane also is the distinct mode of acquisition of this knowledge, however debased the original motivation. Cold blooded (as apart from cool headed) analysis, and rational, reductionist atomization of phenomena, human and nonhuman, were the gifts of both the Baconian and the Cartesian models of science (the probing reader can discover for herself how many of the discoveries of modern, Western, medicine. for examble, owe their origin to systematized violence, cruelty, and abuse against the helpless and the vulnerable. *Contra* modernist propaganda, which adopts a hypocritical pose of horror, Hitler's scientists were proceeding only in well established *European* tracks when they experimented on *live* gypsies, Jews, gays, communists, the poor, the retarded, etc.), with the scientist deliberately situated at a safe remove from the ordinary business of life, much like generals in armies, safely remote from the "theatres" of war.

Indeed, the greater the distance, symbolic and otherwise, between the scientific process and everyday life, the stronger the alienation within the process itself, and the greater the mystique associated with it. The scientist as *hero* is the unique creation of modernism, *his* (in its upper echelons, it is still, predominantly, a *male* profession) exclusivist knowledge premised securely upon the general (and *planned*) ignorance of the vast masses of ordinary humanity. That we all accept, and scientists thrive upon, this invidious separation is an index only of our own generalized condition of "*subalternity*" and subservience to the dominant illusion(s) of the epoch. Effectively, modernism replaced the competing *ideological* authority of the medieval Church with that of Science, once the latter was safely interned within its own *logos* of dominance.

At any rate, analytically dissecting peoples, cultures, and societies, much like bisecting hapless frogs in high schools (European medicine developed on the basis of torture and mutilation of dependent and helpless peoples and species and remains, even today, supernally more intrusive, uncongenial, and discommoding than traditional therapies), as another "scientific" pastime, was only the prelude and accompaniment to the violent destruction of their cherished autonomies in practice. As such, gratuitous, indiscriminate, and *amoral violence* was the vital adjunct of the Euro-project of science from its early modernist beginnings; even to speak of the "*scientific revolution*" as a European, modernist phenomenon is a travesty: *all peoples have engaged in the quality and quantity of science necessary for their survival*—the Bushmen are still here, secure in their "science," though in danger now only from modernist predations on their habitat.

Indeed, as just noted, there's a linear connection between this unsavory heritage and Hitler's misanthropic legion of the loyal *scientist-servant* of the state, something that today is institutionalized far more securely in the sprawling, hegemonic industrial-scientific establishments of the U.S. Leviathan. The conceivers and executors of the horrific devices that fell on Hiroshima—*even the noble Einstein not exempted*—can hardly pretend to be a breed apart from the infamous architects of Auschwitz. *In vice as in virtue, modernism lived, then as now, defiantly, but by the sword.*

However, philosophically speaking, the important issue is not so much the egregious *misanthropy* of modern science, but also its fundamental error(s) of philosophical *method*: but only to the extent to which the matter speaks directly to the squalid *dehumanization* directly stemming from it. *That reason could be thought "superior" to empathy is a modernist conceit that is at the very basis of its alienation.* Understanding that is not hostile and *separatist* in intent does not require the services of a carefully bribed and bred tribe of icy analysts; comprehension of the human lot does not require stark *detachment*, nor the studied pose of *unfeeling* objectivity: indeed the precise opposite. *Feelings and passions are the natural tools with which sentient beings approach each other; and they have been sufficient for millennia to form normal expectations, mutual comprehension, and sustainable ties, between reciprocating beings.*

There is, to state the moral, no anthropic need for a "social science," as it stands today in its modernist guise; we do not know more about ourselves today than our forebears did: and if we do, it is not because of social science but in spite of it. It is merely an elitist policy-driven agenda of modernist domination: it serves neither as a necessary, nor sufficient condition for human empathy let alone human emancipation.

A touch of nature, wrote the effusive Shakespeare, makes all the world kin; a flash of *empathy* does the same for the social world. For all the glitz of wealth, and glare of power, there is precious little that *social science* has discovered in the last three centuries that could not be learned through more convivial means; time travelers in the past learnt more about each other's civilizations, at lower cost, and fewer perils to others, than what the average social scientist, condemned to trivial *micro* analysis of *mini* phenomena, can ever hope to know, feel, or understand. Social science, in its most mature form, is the very embodiment of the philosophical alienation of the modernist *geist.* Even at face value it is a bogglingly chaotic enterprise: we *assume* universalism and employ deductivism in economics, and psychology, but switch to particularism and inductivism in anthropology; that is, we are all *alike* in economics, yet each is *different* in anthropology—the sheer *opportunism* in the choice of epistemics and ontology is as breathtaking as it is bewildering to the bedeviled undergraduate trying, whenever so alerted, to make sense of it all.

Compounding grievous error was egregious insult; the arrogance with which European science condemned alternative epistemologies to perdition in trying to secure for itself a sole *monopoly* of the means to social knowledge, while parasitically devouring the discoveries precisely of these other traditions (as, say, in modern Western pharmacology), is a wonder all in itself. Modern science has posed successfully—given the illiteracy not merely of the average citizen, but the average scientist as well—as the inventor, not just of this and that, but of all knowledge. Indeed, the only acknowledgement ever given to "precursors" is usually to the ancient Greeks, in keeping with the same governing racial prepossession. Just a minor case in point is the theorem of Pythagoras, widely attributed to him, *though it does not appear in any of his surviving writings*; even had he formulated it, instead of learning it from the Egyptians as is just as likely, it would not occur to the racist that other civilizations (Babylonian, Egyptian, Chinese, and Indian, to name but a few) may also have had *independent* access to this fundamental theorem of design, topography and mathematics (as we now know they did, and long before Europe). *And of course to selectively incorporate the accomplishments of Mediterranean civilizations to itself, when and where it serves its own self-image, is another spectacular (north) European feint.*

Only slowly are the astonishing—the surprise is wholly gratuitous, of course, and only on account of the wholesale suppression of such information for so long—scientific achievements of non-European societies coming to light; and they give the dispositive lie to European primacy, let alone supremacy. *Human cultures, if they survive at all, anywhere and everywhere, learn to understand the environment they inhabit: as such, the "scientific temper" is an innate anthropic universal.* At any rate, it is salutary to remind ourselves that the most profound discoveries of human evolution: the wheel, the preservation of fire, writing, enumeration, and agriculture, to name but a few of the momentous discoveries of humankind, *predate European science by aeons.*

Far more importantly, though, the rest of the world, *as much as pre-modernist Europe*, has kept this planet habitable for millenia; it is regrettably modern Europe's special destiny, *well in keeping perhaps with its vaunted historical uniqueness*, to terminally threaten, today, that very habitat, ironically in the name of *progress*. In line with the signal insight of Marx in another domain, the *appropriators*, even in this realm, need to be carefully distinguished from the real *producers*. With each passing day, with each new debacle caused by our ignorance of, and trespass on, nature (such as BSE, for example,) we learn of the astonishing perspicuity of *native* science: in health, in nutrition, in ecological responsibility, it is the "savages" who are become now our prime, pressing, even profound tutors.

Modernist science has been radically *reductionist* in both the social and the natural spheres; in the social sciences, the bias took the form of a *reductionist, positivist, and "determinist,"* rational-critical *materialism* as with the imputation of a hostile, competitive, "economic" motivation to all human behaviors, coupled with the pose of "*objectivism*" that is, treating human subjects as manipulable "*objects.*" This posture was to be duplicated also in the approach to "*nature*" objectified and reduced to an inert, passive, and "dead" ontology. Early classical physics, which dominated the sciences between 1600–1925, serving as template for all the sciences, exhibited both the determinism and the reductionism admirably, with Newtonian mechanics implying that physics was all about dead, rock-like things. Under the Quantum inspiration, after 1925, both epistemic and ontic views did change, albeit slowly, with "*indeterminism*" now admitted, with a newly configured nature now stepping "*out of character*" appearing to be composed more of "*thought-like*," though still unconscious "things" but that collapsed, apparently, into rock-like things again, upon observation. Today (i.e., *post*-1995) *post-Quantum* physics has learnt more about the likely "*self-determining*" nature of reality where *coevolving* "rock-like" and "thought-like" things combine, mysteriously, into *living, self-conscious* "things": thereby "*catching up*" only with the cosmology of Vedic and other ancient civilizations. *The idea of conscious, let alone self-conscious, matter defies the suppositions of classical materialism in all its variants, from physics to philosophy to "social science."* Indeed, given adequate comprehension of such post-quantum subtleties, social science might be well persuaded to give up, amongst other affectations, its chronic "physics-envy."

At any rate, the implication of seeing an impassable *apartness* between "*us*" and "*nature*"—in extending a *mechanical* model of the universe to the social as well, whilst believing nature to be "dead" and expendable, as in classical physics—combined with the metaphysics of modernist materialism, spearheaded the long and uninterrupted history of ruthless despoliation which now threatens the very existence of anthropic, and other, life on this planet. Modernist rulers were to subjugate both nature and weaker societal orders as part of the self-same agenda of exploitation. The point may now be summed up: it is not only that various projects embodying violence and domination found their fitting avenue in *modernist* science (a casual perusal of Baconian tracts containing the so-called "Baconian creed" might be illustrative in this regard): *it is that modernist Science was, ab ovo, a project of like nature all by itself.*

(12)

The key turning point in Europe's relations with the rest of the world, and its own past, auguring the modern era, was the Crusades—itself inspiring a new sense of *Trans-European*, if only *Intra-Christian*, identity. The ideas and motivations that informed that extraordinary set of adventures are not apart from the thrust of the so-called Reformation and the Renaissance that followed. From 1095, when the Council of Clermont promulgated launch of the First Crusade under the rhetorical spell of Pope Urban II, to the eventual debacle of the Seventh and Eighth Crusades (1248, 1270, led by Louis IXth of France) opening the way only to the ultimate surrender of all Christian possessions in the Holy Land (Acre, the last possession falling in 1291), much was learnt, and very swiftly, by Europeans about themselves and the *Other* ("*holy war*" colonialism in the Holy Land presaged, eventually, its formidable successor exploits in the non-European world); from an initial *defensive* posture in relation to Islam to a far more self-confident one, even as the commerce of Genoa, Pisa, and Venice flourished in consequence. *Christianity, and its holy wars, energized north Europe long before the Reformation arrived to succor it.*

Only a few steps later, following in its wake, the Enlightenment and the so-called *Industrial Revolution* (far inferior in critical significance to the *metaphysical* revolution that preceded it) completed the subversion of *pre-capitalist* ideologies and practices, aside from institutionalizing the *great meditated divide* between Europeans and non-Europeans as a permanent one. Few turning points could have been more decisive; and few examples could illustrate the change more succinctly than the novel conception of morals and society (as with Hobbes, for example), which evolved to mature into the standard modernist template of "*civil society*" that economics, and related sciences, adopts so faithfully as its starting point.

Suddenly, the *social form* which had served as the organic matrix of social life for millenia, cemented by relations, valorized by memory, and hallowed by custom, was now viewed as a cool, rational, *contractual entity*—a mere instrumental *tool* of a *universal egoism*—involving only selfishly considered *material* reciprocities. Instead of being *the precondition and outcome of all social actions and reactions*, it was now merely the servitor, the shell, and the abstract *nexus* between "rational," meaning calculating, individuals. Few Europeans today can fathom the depth of this extraordinarily *Great Devolution*—whereas any and all non-Europeans still plying on with their inherited social values intact, regardless of the degree of modernist corruption achieved independently, or imposed upon them by grace of their Western masters, can hardly fail to be, even in this late era of European imperium, endlessly stupefied by it.

Such an attitude toward the mainframe could only invite a similar devaluation of the lesser constituent forms; as such, the very basic building block of human society—the *family*—could similarly be viewed as involving only limited, and limiting, contractual, and commercially dischargeable ties (as with the sorry, latter-day reductionisms of economist Gary Becker). Fortunately, thanks to the grace of Creation, only *nature—the grand Ethos that runs in, around, and through all things and non-things*—has barred the way to a wholesale perversion in this regard, and accounts for the endurance of some, however bare, and scant, semblance of *affective* ties such as still endure within the modernist household (European, or otherwise).

Those who, like Levi-Strauss, marvel at the conquest of *nature* by *culture*—and give high praise to Western civilizational accomplishments (despite the *de rigeuer* genuflection toward a putatively "*savage*" mind) in this area—must wonder also, on a daily basis, at the mixed nature of the blessings of such a lonely path to a doubtful grace. The grand conceit of European ideology is to celebrate culture, much like technology, as a sort of a "victory" over nature, another index of its separatist, sublimatory ideology of *anthropocentrism*, as though humans ceased to be of corporal, and mortal, flesh-and-blood organisms, when engaged in their rarefied *social*, but yet *anthropically driven*, interactions. Only in that misbegotten mindset could it have been contemplated, as with late twentieth century British science, to replace nature with a series of advanced photo-biological reactors.

The Levi-Straussian dichotomization of nature and culture, much like the Cartesian *mind-body* divide was yet another characteristic feature of latter day European ideologies (men–women, white–black, occident–orient: the list of *antinomies*, as befitting an ineffable *misanthropy* unbound, is near endless), with their penchant for simple, and simple-minded, oppositions, between essentially *complementary* elements. *It is this narrowly conceived one-sidedness, structurally unable to transcend the divisive limitations of atomization, that still remains the bane of all European world views.*

At any rate, the pernicious grip of the metaphors of commerce and credit, where contracts may be willfully evoked and revoked, inevitably spilled over into the far less contractible areas of social intercourse, perhaps quite "naturally," meaning imperceptibly; but little effort was made, in the European tradition, even by its so-called conservatives, to restrain the repercussions of such an insidious worldview (despite honorable exceptions of yesteryear like Carlyle, Ruskin, Southey, etc.). The inbuilt rot today, of course, with the generalization of the nefarious ideology of modernist economics, under the new guise of "*neo-liberalism*" has gone almost beyond the possibility of redemption. *Nothing exceeds, one might say, like excess.*

Real, *anthropic* society, in all human constructions other than the regressive, if world conquering, model of so-called "*civil society*" just described, is an organic *complexus* of *affective* relations, the precise antinomy of barren, monist, contractual ties based on simple notions of vulgar, *individuated* self-interest (*the modernist fanfare of moving from "status to contract"—as in Maine, for examble,—or, in that same vein, from "ascription to achievement" is both a sham and a gloss: traditional societies have scope for "achievement" much as they have implicit "contracts" that are far more normatively binding than mere "legal" ones; whilst modernist ones quite unabashedly tread heavily on considerations of merit whilst reneging on contractual obligations as self-interest dictates*). It is this feature, once again *pre-given by natural instinct*, that still sustains *familial ties*—even against the onslaught of modernist inversions—as the very last bulwark against a total atomization of the human prospect. *Contra* the pretensions of modernism, the anthropic family is only an extension of the instinctual one and not an interruption of it; and *in that special sense, the social life is merely an ideologically mediated extension of the natural life, not a rejection or suppression of it.*

At any rate, the Crusades marked the early, still gathering spiritual maturity of this grim European resolve to pacify recalcitrant practices, ideologies, and peoples; and a vitally *recharged* Christianity (if in mockery of the mores of the *First Christian*), that followed, was thereby, however fortuitously, the vital prelude to the eventual conquest of the globe and the concomitant restructuration of all societal obligations, inter-societal discourse, and civilizational covenants in their entirety. It was, therefore, squarely within the contours of *religious* struggles that involved *transnational warfare* that Europe discovered both its special identity and its manifest "*destiny*" that was to prove so momentous to the world at large. To that extent, the *secular* historicism of latter day modernism is quite simply misplaced: *Europe vanquished the world owing to its unrivalled and unflagging will and capacity for conquest*—in these attributes it had no pareils, past or present; but even that primordial force of will was underwritten by its own emergent, and indefatigable, sense of *mission.*

Euro-capitalism was fully institutionalized by a wide-ranging panoply of "pre-requisites" away and beyond *the simpliste,* univalent condition of "*wage-labor*": it could become a world conquering force only in conjunction with protocols as diverse and implacable as the domestication of women, the expropriation of peasants, the exploitation of workers, the subjugation of "Other" noncapitalist economies and the confiscation of their wealth, resources and labor, the real and metaphysical "conquest" of nature (inclusive of other animate life forms), the reduction of human reason to materialism, the deracination of the very bonding *logos* and *esprit* of anthropic society, the replacement of religion, morality, and ethics, by "science," the perfection of a racist *weltanschaaung*, the indoctrination into the mores of anthropocentrism and androcentrism, and the warmly embraced inculcation of the "religious" ideology of a god given mission to rule the planet.

These various modes and mechanisms constituted the *élan vital* of the European "ascent"; small wonder such a tall order was simply out of the question for those emulous regimes in the non-European world which tried, quite pathetically, to "measure up" by submitting themselves to modernist catechisms. Easy to see now that Marx and Weber understood and touched, not incorrectly as much as incompletely, only the bare fringes of this great cataclysm in human affairs. Like the poem-parable of the "*Blind Men of Hindostan*" has it, each, with his own specific set of ideological blinders, saw the parts, but missed, in near spectacular elision, the horrific nature of the whole.

Modernism entered this world clutching the grim manifest of *science, materialism and progress* (i.e., "growth") as its ruling collation of *mantras*: Euro-centrism, thereby, is not merely a centering of all epistemes within European ideas, *en generale*, as an unselfconscious form of ethnocentrism, but is a centering of an encompassing world view based on this specific, indeed historically unique, *formula* constituting a veritable "*syndrome of accumulation*." To the extent this ideology is universalized today we are all (barring the eternal exceptions previously identified), more or less, in various shades and measures, Eurocentred in our ambitions, expectations, and approaches to life. In that highly particularistic, if almost tautological, sense, *modernism is Eurocentrism.*

2. The Utopian Impulse: Mnemonics of Affective Society

One of the more enduring feints of modernist ideology is its lofty pose/posture of *liberalism*, pertaining to the economic domain usually, but also extant in some of its varying political moods (free ranging from outright fascism to a more populist republicanism, depending largely, but not exclusively, *on the extant nature of labor supplies*). In the scope of the specific slogans/victories of the French and American Revolutions, Europe prides itself on its demotic and democratic achievements where the political value rests squarely, or so it is believed, on the "*free citizen*" as the fulcrum of consent and legitimization. Viewed in this gratuitously roseate light, *non-European* polities (past and present), *prima facie*, appear, in contrast, to be abject tyrannies, symptomatic of one or other variant of "*oriental despotism*," another stock obloquy of the enlightenment.

It would be utterly facile, of course, in any serious discourse, to attach credence to such *simpliste* vulgarizations; not being radically *individuated*, and isolated like the typical (i.e., modernist) European, the *non-European*, enmeshed within the *healing bondage* of customary ties, had never, until benighted by modernism, felt any great interest in being thus "*set free*"—that is, *to live and die alone*. The fulsome pride that modernism takes in "individuation"—often setting it up as a high "moral" ideal—is a grievous, even tragic error: *in all human society, inclusive of the most communitarian forms such as tribes, we exist simultaneously both as individuals and as social entities*. Modernism cultivates the one at the virtual expense of the wholesale deracination of the other—thereby severing the social tie *virtually entirely*.

Indeed, the shoe needs be, pointedly, on the other foot. The centrality of an ever interventionist stance of *etatisme*—the very *leitmotiv* of the

European "ascent": from the *absolutist* state that ushered in the modern era of capitalism, much as its successor, the "liberal" state, that was charged by figures as unlike each other as Napoleon and John Stuart Mill with fulfilling the task(s) of human emancipation—to the "progressivist" ideology of modernism is simply indisputable. The European motto has been—and most latter day imperialist interventions in the peripheral world are justified in similar terms—, to quote the prosaic Rousseau: to "*force people to be free*" (we might well title this modernist *Buonapartism*). Even the great John Stuart Mill, in his otherwise passionate, even classic essay on liberty, could readily give his free assent to this first canon of fascism and imperialism alike: it was seen as altogether justifiable to use the might of the state, that is, *brute violence*, to achieve putatively higher order values such as "progress" and "liberty," as understood, that is, by such self-styled lawgivers. That this didn't strike these august framers of constitutions (for others!) as even mildly paradoxical, given the hiatus between the merely noble-*sounding* ends as opposed to the rather patently *ignoble* means, is a fitting tribute to their fundamentally intolerant, unethical, power-driven, and singleminded *zealotry*.

The intellectual *absolutism* that underlies such views may readily be ascertained: *a few were giving themselves the unilateral right to decide for the many* (as indeed Europeans have done for the rest of the world, the seventeenth century onwards). That this pose would *ipso facto* rule out any conception of respect for cultural *difference*, let alone social *autonomy*, did little to daunt their fierce, *monovalent* enthusiasm. In this respect, the modernist slaughterers can hardly claim moral high ground over the ritually disparaged likes of an Attila or a Genghis Khan (when such marauders hail from the "west," they are suitably dignified by grandiose titles; consider just the *tone* of *Attila the Hun* versus Alexander the "*Great*"), particularly in face of the latter's tolerance in the religious and cultural sphere which stands in high relief and in marked contrast to the modernist European totalitarians. At any rate, the *state*, increasingly occupying an abstract, alien, and repressive public space, was blithely charged with performing *nurturing* functions traditionally allocated, in more civil social formations, to *social* ties. Odd indeed that that paradigmatic "individualist" heaven—the United States—requires the maintenance and continuous, annual enlargement, of the *largest structure(s) of state power ever built on the face of this planet*.

The glaring fact that ethnic and religious (or political) minorities were not to share in the slim benefits of individual rights also did precious little to desecrate or debunk these myths. The U.S. constitution (at least some of its, typically unacknowledged, inspiration coming from the great Iroquois confederation that the white conquistadores overran) of "free-born men" was cheerfully consistent with *real*, not metaphorical, *slavery*, even as it was being drafted—much as the Swiss could feign democracy right until the 1980s, while denying *women* formal membership in the polity. Outright blindness, coupled with rank prejudice—such was the burden of modernist rationalism in the political sphere. Typically, all the liberties insecurely and unevenly possessed by the many today (despite the growing inroads of the *techno-fascist* impulse) remain hard won rights claimed—*and still in ever grave need of defense—against* the extant systems of wealth and power, not *because* of them; this as true, of course, for European, much as non-European, but *modernist*, polities. At any rate, the striking fact about *post-enlightenment* ideology is precisely the ubiquity of its generalized state of *structural violence*, anomalously and insecurely located in the highly chimerical peace of civil society, permanently aimed, as it is, against women, workers, and ethnic, religious, and cultural minorities.

In all stark and scandalous simplicity, a few rich and powerful white men set out to tame and subdue the world, confiscating, in the name of civilization and liberty, the birthright of peoples to be *self-directed* and free. *No other minority band of marauders in history has ever been so successful on such an epic scale, in such a short period of time.* Even more astonishing is the encompassing manner in which this facile conquest was ably, even brilliantly, disguised so the *victims*—to this day—remain all but unaware of their own enduring oppressions. It is necessary to note the *reification of domination* achieved in modernist ideology: we can solemnly believe as "constitutionalists" that it was the "US Supreme Court" whose judicial wisdom cut through the impasse of a near dead-heat electoral vote by setting aside an ongoing recount rather than the simple, "deconstructed" truth that less than a dozen, mostly white, elite, men and women, Republican appointees and/or sympathizers, used their statutory power to "elect" George Bush II all by themselves; *the issue is not whom they chose—the issue is the institutional cover of legitimacy provided* for private political agendas to operate behind and within the system of "justice."

In effect, European liberalism was, and still is, an elaborate, effective, overarching ideology of world conquest; in much the same way the bible travelled importunately ahead to pacify the natives prior to the less decorous arrival of carpetbaggers and cannon, liberal progressivism was to numb a capitulating, if still largely uncomprehending, world into a near permanent aphasia of spirit. The unspeakable atrocities of the Belgians in the Congo, Americans in Vietnam, the English in Bengal, and the Spanish in the New World are all cut of the same, wretched, self-righteous, imperial cloth.

As such, it is quite futile today to accept any/all European political categories—*left, right, and centre, or liberal, conservative, or radical*—as constituting genuine *alternatives* to the modernist way; indeed, taken together, *they are the modernist way*. Whilst the conservative steadily stokes the baseline, recreant fires of modernism, the liberal stays for the ride distributing prophylactics against any *real* that is, serious rejection of the great modernist machine. To this day, the true obstacles to a reawakening self-recognition amongst non-Europeans (and the victims of modernization *within* European poles) are, far more than the usual run of material hurdles, the innumerable *ideational traps* of Western liberalism and radicalism, both of which demand the willing subordination of native/traditional manners, and mores, in favor of a sallow dependence on the hegemonic political/ideological traditions of modernist Europe.

The various classes of intelligentsia that participate in such processes (specially the commodity-fetishizing part of it) remain unconscious *neo-colonials*, regardless of political hue, still serving to maintain a permanent European bridgehead—aimed like a dagger at the heart of their societies—in their domestic backyards, a form of direct intellectual occupation that is even more effective (for being cheaper and easier) than a traditionalist landing of the ever-present Marines. Their eventual payment of dues, for such injudicious capitulation at the *individual* level, is even more bitter and painful as the real, inherited social matrix of cheer and benignity slowly recedes, in the face of the encroachments of such ideologies, leaving him/her hopelessly marooned in the modernist wasteland of a lightless sea of commodities.

Paradoxically—indeed a great irony of history—those ingenuously espousing recalcitrant and refractory *native* traditions, *the only provenance of an ultimate rejection of modernism*, are precisely the ones libelled by modernist ideology as archaic, atavistic *reactionaries*, thereby enshrining, within the secure bosom of the modernist, virtually anywhere on earth today, the specifically European image of itself as *the locus of all economic correctness and political virtue*, that is, of progressivism and human rights. All the culturally based *revivalist* movements in the non-European world today (inclusive of *anti-modernist* movements within European metropoles), reacting to the deadening force of European modernism, are blindly branded as retrograde by the elites commanding the modernist polity in these formations—liberal or "left-wing" as the case may be—thereby colluding with the colonial European viewpoint, with not the slightest effort invested in understanding their real, *historical* significance within the *ex-colonial*, but still *neo-colonial*, enclaves and/or societies.

For all their lack of sophistication, such "nativist" movements represent the slow, painful awakening of an independent *self-awareness*, and search for an authentic inner identity on the part of long suppressed cultures, and sub-cultures, from their extended colonial nightmare of ridicule and erasure of indigenous histories, much as they are the inevitable defenses against the more current genre of neoliberalist offensives foisting fabricated, vapid, and hollow ideologies of industrial consumerism worldwide; their time is nigh, and may, surely, not be elided. To state the *moral* simply: *all European political traditions serve only the Modernist Project, in greater or lesser degree; we need to break with their logics, not in part, but in toto—before they break us.*

Important perhaps also to descry that *political* liberalism, contrary to most interpreters including Marxians, did not develop as the *secular* antidote to the absolutism of the *state*, as often projected in modernist discourse, but much earlier in *religious* antagonism to the absolutism, not of the state, but of the *papacy*. As such, oddly enough (and against the stream of the comforting fables of liberal historiography) it is to early *Christian ideology*, again, that we owe the originating impetus of *Euro-liberal* ideas: the relatively obscure Marsilio of Padua, and William of Occam, and others of that ilk, in resisting papal absolutism, originally set in motion the so-called "*liberal*" current, as early as the fourteenth century, long before the far more celebrated Locke and the splendiferous *genii* of the French Revolution took to the field armed with animadversion and invective.

In this vital regard, to be religious (i.e., *Christian*) and to be secular *simultaneously* was the sole privilege of Europeans; in effect, the non-European world was sold a version of secularism that yet safely preserved, and safely reinterpreted *Christian* values. In fact, the European "Reformation" *modernized* and *Westernized* an *eastern* religion, that is, stood it on its head, to the point where it was scarce recognizable. Stated differently, Euro-modernism preserved much of the preexisting, and received, *Euro-traditions*; this select generosity (toward the preservation of *some* Euro-traditions), was not to be extended to the *non-European* vassals of modernism who were compelled, in effect, to reject their own ancestral heritage, *in toto*. At any rate, in the modernist viewpoint, quite unmindful of such subtleties, *Christianity* (as safely *reinterpreted*) *is secularism.*

(14)

Where did European *culture*—as the term is understood today by Europeans—derive from? To modernist Europe's own cherished contentment—that is, within its own *myths of origin* so to speak—Greece is the favored cradle of its proud civilization: a strange supposition for those acquainted with even a preliminary sketch of civilizational, as opposed to *political*, histories. Mercifully, in the gracious works of the early classical Greeks themselves, very little of such self-centred pontification may be discovered; indeed, the self-acknowledged debt of the Greeks to Egyptian civilization, and its culture capital—*Alexandria*—was, in the main, refreshingly free, open, and uncritical. Although today assimilated within the *chauvinist* European mould, Greece, like Egypt, was effectively a *Mediterranean Civilization*—and one should resist incorporating *Mediterranean* civilities into the *North European* context of the glaring *absence* of such phenomena. *The north European pirated Mediterranean ideas much as he plundered non-European domains*—and *Egypt was the mature fount of this civility*, even as the Greeks were, under Egyptian tutelage, learning first and refining later their rudiments of cosmology, statecraft, and science.

On the other hand, the scholarship of Egypt was itself liberally fertilized by seminal ideas originating in India and China, themselves long opulent in the practical and theoretical sciences. Greek outlooks were shaped in that great melting pot of *antiquity*, with Egypt as the delivery point of new ideas (a role only *later* to be assumed by Greece); but this was a *Nubian* Egypt, a *black* African civilization. Curious indeed that *white* European cultures, much as their traditions of science, should have derived, however unwittingly, from rich traditions emanating from Black Africa, the land that the great Hegel, in line with late European prejudice, would claim to be only at the stage of the "primal *infancy*" of humankind ! To the extent that Greek culture was built upon Egyptian founts, *European civilization is the indirect offshoot of Black Africa*, although, again, it's still a case of *North European piracy of Mediterranean niceties*. Add to this the anthropological fact that *homo sapiens* probably evolved out of Africa, prior to migrating out to Europe and Australasia and we get a full measure of the much vaunted "*European*" primacy.

All of this is only a small, if relatively unknown, part of a *Great Story* that still remains to be researched, written and told by generations of independent scholarship yet to come. Just one other minor part—a case in point—even more obscured by ethnocentric European scholarship, is the specific linguistic contribution of *Vedic* India (not to be loosely confused with the *political* entity that is modern India today): *as is well known, Sanskrit is the mother language to several so-called "European" languages* (the term "*Indo-European*" is a canny bit of fudging, adding a European suffix to an otherwise *independent* term). The full implications of this linguistic paternalism of classical *"Aryan"* (i.e., *Vedic*) culture to the development of the European psyche has rarely been explored with any degree of merit. It is suffice to suggest that, as with the Gypsies, that are now firmly believed to have originated in northwestern India, many European tribes also owe their cultural origins/evolution to the engendering, and enriching matrix of the Indus Valley civilization. The fact that even European myths of their putatively "*Caucasian*" heritage place its origins oft-times in the elysian Vale for Kashmir is food for thought in this regard.

As such, it may well be safe to speculate (*and this is only educated speculation)—as a necessary epistemic balance against the self-serving speculations of European scholarship in another direction—that the so-called "Caucasian," the ruling demiurge of this planet today, derives in part civilizationally (aside from his African roots) from the seminal troves of the Aryan "India" of Vedic Antiquity, and not from some mythical "Central European" zone* as designated in the many received variants of the modernist tradition. *Language is not merely a "medium" of communication: it embodies within itself the very abiding nucleus of cultural norms*—self-titled *Europeans* could not have "*shared*" a linguistic structure fortuitously without carrying as coevals, in a *Wittgensteinian* sense, many of its concomitants with them.

What a profound, if fitting, irony that the English conquistadores arrived in latter-day India, lofty and superior, but speaking a *Vedic* language; one has only to compare, linguistically speaking, the sublime order of Sanskrit with the arbitrary fickleness, and maladroit idiosyncrasies, of the English language to assess quite swiftly, in simple logical terms alone, the issue of "superiority" (for those to whom such a hierarchy is important to establish!). Wisdom from Africa; languages, even so-called "modern" *mathematical analysis* (everything from logarithms, to calculus, to set theory), normally *arrogated to Europeans by Europeans* but which dates, incidentally, *centuries* prior, among others, to the brilliant work of mathematicians such as Madhava, from the southern state of Kerala in India. Already, it might seem, "Europe" starts to dwindle in independent significance to its more appropriate placement on the civilizational scale.

Perhaps, speaking speculatively, given only its lapidary lateness, and fledgling status as a civilizational player on the stage of world history did it become incumbent upon the European psyche to conquer the world so as to establish (by way of convincing itself) a self-proclaimed and rather unself-confident "superiority." As the noble Gandhi once told a Western journalist, in the midst of the carnage of "World War II," only half-jokingly, "*Western civilization*" would be, if introduced at all, a "*very good idea*" (and it remains so still—not merely as a pious hope, but as a fervent prayer, if this planet is to be preserved, for now more than ever *the European is its principal, if radically irresponsible, custodian*), fully aware that *the rise of modernism had extinguished the very possibility* of a *European* civilization (other than the preexisting civility of its *internal, and eternal, "Other": women, workers, and native peoples engrossed in their perennial moral economies*).

In fact, given the penchant of European historians to contentedly attribute a central *European* homeland to the so-called *Aryans*, believed to have authored *Sanskritic* civilization, the putative "*Caucasians*" (a self-designation in the United States of peoples of European, white, descent mythically originating from the "Caucusus Mountains"), if such a category is real at all, might well have originated in the Vedic geo-cultural perimeter, rather than elsewhere, a hypothesis that may only be satisfactorily researched by a new generation of *non-Eurocentred* scholarship freed from the bonds of Western tutelage and presuppositions. Even further—and far less speculatively—European accounts of the *dating* of Vedic civilization, and their handling of the *primacy of Sanskrit*, needs be set aside, or at least critically reevaluated; as and when the real facts appear, employing perhaps *astronomical*, instead of *ideological*, dating and data, it is conceivable that the *antiquity* of the Vedic period would be pushed back by millennia highlighting its originality even more effectively: and *Europe, incidentally, would, then, be revealed as a rather late riser in the universal scheme of things.*

Even received biblical accounts of the life of Christ himself may be in real need of amendment (the Books of the so-called *Apocrypha* edited out in later editions of the classical Bible themselves raise some oblique questions in this regard as to the received view). A growing strain of increasingly serious scholarship points to the significant travels of the historical Jesus of Nazareth in various regions of India, Tibet and, possibly, even China: even more startlingly, many accounts point to his final entombment in the empyrean vale of Kashmir, gainsaying the legend of his expiry on the cross, wherein a mausoleum bearing his Aramaic name—*Isa*—still exists. The challenge this set of facts, if fully confirmed, poses to received Eurocentred *theology* on the life of Jesus, and the provenance of his many ideas, may well be imagined. Not merely modernist science but modernist *theology* also may be in need of some vital correction(s).

It is perhaps given such haunting visions of the *real* placement of Europe in history that there exists such a powerful need amongst Europeans, and their cultural dependencies—matched in its scale of self-conscious *exclusivism* today only by the *equally materialist*, but far more self-confident, modern China (in many senses China is the ultimate, the perennial, and perhaps even the providential, *antipode* of Europe)—to maintain an array of nuclear warheads far ahead of any real "*defense*" needs (the continued existence of NATO today, with the wholesale disappearance of any/all cold war provocations, is a powerful index of the old European ambition of an *armed camp of Europeans* standing tall against the non-European world). It helps maintain and secure, in real terms, their requisite *illusion of separateness and superiority*—at least in one, base, misanthropic, sphere if in the face of severely recalcitrant cultural and social facts of plain dependence and laggardness.

At any rate, the Enlightenment produced, in near final form, the now consecrated myth of European *priority* in all the sciences, from "discovery" of putative "Pythagorean" theorems to the principle of gravitation (despite their patent, even abject, falsity), a prepossession that grew stronger and bolder with their colonial conquests of non-European peoples; *alternative explanations could only abide if alternatives had a voice, space, and identity of their own* (such autonomies, on the rise since the process of formal *decolonization*, are, ominously, once again being stilled today by the advancing onslaughts of the global agenda of *neo-liberalism*). At any rate, suffice to say that European self-assurance grew proportionately with their carefully cultivated, and self-induced, hebetude about the nature and meaning of civilizations other than their own, once the latter had been safely conquered.

As against this arrogance, it may well be instructive to indicate *that there is no major idea originating in the European Enlightenment, whether in science or in philosophy, that had not been anticipated, somewhere or other, in the reflections of Other, preceding, civilizations* (or even in Europe's own distinguished *premodernist traditions*: such as that of the ancient *Celts*, for example, itself but one of many such). From the "discovery" of gravity, or the principle of the circulation of blood, and many such other ephemera, non-European *precursors* exist, only to be gratuitously ignored by European histories, and historians, of science.

Similarly, only by wilfully ignoring and/or suppressing ancient lineages in the philosophical evolution of humankind can we eulogize, as in European tradition, the work of a Kant, a Descartes, or a Hegel, as inaugurating *nouvelle* ideas in the history of humankind, *de novo*, which is the symmetrical complement of believing philosophy to have *originated* with the likes of Plato and Aristotle. The myths of *Eurocentrism* are legion; from claims of scientific and technological priority, to peerless prowess in moral and physical accomplishments: and they are, one and all, a spectacular sham. *Histories are written, wily nilly, by conquerors*: and since the European was to excel in that latter department as no other, they could only script their fantastic confabulations in a very fine frenzy.

(15)

Five hundred years after the Crusades, that energized a subcontinent, and connected it to the vital commerce of the Mediterranean, an ill-developed, rough-hewn, peasant society of bickering warlords transformed itself, by guile, force, skill, and an iron determination (which would be admirable were its motives less murky) into a modernist social formation vested with the ominously incendiary potential to transform the world. Struggles between secular and clerical barons (other than peasant revolutions at least partly inspired by the insecurities at the political apex), were possibly the operative media for the historical transitions that were to prove so momentous, *but only at the last remove.* Religion, as Namier observed a long time ago, was a sixteenth century name for *nationalism*; but it was also more, much more than that—it was, additionally, the powerful, sublating force for cross-national and supranational bondings.

The ideological unity of *Euro-feudalism* was always *doctrinal,* even where the church was unable to directly exercise total political and military domination. Of course, all this is confirmed in the so-called Reformation itself which, although technically a doctrinal dispute within the Church, dragged into the maelstrom of conflict, national, tribal, baronial, and class ambitions. Marx was right when he wrote that religion was the dominant social force in medieval Europe, although his epigones were to dissolve this vital insight in the fetid swamp of barren materialist dialectics.

In this important sense, the Reformation not only preceded the Enlightenment chronologically but was one of its operative stimuli (the other being the colossal, and *quite unilateral, transfer of values,* including ideational ones, in the *Great Colonial Encounter*); prior to the latter divide, European intellectual and philosophical debates were all purely doctrinal debates within Christian ideology. The new *secularism* of the Enlightenment was principally a position aimed at the Church (a *pre-Modernist* church that, for all its varied corruptions, still held nominally to the "classical" messages of Christ which proved so inutile and obstructionist to incipient modernist motivations) so as to divest it of a direct, and determining, role in political and societal matters. Accordingly, late European secularism, in its formative stages, was never based on any serious adoption of *agnosticism,* as for instance in many ancient Vedic or post-Vedic philosophical systems loosely connected with Hinduism; rather, it was, in the main a matter of a simple *delineation of domains.*

The much vaunted modernist separation of Church and State was, therefore, only that: *a politic division of domain between secular and ecclesiastical ruling elites*; it didn't imply any real derogation of the role of the Church, now granted valency in a domain autonomous (somewhat on the lines of a Kantian separation of domains between *phenomena* and *noumena*), except among fringe groups. *The fact that the true Calvinist saw his strictly acquisitive activities as the preferred means of serving God is illustrative of the dominance of an exclusively Christian ethic within the very bosom of the bourgeois revolution, normally thought to be independent of such influences.*

This is a highly important fact elided systematically by secular historians, a pretermission that obscures many vital clues to the *logos* of capitalist development. The unsplendid merchant ship and gunboat—trade and flag—are well documented in such histories; the fact that the cross was never too far behind either to be entirely obscured is what makes the process so highly significant. Cadences of Moses and the prophets informed all European expansions to the extent that *the Judeo-Christian ethic (in its revised form) was the unwritten code of European culture that informed all its actions and reactions.* It was the unique, pragmatic and *venturist* secularism of this "reformed" Christianity that made it such an all conquering global force.

It is this important fact that separates Europe from its clones and near-clones within its multiplex dependencies; with some exaggeration it may be usefully said that *European capitalism was merely the secular, temporal form of an activist, expansionary, missionary, and zealous* (though reformulated) *Christianity*: as such, Europe could, without contradiction, maintain a happy, if quite dubious, continuity within Judeo-Christian traditions—that is, with its own *past*—while still serving as the proud exemplar of secular progress. In contrast, Non-Europeans could only be rational and capitalist by dint of *denying* their received culture, heritage, and religion(s).

The dilemma is painfully tragic: the non-European participates in global capitalism today only by means of a crippling trial of various *rites of passage* of self-denial and identity rejection; that is, in her case a new, and artificial, cultural identity has to be created, but strictly on the lines of a template that is European in provenance. The implications of this for character building, self-expression, and self-confidence, can well be imagined; and the eternal dependency on European culture for philosophical and cultural expression—despite cultural and political feints to the contrary—is easily visible in those ex-colonial dependencies that were, and/or remain, closest in tutelage to European capital, for example, Thailand, erstwhile Hong Kong, Singapore, *etc.*

Indeed, reverting to the colonial era, the picture gets even starker when it is noted that even to be treated nominally as a *second class subject*, formal membership of the Christian church was quite often a necessary prerequisite (many converts to Christianity during the colonial era served eagerly as a *buffer* between colonizer and colonized, earning the gratitude of neither). The gathering Islamic storm of the current period, potentially as important as the global Euro-crusade of Neoliberalism, if aimed in an opposite direction, the portentous *bellwether* of more such revolts to follow, is an indication of the growing rejection of European modernist values amongst at least some of Europe's dependencies and ex-colonies: as such, the Crusades are now being re-fought, if as yet only on a cultural plane, all over again. The real war between Europeans and non-Europeans, then as now, despite the many economic and political mediations, was perhaps always purely a deeply cultural, and philosophical, one. At any rate, classic European colonialism was as much driven by the fires of *moral* (however *amoral*, or even immoral in content), much as *material*, passions.

(16)

It is only in the modern epoch that Europeans thought warmly of themselves as embodying "*progress*" in all spheres of life: science, culture, the arts, technologies, and so on. The idea of *change*, and particularly change for the "better," evolved in the crucible of its revolutionary epoch, was to be enshrined in popular ideology almost as a motto, both social and personal; between the classical conservative and the liberal, the struggle, dubious as it was, was not the whether/why of change but simply the pace and trajectory of the changes involved. Columbus' facile and remorseless extirpations of the hapless aboriginals of central America, to be duplicated by others similarly poised, enhanced the gathering European sense of their own superiority, in the material/military sphere first, and then, by extension, to all domains afterwards. The wealth (material and scientific) and cultural splendors of India and China, that had held previous generations of Europeans in thrall, were suddenly devalued, and transmogrified into dross, when it was discovered how artlessly they could be conquered, subjugated, and pressed into servitude and/or into unfavorable treaties of commerce.

Progress, as per European self-definitions, was self assuredly assumed to be a European commodity in sole ownership; "*Other cultures*" were, in contrast, so savage and barbarian such that a veritable *nouvelle* science—"*anthropology*"—had to be developed to study their idiosyncrasies, much as the globe's flora and fauna, anywhere and everywhere, had previously come under painstaking technical scrutiny in the hungry search for commercial advantage. Even when not directly a tool of imperial expansion, the very motivation to study "*others*" was a nefarious one; the European was not seeking information out of any empyrean love of knowledge of the opulent diversity of the peoples of this planet, but rather, an accurate, if

Machiavellian, measure of the alleged *distance* between himself and other species (indeed one of the original impulses of European anthropology was to establish a classification of the *appropriate* "hierarchy" between the "races").

If Darwinian ideas quite unexpectedly, and virtually irrefutably, pledged the indelible *connection* between the European and other species, much to popular chagrin, anthropology could still provide a levelling, *counteractive* measure of the *evolutionary dissonance/distance* between Europe and other continents. Progress was not merely a capitalist measure of the *marketization* and *capitalization* of productive forces, but also a contented European evaluation of the superior legacy of *whiteness* (in an otherwise gratefully *colorful* world).

Not only were Europeans the best; they were getting better all the time (Condorcet, Turgot, Tylor, Frazer, Morgan, Lubbock, Maine, Durkheim, Spencer—the list of canonical figures in the modernist tradition, in spirit similarly imbued, is monotonously endless in this tendentious project), ever increasing their social and temporal distance from others. Such was the real meaning of the *progressivist* current of the Enlightenment; but, tragically, for others, the Europeans were not prone to rest content within their borders with their smug, if also *sullen*, *apartness*, which might have served the cause of humanity admirably—instead, a consumptive sense of apparent (and manifest) *destiny* would propel them to seek to "*uplift*," perforce, the less fortunate under the guise of the notion of the *white man's burden*.

Only partly was this the *excuse* for colonial conquest, no matter how insistent mercantile interests might have been; the true faith that delivered colonialism, as state policy, *contra* materialist explanations, was a fairly widespread determination that the white man truly had a god-given mission to civilize and save the world, an idea which still flourishes, if only implicitly, in all European social formations. Of course, today, the G8 nations, if one ignores the highly marginal and anomalous role of Japan in its midst, who virtually dictate global policies along with their Transnational Corporate entities, enshrine this hoary vision in the reality of Europe's ownership and/or control over the world's resources and populations. European dreams of global conquest, from its humble beginnings, have only now, in this dangerous new millennium, come to an awesome fruition.

The other side to progressivism as *state ideology* was the restless effulgence of Europeans expressing their ritualized discontent in the continuous transformation of all things, and many *non-things*. The *technological fetishism* that marks the current epoch of the *fabricated* capitalist cultural milieu (and its political correlate of *Techno-fascism*) is not merely the inevitable concomitant of the trajectory of capitalist competition, but a vital form of self expression of this very discontent. *When the soul is not at rest, it seeks perpetual change in its total environs*; hence the need in European society—not at all the case in equally capitalist but *non-European* formations—to endlessly reinvent and redesign identity, personality, and ego, seeking rest but unable to find it in their chosen avenues of expression and dialogue. To define this hopeless effulgence, and its various expressions, stemming from an essential lack of peace, as but so many venerable *momenta* on the uplifting path *to progress* is, of course, another grandiose delusion of modernism.

Recognizing no higher ends in themselves—matters confined to the dustbins of history earlier on—all things and non-things, can only serve as means to another set of means; given this infinite regress, social forms become devoid of *content*, that is, become, quite literally, *meaningless*. The senselessness of many varieties of crime in the United States today, and the catastrophic emptiness of daily life when not connected, indeed crammed, with commodities, reflect *this absence of a center of cultural gravity to all institutions*, all stripped of their affective, human content, and instead rendered cold, rational, and calculable—but, alas, also profoundly unfulfilling.

Progress required a shining standard: Europe provided its own modernist institutions as such a gleaming benchmark. It required a touchstone, and a materialist ideology delivered continuing, unstinted capital accumulation as synonymous with the welfare of this world and its peoples. It required an enduring merit badge of abject failure to set off its own supernal success in high relief, and so the non-European "Other" was duly wrapped in the black flag of the permanent disgrace of (an ill-conceived and miscalculated) underachievement.

(17)

Few European ideas have greater currency today than the ideology of near-absolute personal freedom and liberty, also developed during the era of the Enlightenment and worked into secular religion by the reckless ilk of John Stuart Mill and Spencer. In its uniquely capitalist form, it boils down usually to the freedom of trade or/and freedom of investor/consumer choice, upon which the carefully constructed structure of all other, quite secondary, freedoms rest. Although the energetic partisans of the idea had little awareness of this insight, essentially the European notion of freedom was *release* not from social, but *moral* restraints (the *defining* artefact of precapitalist, premodernist, social formations); the *real* opposition that European individualism generates is not between the *individual* and *society*, as mistakenly argued by Marxists and various materialists, *but between wilfully asocial individuals and extant canons of culturally mediated morality*. Individualism was but another name for the sacralized abandonment, acquittance, and abnegation of *co-respective* responsibilities for one's fellow creatures (to say nothing of the now haplessly *dependent* species, and all the "*other*" planetary life forms).

Conventionally given morality and ethics set bounds to all actions, social and personal; in trying to shake itself loose from such inexpugnable restraints, the European was to take a fateful step on the possibly irreversible path of dissolution of all social ties. *Societies are not "contractual" entities, as the squalid soothsayers of the Enlightenment would have it, but moral organisms* (much like the family, tribe, etc.) *grounded in the arcana of anthropic evolution*; once the moral cement is eroded, systematically as in the case of Europe, the social loses its efficacy as a *totality* involving, as it does, a delicately balanced set of rights and responsibilities. In place of the *positive responsibility* of a moral society, enshrined in its unwritten codes, the European invented, with much fanfare, the *negative dialectic* of modern law—enjoining one merely not to endanger the property and person of others (except when the ruling caste, class, and state had need to do just that). Consensus, based on felicity, trust and fellowship, on the other hand, has no need for "contracts" (or passionless pieties inscribed permanently on parchment).

The striking difference between European and non-European concepts of *liberty* lies in the material fact that *non-Europeans* still possess (though in ever diminishing degree) a culturally sanctioned, if politically mediated, notion of *freedom* that is often far more permissive (compare, e.g., the genuine *anarchy* of rural Indian every-day life to its American counterpart to get a measure of this "laxity") than its European equivalent. In the case of Europe, this normative culture of creatively inchoate *traditional* liberties was eradicated as a force and carefully replaced by the precisely delineated, and hence supremely *repressive*, *formalisms* of *capitalist* law and order, by the modernist revolution, so that freedom could be constitutionally confined to the abiding and indefectible context of capital accumulation.

The critical *psychic surplus*, of *freedom from definition*, so symptomatic a condition of simple societies, was being captured by the *annexationist* impulse of corporate modernism. Stated differently, to leave freedom *undefined* might have run the risk of thwarting accumulation as a process (cultural *resistance* to the normal processes of capitalist accumulation is a multi-faceted, near universal disposition, in *all* world cultures not succumbed to the wares of a *fabricated, industrialist, mass culture*; industrialization and proletarianization were resisted, even in Europe, by a strong sense not merely of material dispossession but of an even stronger sense of unacceptable encroachments on preexisting liberties): any such possibility of a *populist* definition of freedom, as, say, with the Diggers and Levellers of the English Revolution, had, therefore, to be rejected *a priori.*

Viewed this way, putatively *democratic* constitutions, the pride of modernist America and Europe, are not the openly *enabling* instruments of popular imagination, but are, in principle, supremely *annexationist* organs, and are, to that extent, profoundly *conservative* in intent and agency. When constitutions, brimming over with recondite ideas, designed by elite professionals, take precedence over culturally mandated, evolutionary, comprehensible, and living norms, the promise of an artificial, barren, cold, and *anomic* social ordering (where formal "laws" are made by a few and sullenly accepted by the many)—as per the apocalyptic vision of classical Hobbesian misanthropy—becomes strictly, and severely, fulfilled.

However, it is necessary to point out a dialectic here; the very fact of denying cultural specificity has the self-fulfilling effect of destroying it, and leaving a vacuum that may be filled as easily with beer as with Beethoven (culturally, this is about the average measure of *consumptive distance* between modernist elites and nonelites). The corollary of the wholesale denigration of *values* (as in latter-day America, a veritable wasteland in this regard) is, in effect, a vital ignorance of the *value of values* itself; from being an essentialist heirarchical ordering, values then become horizontally placed on an undulating standard of equivalence (as in the notorious, Benthamite, "pushpin is as good as poetry" idea). This leveling downwards "race to the bottom," in manners and mores, is then proudly exhibited as embodying "democratic" ideals thereby making a virtue out of an abject debasement.

As such, the historical *closure* to social innovation thoughtfully attempted with, by, and through *written* constitutions is, ultimately, a weak and vapid one; when people are demystified and/or enraged sufficiently, constitutions, like money under hyperinflations, are instantly devalued. Lacking any special sanctity in a *desacralized* world, as compared with the hallowed sanctity of age-old, customary, cultural restraints, they present empty armor against any real social change *that, however, now perforce has to be extra-constitutional and eruptive by its very nature.* It is this that makes a modernist society perpetually *entropic* as against the inherent *co-respective,* and long-enduring stability of the tribal formation.

The rational, formal, *depersonalization* of modern society makes of it an empty shell that can neither sustain nor succor those it seeks to confine permanently within its intrusive and enclosionary bounds. And, as such, the grim repression of the *rational-modernist* grid stands put to invite only a spontaneously lit cataclysmic upheaval as the *modus* of any real, substantive change aimed against its corruptive *logos*. Few modernist citizens can be presumed to go contentedly to their graves clutching copies of their constitutions; the *real* social contract, in human history, has always been a deeply emotive, not an empty formalist one. *Afghan tribals are* (i.e. constitute) *an organic society, no matter how rent with conflict; modern Americans are not, despite a more than equivalent level of strife.*

Precisely *contra* the hallucinations of a Durkheim, the so-called "*organic solidarity*" of modern society, is only a shell compared to the ontic depth of what he despised as "*mechanical*" solidarity. *The "division of labor," once generalized on the basis of an engineered "civil" society, spells the certain extinction of the "moral" society.* The great Adam Smith, who understood this difference, nonetheless, couldn't bring himself to accept the notion that *empathy* (as vividly described in his *Theory of Moral Sentiments*) could collate within itself, as in tribal society, the necessary premises of the economic (i.e., *material*) life. Thus European materialism was to create and maintain a social form, in line with the deleterious precepts of the *Wealth of Nations*, where wealth could safely be amassed apart, and away, from the gestational values of nurturance, altruism, and affection.

(18)

One great contribution of the Enlightenment to the modernist outlook was the ideology of abstract equality—*egalitarianism*—which, despite (or perhaps because of) its ubiquitous defaults in *praxis* remains yet an inspirational, if ultimately pharisaic, political idea (or, to lend it a degree of realism, a "*political formula*," as Mosca might have termed it). The fact that this ideology arose as a dissembling slogan on the part of classes duly disinherited by the *ancien regime*, and the fact that the very same classes employing the slogan, in all revolutionary enthusiasm, were to go on, similarly, to deny it to lower orders when they, in turn, seized power is little discussed today. Just like vulgarized Calvinism, and the notion of the "White Man's Burden," the doctrine of equality is around simply for having been around; steeped in self-congratulatory idioms as they are, few amongst the modernists today reflectively query the issue of the real-life existence of the empirical basis/counterparts of their own beliefs (it would be far too traumatic to discover the vacuous truth therein).

It remains something of a mystery how such an ideology can survive in the face of such strong, daily doses of, empirical confutation by the elementary facts of the capitalist life. In the United States, where differentials of wealth and power now bid fair to exceed the degree of skew amongst the very poorest of peripheral economies today, and every bit as ugly to the naked eye, the ideology is perhaps the strongest; and yet in the modernist outlook, a dumb, child-like faith in the ideology is the effective substitute for any project of serious, concrete, empirical steps to achieve/attain it (there are no presidential or royal commissions charged with the missions of achieving "equality," "freedom," or any other such bunkum). On such flimsy *ontic* grounds, the Europhile can routinely decry the tawdry heirarchies of non-European societies for not subscribing to this defining *mantra* of Euro-liberalism, despite the fact that *real differentials in wealth and power may in fact be far more minimal in the latter regimes.*

In sum, the practical impact and import of this ideology has been minimal even within European societies; in the United States, it has served only to produce a *non-deferential society*, which—though interesting and important—is hardly the same thing. Of course, the fact that the commitment to equality in the American constitution was to be conceived—in the ultimate insult to the *non-Europeans* who, in all wretchedness, constituted the latter—*within the very womb of a despotic slave society* has done little to impart a sense of realism, or even dignity, to the idea. And the additional fact that women, minorities, workers, and the poor, still have to struggle, on a continuous, daily, and endless basis to attain such *de facto*, and *de jure*, equal rights, is another indication of the sham and specious nature of such capitalist equalities.

Incidentally, the real-life absence of any appreciable material equality in either opportunity or circumstance is *not* the primary issue as regards the doctrine of equality: nor does that mundane species of pretermission exhaust the real lesions in the problematic of the *ideal* of equality, which still remain to be discussed. I will be arguing that the modernist notion of equality, barring a few abstract spheres, is in fact a baneful, reactionary, even an *asocial*, idea that does little to dim the tensions of modernism even when respected in the *observance*, and not in the breach, as is far more customary. *Indeed, we might well ponder, en passant, the sheer social largesse of being treated "unequally," meaning more than equally, which is the norm of hospitality in traditional and tribal cultures to understand the potential and possible benignities of "inequality."*

(19)

Although popularly attributed to Bentham (despite several equally unworthy precursors), the imputed *behavioral* psychology of humans, but only as fitted within a *utilitarian* calculus, that is with us to this day was another great (in the sense only of being enormous rather than venerable) and dubious gift of the Enlightenment. Oddly enough, the life-chances of an average person located in the brutish context of Shakespearean England were to be transmogrified by Hobbes as the basis for an indictment of the *normal* life of "*man*" in the so-called "*state of nature*" (held up as, nasty, brutish, solitary, and short—as though nature itself was an echo chamber of a purely *English* reality). From Hobbes, it is but a short cut to Bentham in viewing the aversion to pain and the pursuit of pleasure as the *alpha* and *omega* of (a similarly brute-like) human existence.

Only through disbelieving non-European/non-modernist eyes could such a perversion of the human aspect be seen for what it is: *a sheer libel upon the human race*, as Marx might have put it. Western ideologies—economics specially—routinely, and ritualistically, institutionalize these retrograde premises in their vapid assumptions about the mainsprings of human conduct. In all irony, a brutish *hedonism*, usually decried as a heathen, pagan, and plebeian attribute, is in truth the definitive modernist, and European, *genre* to the point of being their only reliable, secular, and comprehensible religion (as opposed to Christianity which is now only their *ritual* ideology, leastways on sundays).

One wonders, in dull astonishment, how the truth of such propositions was ever gauged, in the *chic* gentlemen's clubs where they were first proposed, even in the netherland of wild ideological constructions; of course, possibly, the matter was seen as a tautological one not requiring any further intellectual effort beyond a blunt, Johnsonian assertion of dogma. Certainly, there is no evidence in Benthamite writings (any more than in the works of the political economists) of any deep, *empirical* study of social, or even animal, behavior. Matters were settled, apparently, on the secure basis of *inspired introspection* (the elite Englishman probed deeply into his barren soul, and found nothing but embalming capitalist contentment nesting within a now innate sense of superiority to all peoples). However, the fact that even the American constitution is compelled to underwrite, even *decree*, the lifelong pursuit of pleasure, by means of a solemn declaration (nay, an *injunction!*), would seem, *prima facie*, to indicate the lack of any real conviction in any natural law, or other pregiven propensities, that automatically, and or effortlessly ordained such ambitiously *asocial* behavior.

Indeed, the truth is otherwise; if one sidesteps the mystagogy of the so-called Benthamite calculus, and searches for some such overarchingly trans-historical, and enveloping model of universal behavior (though any such search should itself be suspect), the fact is that there is a far more convincing candidate: *an apparent law of nature (in all life forms), if you will, which society is little able to sublimate, that seeks autonomy* (defined, of course, conventionally) *and resists intrusion*. How much of social, and natural, behavior becomes readily transparent when this simple idea is substituted for the egregious distortions of Benthamite fantasies!

In fact, pressing this idea forward, pain and pleasure of the Benthamite definition refers really only to the *physiological* domain (it is a species, therefore, of *physiological reductionism*); what I am proposing is far more safely located in the much wider domain of *general* human (and most animal) *behavior*, both societally and individually. Of course, this is not to suggest that there are no other principles governing social interaction; merely to point out that, such simple, and inherently repressive, *reductionisms*, if they are to be indulged, or indulged in, at all, are better located in facts and near-facts than in dire, misanthropic fantasy.

(20)

Conquest and colonialism, as accompanied the establishment of capitalist social relations, mores and attitudes, not merely in the ruling orders, but amongst all strata educed the requirement of continuous *intelligence*, that is, practical information requisite for the subjugation of subaltern orders of the populace both within and without the European social order. This unedifying task—of assuring *hegemony*—fell to the newly emergent *political* project that, for want of a more suitable phrase, we might call *social science*. Struggles against the *ancien regime* had already produced a frowsty tribe of scribblers—the *philosophes*—whose irresponsible imaginations ran riot, warming up red and hot as they approached the grim context of the French Revolution. Against the established orthodoxy provided by the ideologues of the church, these indefatigable *counter-missionaries*—calmly unhampered by any practical experience in social administration—gaily authored and advanced both *nouvelle* ideals and novel practices, as untethered imaginations bolstered only with the refreshment of claret could be expected to supply.

Although clad loosely in such daunting raiment, the "*science*" part of their corybantics was a splendid lie; in truth, they were politically inspired propagandists, nay ideologues, whose acquaintance with facts was but only slight and *en passant*. *Avant garde* advocates of a new regime in which they hoped to occupy a special, even honorific, place, they were a predacious priesthood even more implacable and intolerant than the hoary caste of Church scholastics they were trying to retire by means of glib rhetoric and coarse invective. Despite elaborate lip service—and men do wax eloquent whilst dreaming of power!—and ritualistic genuflection to the grossly inflated ideals of reason and empirical evidence, they had, in truth, little respect for either, except where it suited their singular political ambitions.

To this day, *modern social science, their direct heir and lineal descendant, as regulated by the varying requirements of state policy, is simply the subtile artifice of legitimation for virtually anything policy makers desire to perpetrate.* The fact that dissenting radicals, where admitted into such spheres at all, take recourse frequently to the selfsame instrument to criticize the establishment, usually without pronounced effect, is really of little valency or solace.

Revolutionaries, that is, dispossessed or disempowered men, above all things, seek power; and the Enlightenment in that sense was a revolutionary social phenomenenon. Whether in Smith, Ricardo, or Mill, the castigation of the old order was merely tendentious, motivated, programmatic, and partisan pleading for a new pattern of accumulation and a social order that would automatically succor it (and themselves within it); the mantle of *science*, accordingly, was a highly selective one, to validate but a specific set of socio-political pretensions. In effect, capitalist discontent with the refractory mores and ordinances of the *ancien regime* was being given a grandiose name, hoping to validate crass apologetics with the splendid aphorisms and high gloss of science (wherein classical physics and mathematics stood at the apex: economists like Malthus went out of their way, accordingly, to dress their facile fabrications with the high trumpery of *numbers*, the better to deceive the semi-literates—it was, henceforth, to be the dissimulating *Age of Quantity*).

The hapless wards, victims and subjects of these new, relentless, political titans offered heroic resistance to such pretensions, but were eventually to be routed, silenced, and/or grievously marginalized; and as such, the grand ideology of the European, capitalist enlightenment was to saturate all of the social space—and it craved it all—that it sought to subjugate.

To this day, the political establishments of Western capital survive as much through the auxiliary services of social science as they do from their well equipped *swat* teams; and neither set of hired prizefighters are likely, of course, to tolerate the slightest dissent from the ruling premises of the dominant paradigm. Those under the impression that the arena of social science is a "*liberal*" one of open debate, discussion, and rational advancement of ideas, labor therefore under a particularly naive delusion, whose denouement is ever fated to be in a morass of painful disaffection. It would be a preternatural measure of their ingenuous credulity to note that social science, as a *corpus* of thought, has not registered a single major advance in any direction (other than in the old standby field, possibly, *of riot control*) since the "*founding fathers*" (and they were, as befitting the modus of *patriarchy*, all *fathers*) sounded off their imperious, *ex cathedra*, pronouncements between the eighteenth and nineteenth centuries (not a major idea extant today but was spawned in the great, seminal *Genesis* of the Enlightenment).

We still canonize these founding patron saints, who oddly enough were free to proclaim their novel ideas precisely because the *ancien regime* allowed them, positively or negatively, such tolerance; the fact that they have few substitutes today suggests the extent to which we live *now, and not then*, in a relentlessly repressive and intolerant environment of conventional propriety and duly (state) sanctified ideologies.

The whole stadial enterprise of social science is geared to endlessly *reprocessing*, reflecting altering political moods, the classical ideas of the canonical tradition (a thousand years from now, the abject *servant-social-scientist* will still be debating, with an air of effusive seriousness one or other throwaway idea/remark in Durkheim, Smith or Freud); rather like the church, one might note, endlessly debating the lives of the saints and the apostles. At least in the case of the church, new saints, if not apostles, remain possible; in social science, no such novelty is ever to be permitted. *We know all that we ever need to know*; all incoming ideas need to be vetted, formatted, expurgated, and then safely incarcerated—that is, entombed—in carefully sterilized and prescreened cells.

The philosophy of the Enlightenment was but an *instrumentalist* one caught up in the great epochal struggles of the time; even the great Hegel and Kant were debating only, but in oblique terms, the merits of the *ancien regime* and the French Revolution, when they were not distinguishing themselves grandiosely from *non-European* ideas. It is this *topical*, practical quality that debases European philosophy (with the usual run of honorable exceptions) and makes of it a rather pedestrian affair, narrow, self referential, and anything but inspirational. One only has to compare any tome of Enlightenment philosophy with an equivalent classic from, say ancient *Vedic* philosophy, to discover the astonishing epistemic distance that separates them: the distance that, put bluntly, separates the sublime from the trivial.

One great impetus to high philosophizing in Europe in this period was given by the *colonial encounter* itself, which brought with it, as the reapings of colonialism, the riches of exposure to *ancient* knowledge. In that important sense, the dramatically sudden intellectual effulgence of the European Enlightenment is also *the inadvertent gift of non-Europeans*. At any rate, the more ponderous and unreadable—and Kant and Hegel almost went out of their Germanic way to be resplendently opaque—they were (indeed the sheer gibberish of much of Hegelian writings defies description), the less they could address any perennial issue of the human condition.

To this day Western philosophy (if one leaves the Greeks out, as one should; placed in the context of their times the Greeks were no more "*Western*" than the Egyptians) is structurally incapable of offering any real solace to the ills of human beings, east or west, permanently imprisoned between the modernist bounds of vulgar positivism and/or rationalism in one direction, and dire existential despair in the other. As the biblical trope has it, and the market for itinerant Gurus in the United states still reveals, the true caste of "wise" ("men") still hail from the *East*.

The honorable few who rose above this condition, like a Schopenhauer, or a Schlegel (quite remarkably, it was left to the Germans to translate, study, and carry over *Vedic* philosophical texts *en masse*; in fact, outside of the politics of the French Revolution, the major influence on the German philosophical renaissance was the inspirational gnosis of the so-called "*Orient*") were precisely those who took their inspiration from the non-European philosophical systems of *Eastern* antiquity, to be marginalized accordingly as oddball apostates. In effect, the medieval intolerance of Western *theology* (echoed in all vigor by Western *science*, its progeny) was to be replicated duly in its secular metaphysics, fundamentally arid, cold, and cadaverous, in all of its barren discoveries. The mainstream tradition in the Enlightenment did little to warm the human heart or nurture its spirit with benign healings or even with impassioned inquiry; its trust in the apparent clarity and certainty of the mundane fruits of (a reductionist, materialist) reason was to expunge the primal founts of social empathy from which meaningful social bondings are woven.

(21)

The firearm, the printing press, paper, and the compass were to become the prime tools of Western domination of non-Western cultures; today, in the golden era of neoliberalist finance, one might add only commerce and credit—that is, trade and financial dependency—as the other set of allied mechanisms. The simple, if ironic, fact that *all of these were originally non-European inventions* must be a sobering thought to those prone to genuflect before the putative superiority, and originality, of modernist science. It might also be noted that the (putative) absence of a compass did not inhibit navigation on the part of several non-European peoples who engaged in explorations not of necessity confluent with the motives of trade and conquest. It was not a state of mind, nor a penchant for reflection, that furthered the rapid development of European natural science (although the entire effort was located within the metaphysical matrix of *anthropocentrism*) but rather *dire industrial necessity in the context of, desperate international, and internecine, rivalry and war*, features that have but little changed in the modern period where most research that is amply funded is still of the *strategic* kind.

If one but adds *commercial greed*, to industrial need, then we effectively sum up the driving *ethos*—the colossal strengths and weakness—of European science. Salutary to note, in this regard, that neither Vedic wisdom, wherein science and ethics were combined, nor Buddhist or Jain explorations in mathematics, were either provoked by, or were concomitants of, conquest and accumulation but bore a purity of ardor and endeavor that has simply no modernist European equivalent leastways in the classical period of the Enlightenment (this does not mean that the later post-Vedic tradition did not inculcate *philosophy as statecraft*: Kautilya's *Arthashastra*, in that regard, compares favorably with, if long prior to, Machiavelli's ideas).

However, the new scientific outlook of the Enlightenment was not engendered unopposed and had to fight it way over the back of older traditions of science that were far more hospitable to humbler social needs and necessities, that is, they were not driven solely by greed or power. Much as the ideas of liberalism triumphed over church ideology by virtue not of better argument or better evidence, contrary to modernist legend, but *the power of better organized force* (as instanced in the politics of Galileo in *success*, and the lost crusade of the great Paracelsus, in *failure*), the new sciences simply expelled the old arts and pushed them to the outer margins of existence.

Superior force, organization, and iron discipline were the redoubtable tools of European mastery, but even they, in themselves, may not have sufficed to effect the supreme dominance that is visible today in all corners of the world (excepting China, which remains the least Europeanized of any modernist social formation) were this force not to be supplemented with a *philosophy of domination* that, to this day, has no pareil in the history of human endeavors. Non-European empires, faced with the European peril, had to learn the hard way that guns without arguments almost fail to fire altogether. Somewhere in the Renaissance, Europe possessed itself of such an inexorable ideology, a veritable *manifest, of conquest* of all things—and peoples.

The very spirit of the ruling European (and his North-American counterparts) today is informed with this wantonly conquistadorean, carpetbagging, temper, still seeking gullible *subjects cum consumers*, wherever possible, still seeking to take without giving, to rule without consent, ready to cheat on treaties, renege on friends, and exact from the weak and the helpless. The craven U.S. invasion of Grenada, infamous act of state piracy apart, where the mightiest force on earth trampled on the poorest little island imaginable, and then awarded themselves a glittering gallery of medals—more than one medal each for every soldier, sailor, and marine landed (and many who never landed incidentally)—can convey but a very small appreciation of just how far from even the very simplest norms of *morality* European "civilization" has traversed in but a few centuries (equally linear and unbroken is the red line of infamy that connects the atrocities of the Europeans in Africa and the technology driven savagery of Americans in Vietnam).

Indeed, the very word itself today has no readily agreed upon meaning or significance in modernist society—just as similarly, *economics*, the ruling *logos* of modernism, has no place for, and comprehension of, the idea of *fairness* or *justice*, terms which are *literally meaningless* within that discourse. With the destruction of normative ties, the social basis of morality erodes and becomes privatized (small wonder that the U.S. Supreme Court deems, with much relief, morality a local, community resource subject to local adjudications and alterations of fashions). Morality, like ethics, becomes merely an *option*, among many choices, for the ordinary person, to be exercised when it involves the least cost to the practitioner; like *faith*, its close country cousin, it has become effectively dispensable, and quite sub-optimal, as a workable code for conduct. Once again, the United States (where bad guys win with a grim, degrading, monotony), the most degenerately advanced in these directions, is living testimony to the simple rectitude of these propositions, whose truth is confirmable by simple, direct observation alone.

(22)

The so-called *Dark Ages*, to the non-Eurocentred imagination, if true to their name at all, will now take on special significance for representing a happily anomalous phase in the evolution of Europeans to their modernist present. Far from being a barren time-warp of sloth and inactivity characterized by some ill-assumed torpor, as is the impression usually created in the canonical texts when compared with the more "dynamic" history to follow, it was precisely the period when Europe, thanks to the grace of a merciful providence, lived *perhaps* much like the rest of the world within parochial, but consilient, dreams of modest self-fulfilment not attached to the phantoms of conquest and world domination. Only a modernist mindset that, unbeknownst to itself, values hothouse growth, primitive accumulation, and global vandalism, could view those allegedly uneventful times with scorn and contempt. Indeed, situated between two violently bloodthirsy empires, the Roman, and the several European ones to follow, one could actually credit the European in this time with a relative *introversion* that, no matter what the cause, is well worth emulating all over again.

For the *non-European*, the "Dark Ages" are the blessed time when the fires of *Euro-chauvinism* had not yet been decisively lit; there was neither torpor nor slumber, as the vain, glorified imagery of the Renaissance would have us believe—but a period inured to the vacuous ideologies of expansion that both modernist radicals and liberals, *birds of the same feather*, find so irresistible. That modern Europe finds that relatively mild era, wherein slavery was being transformed into serfdom, quite unheroic—finding its quietude almost an embarrassment—is a testament to the predatory values it subsists on in the modern period.

Nonetheless, regrettably, the respite, such as it was, was shortlived; within but a short interval, Europe would catapult itself from simple savagery straight into a modernist, technologically driven barbarism. The force that was to fire this new vision of itself would be a *recharged Christianity*—as Hobbes had seen it, the Christian Church was the ghost of the Holy Roman Empire—now anxious to define itself against the growing influence and power of Islam. As such, the contours of world history were to change because of the clash of these two equally relentless desert-born faiths. The Crusades, thereby, mark the great watershed in European history, of more importance than the industrial revolution in stoking the fires of European identity. It is necessary to note that long before secular science was recruited to aid the effort, primal *faith* had already cajoled Europe to first identify, then glorify itself. Only few might choose to recognize it in such terms, but the Crusades are on again today with Islam now sullenly taken to the field charged with a primal faith of its own—but backed by the power of petroleum rather than secular science. Whether this latter-day ontological support, is more, or less, effective than the latter epistemic force remains still to be seen.

Civilizations are revealed to the careful surveyor both in their practices and their ideas; but in ideas more so, because ideas are always necessarily more complete than practices which always remain compromised by material and other relational constraints, that is, by the mechanics of *praxis*. The ideas that dominated the Crusading spirit are worthy of study, much as the radical reformulation of Christian tenets that followed upon the success of those ventures (5 major Crusades were launched between 1098 and 1250, even as, between 1150 and 1280, 80 cathedrals were to be erected in France echoing in stadial and grandiose masonry the lofty spirit of those adventures). Many of the dominant tenets of the Euro-capitalist spirit, that are now part of both history and folklore, individualism, acquisitiveness, and a reductionist rationality, are also related to, and reflections of, this *reformulated* Christian ethic. At any rate, the ancient Mediterranean peoples who had overrun northern Europe, under the guise of the Roman empire, were now to be pacified, in turn, by the Northerners. The north, historically—in modernist terms—*backward, resource poor, and lacking cultivation*, was to prevail over the south, not just ephemerally in this or that particular saga but forever after in an epic age of domination about to commence.

Given its numerous tribes, Europe could be integrated in many ways, materially, politically and ideologically; by far, the last bonding was the strongest, and despite the considerable economic and political and military power of the church, it is still its *ideological* cement that bonded Europeans and gave them that marked feeling of separation and *distance* from others—that is, a certain internal *coherence* (necessary, one would imagine, for the regular conduct of trade, finance, markets, amongst other forms of social intercourse). Christian ascetiscism, not wholly disparaged even in the Reformation, provided a secure cloister for science and bookkeeping, even as the military and economic needs of the Church—which Gibbon argued had quite felled the Roman Empire—allowed for sustenance of trade and production.

Of course it was also handy that the Church, being an empire on its own, could forestall the growth of rival, secular empires for a long period in European history. *Islam and Hinduism were never organized as transnational ecclesiastical powers on the style of the Church of Rome*, and thus could hardly have had the same political and planetary consequences as with the case of Europeans (at least until recently): their chauvinisms were to remain insular and insulating rather than *extraverted* and all-conquering (despite the admittedly uneven record of Islamic empires in this respect). The key institution that continues unchecked between Europe's modernist and premodernist history is thereby *religious* sentiment; as such, Euro-modernism is merely Christian ideology solidified with the modernist traits of *technological* fetishism (a latter day appendage), material greed, and the politics of expediency.

(23)

Religion is normally conceived as being of, and belonging to, the *sacral* domain, as per classical Durkheimian formulations, far above the banalities of the profane world. However, Christianity not merely abandoned the sanctuary of its sacral cloisters, but ventured mettlesomely abroad to conquer and subdue, driven by secular as much as sacral prepossessions (*cuius regio, eius religio*, as the saying goes). In that received vein, the *secular humanism professed by many in the west is simply a mundane form of uncharismatic Christianity*, and largely understood as such by those given to reflexive reflection upon such matters. The great European contribution to civilization was the *quantification* of social life, and the intemperate worship of *idola quantitatis*; as such, latter day *Christian materialism*, or Calvinism as Weber saw it, is quite indistinguishable from the day to day premises of political and economic liberalism.

Aside from the radical denudation of the human prospect, which is the ultimate reflux of such ideas, and the abject derogation of premodernist values of care, compassion, and consideration, which they ultimately presuppose, the *calculus of discontent* that they have imposed on the world is the *fons et origio* of the spiritual squalor and the day to day misery of the average citizen that is visible no matter where on earth one travels today in the zones where Europe has cast its calamitous shadow.

That at least the shadow of such prepossessions are discernible and evident even to the ruling mainstream is witnessed in the brief currency of the well known, if misinterpreted, notion of the "*revolution of rising expectations*" that flourished in the volatile sixties, and seventies, when the "*third world*" was being assiduously studied for its potential *political* utility *vis à vis* the cold war. Mass discontent, turbulence and turmoil, was being noted, but only to be misread as signifying the need for more modernization, not less (what chastened the enthusiasm of the modernizers was not the revolution of rising expectations as much as the *rising expectation of revolution!*). To dispossess the vast populace of traditional recourse to resources, in the name of *progress*, to invest them with the bare harvest of economic *extraversion*, and then credit them with the bad faith of exaggerated claims upon the future would seem a cruel enough joke; but far worse the case when the very victims of such deceptions start to believe in the delusion of their own permanent, helpless dependency upon the modernist trio of capitalist, bureaucrat, and expert scientist. As such, the "*third world*" (*a latently racist, ideological construction*) was the ontic and epistemic creation of European ideas and practices in *two* very distinct senses.

On the one hand, European commercial penetration into the hinterland of indigenous peoples explosively disrupted the even skein of their social and material ecologies, thereby creating in an *absolutist* sense, *real* deprivations and privations (as opposed to merely *culturally perceived* "poverty") over and above the traditional well understood ones of natural ravages and human rapine. In this sense, material and ecological disarticulation in the European world had an all too "*real*" existence directly owed to the machinations of the tribe of modernist depredators (whether metropolitan or satellite inspired). But the tragedy of the peripheral world went far beyond the schemata of *material* privation; it was compounded, and made well nigh irremediable, when, as a follow through to conquest, the feckless ideology of the modernist was forcibly injected into the psyches of simple societies—through force, fraud, bribery, and chicanery.

Suddenly, *enough was not enough: more was better*—in a fetid swoop, so to speak, a new culturally perceived *relative deprivation* supplanted imaginations long accustomed to self-sufficiency, self-organization, and self-provisioning. Now, nothing seemed possible without the modernist presence of market and state, mediating needs, customs, and ways of life. In one stroke of radical severance, sentient beings, who had, with skill and ingenuity, survived millenia of evolution, were dispossessed of their rights, rituals, practices, and, most of all, *self-respect*—rendered helpless, dependent and reliant on *external* sources of sustenance, which could only be capricious and unreliable.

On the spiritual side of this process, and one may speak of this as a species of a *mortal corruption of the soul*, went a debasement that the European first suffered himself and then forcibly transplanted the world over in restless hot-house fashion. Eventually, this was to prove a far more potent force of assuring the decay of simple societies than the military and commercial wars of conquest or the unequal contracts and treaties thrust upon them.

The stupefying drug of *crass* materialism (Chinese philosophy of the Confucian kind was materialist enough, and formidably so, but yet remained a *bounded* materialism) was more potent than the opium chests dumped on the unwilling Chinese, more effective in securing the unforced submission of entire peoples to the path of modernist perdition as they streaked dully, but dutifully, into the thoughtfully ill-designed factories, cinderblock apartment-hutches, and the mockturtle machinery of abstract, *formal* democracy (boiling down only to voting rules and rituals) that was waiting to absorb them into its warped genius. Perhaps a few of us flew there aloft on the wings of joyous, if misguided, enthusiasm; but most found themselves, when self-discovery was possible at all, like hapless tribes of lemmings, playing follow the invisible leader in earnest, and to the point of near-extinction.

The derogation of *use values* (Marx fully understood the radical hiatus that separates the world of *use values* from the universe of *exchange values*, but mistakenly believed that the generalization of the latter was a necessary prelude to the progressive evolution of humankind, a belief that he was in later life, in relation to the so-called "*Russian Road*," but apparently too late for his epigones, to modify) and their systematic vilification and debasement is the progressivist story of the *Great Modernist Ascent*; *vis à vis* simple societies, this meant a rank inability to detect their opulent contours of non-saleable wealth and inalienable affluence. Societies far richer than their conquerors in terms of their *self-provisioning* of *needs* and *self-determination* of social *ends* were then systematically stripped of their *real* resources on the pretext of *developing* them, denuded eventually of both natural and social assets, and left only with the corrugating innovations of the cash nexus and market/state dependency as the prizes of their perilous descent into European worthfulness measured in terms of the chicanery of exchange values and the fraud of market valuations. The fact that such radical devolutions of the social condition, in the modern era, have always been sold to the hapless victims in terms of idiot declarations of amelioration in public drainage and improvement in sanitation makes the story only that much more poignant.

Ancient, and self-sufficing, *moral* economies in Asia, Africa, and Latin America, were ruthlessly overrun, as need dictated (human in one case, material in another) and left to rot in slow, inarticulate decay; next, they were rediscovered as "backward" entities, again when choice so dictated, fit for redemption only through infusion of modernist ideas and capital so as to uplift them that is, maintain them in permanent and chronic dependency on their new-fangled "saviors." The historic irony of this drama was exceeded only by the unprecedented, operatic tragedy of debacle and disaster visited upon these hapless formations.

The transition from a *needs-based society to a want* (i.e. *greed* based) *based* one was not an European invention in the first instance, since class societies have always been *dualistic* in that regard—*ruling elites being wedded to wasteful indulgence and the humble to the more parsimonious norms of sustainable subsistence*. However, it is precisely *Euro-modernism* that *generalized* this fateful set of motivations and attributes to the level of a hegemonic driving force that would henceforth envelop the social in *all* of its dimensions. The putatively "*socialist*" experiments of Eastern Europe, and elsewhere, for all their ruthless and tyrannical ways, were a lack-luster attempt to recapture the essence of such a *needs-based* societal system, only to be more or less forced to fail by the determined forces of *capitalist* modernism, aside from their own spectacular infelicities of economic and political policy.

At any rate, the expiration of contentment and self-worth, once such foreign Byzantine values and standards have been internalized, is the story of the neoliberalist world today as it daily walks the speeded-up treadmill of extended and intensive "*work*," succumbed to the meretricious allure of a glittering, shiny, commodity driven universe where a lifetime of ungratifying labor is the lot of the many while vain, even crass, luxury the prefectiture of a few that preside over the revels from a suitable distance (today's income distribution data reflect this story in dramatic detail: *2.8 billion live on less than 2 dollars a day*, sharing the same capitalist world where a few billionaires virtually own it all). It is a world that is managed, organized, and planned, *for* all of us, if not *by* all of us, modernism, like nature itself, abhorring a vacuum.

The struggle, therefore, to maintain the shrinking but sovereign sphere of *personal autonomy and private space* under the relentless encroachments of state and (corporatist, contractual) society takes on now, for myriads, a life and death aspect. Given the sordid, but real, prospect of a near unlimited expansion of the modernist wasteland at the expense of traditional autonomies, leisure, and convivial cultural relations, it may well be reassuring to remember that while *extortionist regimes of order are always a socially imposed ontic condition, the natural episteme of the species, with or without self-awareness, is to pursue its own purposes in an autonomist way*, albeit within a consensual domain of established values. *This yearning for autonomy is as real as modernist "freedom" (within the stockade of "civil society") is chimerical.* As such, emancipation from European grids, in the domain of science much as society, is a matter merely of *rediscovery* of (recently) lost graces, rather than the fanciful invention of *nouvelle* utopias.

(24)

The nescient *progressivism* of the Enlightenment expressed itself in the primacy of the *three* slogans that have now become the neoteric *liturgy* of modernism: *equality*, *justice*, and the *rule of law*. The most vapid of these slogans is the chimera of equality, in the stark and rabid face, especially, of its striking *absence* from almost all sectors of modern life. But the notion is weakest not in its *application*, which a casual glance at the modernist universe can confirm anywhere, but in its very *constitution*. *There is no convivial society on earth that got there by insisting upon equality as a precondition:* in fact, the most blessed human societal form, the most fundamental unit of social mechanics, the *family*, is blissfully free of any such nonsensical, and patently *contra*-factual, ideological requirement.

To be coldly, and distantly, the equal of someone else confers bliss only to the dreary, lost, and lonely crowds of the modernist wasteland; human beings, in the richness of their sentience, crave, being *mammals*, warmth, humanity and love which cannot be premised upon anything so mechanical, artless, objectivist, and uniform, as *equality*. Equality, in its modernist form, and the passion that engenders it, is the measure of the *distance* of living beings from one another, their wanton lack of connection, their paucity of affection, and their dearth of feeling. As such, the demand for formal equality, as ill requital for the loss of nurture and the enveloping warmth of the social skein, is another sorry, and alienating, index of the dull formalism of the modernist state and society and the cadaverous barrenness of its progressivist integument.

Justice is another holy grail of the modernist empire usually represented in modernist imagery precisely for what it is: stern, unbending, cold, blind, and dry. Much like equality, its formalisms, and its regnant detachments, are a safe index of the demoralization of a society with cleavages so deep that only an agency standing *outside* its social relations can sit in abstract judgment over them. The more uniform and general its jurisdictions, and formalized its rules, the more it violates the principle of *difference*, connection, and context upon which the *organon* of social life is premised. Marx articulated the easy part of the critique which is to suggest that *there can be no justice between unequals*; but this is hardly to imply that formal equality, *per se*, does away with injustice. In fact, much like formal equality, formal justice fails for its own self-appointed, patriarchical, *impersonality*; it is altogether simple to conceive of far more benign, and sentient, (even, one might say, "*feminine*") forms of the impulse of equity: charity, mercy, compassion, pity, forgiveness, and so on, which are far superior to the purely *masculinist* urge to "*mete out justice*," as the hoary expression goes, but find little place in the juridical lexicon of modernism.

Consider for a moment how the idea of justice and/or equality might operate in context of *familial* relations, and one can readily evaluate its caricature within the modernist ethos; in a family one (usually) seeks not *retribution* (justice as *vengeance*, a precapitalist, and *androcentric* idea), nor *restitution* (justice as recovery of property or damages: a "capitalist" notion) but *reconciliation* (to find common ground, minimize frictions, and keep the original *corpus* of social norms alive: i.e. *convivialism*). Only in a social form seriously out of accord with its own *essence* can such a gross violation of the benevolent norms of affective *familiality* pass for the dispensation of an *ideal* form of justice. And yet the great, cheerless halls of judicial process in the modernist polity, as grey, dark, and forbidding as they are imperious and arrogant, shut out the healing light of convivial relations and make putatively "just" outcomes rest on cold, adversarial, and calculating processes that denude the social tie and render otiose the very relations that nurture and succor the elemental forces of the social life. Indeed, in the last analysis, modernist "justice" has devolved only into the delivery of a corrupt and dessicated "*legality*" that daily mocks the turgid platitudes of the former (*Summum ius*, one might say, *summa inuria*).

"Law and Order," imposed from above, is an old, dissimulating slogan of ruling orders, past, and present, but modernism turns it into a fetish of its own. It is another widely accepted modernist myth that legality and order are its own, private contributions to civilizational values, instead of being as they are part of *the very ingrained fabric of all human society*. Indeed, *anarchy* in a human society, much as sheer arbitrariness in public allocations, is always an anomalous condition of very exceptional times; the *norm* in human society is one of shared values and widely instituted and accepted conventions of conduct.

This is not to deny that *iniquity* and lack of "fairness," as perceived from an *outside* point of view, do not vary widely, but through trial and error, reform and revolt, these matters sort out, in all societies, over historical, and cultural, time. Indeed, it is a measure of the grace of *premodernist* cultures to have arrived at, over evolutionary epochs, a (self) satisfactory mean with respect to broadly accepted codes of mutual conduct. The modernist polity, being an *artificial* entity usually built upon abstract (and tendentious), and imposed, ideals has little of that co-respecting *organon*, and instead remains a seething cauldron of competing interests and agendas teetering upon shaky, shifting, and ever contested, and shifting, terrain.

The modern polity boasts of legions of well heeled lawmakers and lawgivers who daily add to the legislative burdens of the social form largely, in capitalist forms of modernism, to allow for cupidity and venality to prevail: that is, laws are made for lawyers to interpret and profit from, while being usually intrusive impositions on the many who have little to do with it except by way of a resigned sufferance. When and where such prescriptive *schemata* are well-intentioned, the dilemma is no better because it involves a *corporatization* of life where all the empty spaces that allow for creativity and social imagination, are perforce captured, sullenly producing uniform *gulags* where there is an *anticipatory* law governing all social space, public and private.

Indeed, this elite, legal conquest of popular social space (another kind of an annexationist "*enclosure*" movement) is a process that has accelerated in current times with the *globalization* of corporatist forms of polity. In fact, the old dream of a world government, but in profoundly reactionary form, may well be approached, if the machinery of the United Nations is successfully suborned to that effect by present, ongoing, joint U.S.–EC initiatives, given their conjoint honeymoon with neoliberalist corporatism in our era: *the WEF and the WTO, are today the corporate versions of an emergent shadow world government being instituted, aggressively, by private interests.*Fortunately, the normal, and enduring, state of competitive distrust between the major Blocs, in an emergent *tri-polar* world, now pitting the

United States, its Anglo-Saxon satellites, and Japan at one end, and France, Germany, and Russia at the other, with China a stand alone giant at a third pole, obstructs an easy and smooth passage to that invidious climacteric. What all this augurs for the future, in particular for the lesser, humbler denizens of this planet is not, in the nature of things, an amiable domain for speculation.

What has been lost, in the modernist conquest of history, may well appear irretrievable: the process of *give and take*, and other convivial reciprocities, where social beings test, measure, and verify their affections, and their mutual loyalties, on a continuing basis (consider social life as an amicable, buzzing *bazaar* instead of a cold and sullen and still boardroom: and the different tropes will speak to the radical difference between something vibrantly alive and something quite inert and lifeless). Such is the nature of convention and custom, consilient and consensual processes, that modernism destroys in its alienating wake, now compelled to succumb to the estrangement of abstract laws made by specialized experts standing over and above the ordinary processes of everyday life.

In effect, the law and order commissars destroy the very possibility of *creative anarchy* which is what enabled, one must remember, the critical parturition that allowed the modernist way to emerge in the first place, from the womb of traditional society. *Endogenous* experiment and invention, *or the popular participation of peoples in their own self-regulation*, is thereby sacrificed to *exogenously* given demands of corporatist, bureaucratic drives reinforcing the hollow, managed, and crippling cretinism of the regulated *industrial life*—tying us to the wheel of endless labors—which is the imposed ontic condition of modernism.

Opposed to this desolating catechism of *alien* law and order, imposed by *fiat* and obeyed by fear, is the everpresent and universal *modus* of *self-regulation* and *self-direction* where *customary* relations bless and sanctify meaningful norms whose first premise is the *organic bonding* of social ties between reciprocating human beings. Modernism fails to connect precisely for its deliberate placement of deep distance and radical dissonance, between itself and the nurturing founts of familial and affective ties. The rank alienation of the modernist universe is a direct, and dire, consequence of its departure from the life-sustaining mores that inform the *anthropic* family—regardless of how it is constituted—as an *emotive* entity.

Then there is the reigning ideology of *liberty*—in its most pernicious social form of "liberating" (i.e., *dispossessing*) wholly *individuated* humans from the enveloping warmth of society, morality, and norms. Few who share in modernist mythology can be supposed to ponder the *negative* heuristic of liberty: the grateful abnegation on the part of state and society of their responsibility to *care* for the now *atomized* and individuated citizenry asked to see life as a lottery and/or a desperate struggle for survival. Individuals are "*free*," in a sense, because *they do not matter*, and do not count.

Freedom, of that order, is the birthright of every tramp, derelict, and deadbeat, of modern society, and such "rights" are readily available (but only so long as such species of citizenry do not get in the way of the well regulated channels of *Accumulation*). Only the most misanthropic of social imaginations could ever view this form of liberty—that is, *freedom from* social care, recognition, and identity—as desirable. Outside the limited elites of wealth and power who are, within their charmed circle, keenly "social" players, the numbers of such excommunicated "libertines" is daily increasing under the pressures of contemporary Social-Darwinist neoliberal policies.

The current phase of the eclipse of the so-called "*welfare state*" (a curious oxymoron), only completes the historical agenda of that form of *anomic*, that is, separatist, and deracinating, libertarianism. Liberty, in the classically vulgar age of the political economist, originally implied little other than freedom of trade and capital movement (accordingly, in England, whilst village *serfdom*, in its new form of the *Speenhamland Amendment* to the *Poor Laws*, still tied paupers to the soil, trade was nonetheless being "liberalized" under the guidance of ideas from Smith, Ricardo, etc.): as such, it was little other than the motivated, and temerarious, ideology of the capitalist class, seeking selfish space for itself, locked, as it was, in mortal feud with aristocratic protectionists.

Under radical and demotic pressures, the concept was forcibly extended to other spheres but rarely ever departing from its original inspiration. Even today, when all other personal and political liberties are suspended, as with fascist and neo-fascist states, and some military dictatorships, it is easy to see the principle of *freedom of trade* and capital flows still being quite properly retained (as in Chile, e.g., after the engineered fall of Allende: similarly, Singapore, for all its draconian political restrictions nonetheless boasts of an exemplary free trade regime). It is no exaggeration, therefore, to suggest that the capitalist passion for freedom pertains vitally to this domain—that is, to *entrepreneurial freedom—first*, before finding application in other residual, and marginal, areas of social life (and then only under pressure from *below*).

The predilection for *democracy* amongst ruling orders persists, similarly, only in so far as the former is consistent with the premises of uninterrupted capital accumulation. Indeed, a perfectly functioning democracy which barred capitalist practices, as is perfectly conceivable, would be anathema to the Euro-capitalist spirit which values *materialism* above all other values; so it is not merely the nature of the political *process* that is at issue, but the *necessary end* it leads to—a democracy that delivered, say Buddhist ideals, perchance, would be quite unsustainable in that logic. This is much the import of the erstwhile Jeanne Kirkpatrick-inspired U.S. doctrine which argued baldly that dictatorships were acceptable so long as they supported the West. Finally, even were liberty to live up to the grand flourish of John Stuart Mill, it would still be barren: for liberty without psychic succor is as meaningless as equality without nurturance. Of course, the European is free, in many regards, but he is also, and in equal measure, bereft and bereaved: estranged from the roots of his own *species-being*, and left only with the cold comfort of the commodification of his few, and fast dwindling, joys.

Of course, the factitious diadem of *democracy*, the easy icon of everyone, is another premodernist artefact today cheerfully appropriated by Europe to herself. If her historians are to be believed, the Greeks invented it, the English perfected it, and America took it to its usual unsavory extremes. Once again, historical truth gainsays such self-anointing flourishes. Self-government—or better still *self-regulation*—is a principle immanent in the *self-organization* of all simple societies, and is an *anthropic universal*, no matter how defiled and usurped by the deformities of rank, power, and privilege of more stratified societies. As such, the idea of democracy—*whose ideational crux is really governance by some modus of consent*—is a near universal in societal forms, if one dispenses with the singular "*majority rule*" corruption it acquired at late European hands.

Indeed, there is little about majority right that can be metaphysically sustained except within the charlatanry of the *utilitarian* mindset that counts heads much like it counts coins (think of the banal Benthamite notion of the "*greatest happiness of the greatest number*," for example). In the European context of a deep fissure between state and civil society, the very defining feature of a profoundly alienated society, such a voting "rule" may well be the least offensive option out of a docket of bad choices; but, on any other, *elevated* human scale, which values *qualities*, the notion is egregiously refractory to the formation of a consilient order.

I offer the *heuristic-modus* of the *human family* (typified in the *tribal form*) again as an illustrative example. A *family*, at its modal best, is a community not of equals but of co-respecting and mutually caring *participants* who share *affective* norms in common; a contented family proceeds on the basis of building a *consensus* rather than mechanically and adversarially "voting" itself into situations that the some or the many might dislike. *Consensus*, which involves the investment of patience, love, care, and sacrifice of self-interest for the sake of the common good, is inherently far superior to any vulgar notion of majority rule or right.

Importantly, consensus is the unwritten frame of this founding, *anthropic* social unit, which may in practice exhibit all manner of ideological and other differences; as such, the human family presents a social vision of a society where unavoidable *cleavage* is overcome by the patient exercise of a *nonexclusionary affection*, and an acute dearth of what might be termed *judgmental haste*. The *natural* tie of kinship undoubtedly plays an important, anthropic part in cementing and underwriting familial relations, but a tribal *society* is able successfully to extend this kinship based model to society at large (through the invocation of *fictitious* kinship) thereby holding out the promise of quite elaborate social constructs built upon an *affective*, anthropic ideology of bonding.

Once again, in stark contrast, the abstract formalism of the "democratic" instruments of modernist society produces in its effects only generalized discontent, conflict, and anger. Most ancient civilizations, and almost all so-called simple tribal societies proceeded on the premise of *building* (not necessarily to be confused with *achieving*) a consensual or near-consensual value system that accepted various *inequalities*, ascriptive or functional, as unavoidable; but it is as if the *cosmic logos* underlying, and invested in, such intricately designed orders knowingly enmeshed both inequalities, and the heirarchies they presupposed, within a pliant and supple *countervailing* system of reciprocities, responsibilities, affections, and mutual rights. The traditional Hindu caste system of Aryan antiquity is a phenomenal case in point, though hopelessly distorted in its latter-day *modernist* visage (which is the conveniently hideous form in which latter-day progressives, and "anthropologists" both encounter and criticize it, with very little comprehension of its original metaphysical rationale, history, functioning, and meaning).

The modernist state and society are both deformed *mutants* of truly anthropic societies—the latter aiming at a far higher order of communality than achievable by *contract*—fundamentally entranced by the *nexus* of commodities, commerce, and cash, rather than caring, cooperation, or coexistence. Given that context, the existence of "democracy," much like liberty or equality, can do little to ease the pain of that original, even fundamental, elision. *When society is not organically linked by the seamless web of affective interactions, there can be no political, or philosophical, anodyne that soothes, nurtures, or heals the deadly breaches that unnaturally divide and separate humans from each other.*

It may also be useful to remember that, despite the ever expanding paraphernalia of quasi-democratic instruments, as say in the United States, power has never been more efficiently centralized and divorced from the peoples it is usually directed against: indeed, despite the nascent populism of the political right in recent years, the United States may be said to have the most politically quiescent populace living under *modernist authoritarianism* on this planet outside of outright dictatorships with the condition of *subalternity* generalized to all of the *mass society* of nonelites. How much of this is due to the deliberately trigger-happy instruments of state power as developed in the raw ethos of a *settler* state, and how much to the tyranny of the *one-dimensional* ideology spewed out by the relentless propaganda machine of the mass media, in the near fifty year context of running a cold war, is a matter that can only be left to speculation at this late juncture.

It may not at all be a hyperbole to maintain, therefore, that, for all their affronts to modernist values, and their rough-hewn ways, Afghan tribals are possibly more "democratic," *in that original sense of governing by consensual values*, than any modernist, European nation-state today, and genuinely closer to the lived *geist* of their own people. *By deifying form, modernism successfully, and systematically, in all spheres, suborns content*; *a voting rule is, after all, only a voting rule.* And, to the extent that liberalism, conservatism, and all forms of European radicalism, premise their political visions on the extant forms of the *nation-state* and "civil society," *the archetypically modernist creations of the ruling classes*, they are all subject to the same abject corruption and nescience, and need to be rejected *in toto.*

All the conceits of modernist politics, structures, and political alternatives, need to be abandoned, not least by Europeans themselves, if there is to be any hope of retrieving the receding promise of a *convivial* society. *There is no emancipatory impulse, in short, that can be built on modernist urges.* The Utopian impulse in the era of the Enlightenment stemmed from the self-realization, on the part of the sensitive and the wounded, of a real world of nurturance that had been lost in the rabid fever of revolution and rhetoric: the aborted attempts to "find" it, or recreate it in the arid desert of "civil society," from More to Marx, is simply the story of the tragic failure to comprehend the fundamentals of anthropic life.

II. Against Modernism: [Therapeutics, Salves, and Antidotes to the Modernist Distemper]

3. The Fatal Conceit: Elisions of Materialism

The Enlightenment offered the world the arid, and seemingly ineluctable, gifts of *science*, *materialism*, and *progress* (i.e., Modernism, in a nutshell). Indeed, today, it is almost impossible to believe in any one of these elements without swearing fealty to the *triad* as a whole. Science was the instrument of deliverance of material wealth, and progress was measured by the incremental growth of that very wealth: as such, materialism was simply the grand ethos that legitimized the banal process shackling human labor, in perpetuity, to the wheel of endless accumulation. From the industrial revolution onwards, this omnipotent ideology of the Enlightenment gathered steam and grew in confidence and power with *Political Economy* as its *Great Propagator*, enshrining, in most of its variants, this unholy triumvirate of mistaken ideas in its entirety.

As such, it would be useful to title modernism the *Age of the Economist*, and *his* (the species was, largely, *male*) false, baneful, nostrums. Little wonder that the Swedish Nobel Committee, itself the *avant garde* so to speak of modernist ideology, decided to award it the status of a "*science*" worthy of receipt of an annual Prize, alone amongst the social sciences. Of course, logically, the only way such a Prize could be claimed would be for the subject (*where a modernist micro ideology combines with a capitalist macro policy to masquerade as universal science*!) to separate itself as much as possible from the *social* sciences: and this latter-day political economy succeeded in doing admirably, *fetishizing the economy, naturalizing so-called economic behavior, and "socializing" only its terrible tolls on the human spirit.*

All cultures produce and consume: but the European innovation in this domain was to *reify* production and *fetishize* consumption as the pre-eminently overriding forms/domains of human activity. We live today, thereby, near universally, perforce, in a purely *productivist/consumptivist* ethos with the intrinsic debasement of all activities unconnected with these two Great Urges of capitalist corporatism. Indeed, the palatial shopping mall of today plays a part roughly equivalent to the role of the medieval cathedral with one important difference: it gives only meretricious, and delusive hope to the wretched, unlike the stately cathedral which held out, at its best, some quantum of perhaps real hope for their salvation (if one takes up Pascal's wager in earnest). That life, not merely social life, may have other, far more opulent avenues and spheres for human exploration was lost in this crass celebration of *consumerism*, and the slatternly *commodification* of all values.

It was open only for the *few*, *victims* largely, to discern the rampant *destructivism*, to say nothing of its implications for the extension of human drudgery, undergirding this *productivist* pose; progress was being "measured" now in exclusively productivist tropes, ontically implying the forcible, and necessary, *destruction* of habitat, ways of life, and resources, as sacrifice to this ravenously insatiable deity. After all, a standing forest was not a resource until logged and sold as timber, a river of no "use" until dammed and turned into coolant for factories, and so on. Tragic irony that this process of the radical annihilation of human and social utilities—a rampant "*culture of death*," to adopt a telling phrase of ecologist Vandana Shiva—was to be sacralized as "development" and foisted upon the weak and/or the gullible the world over.

Being was sacrificed to endless *becoming*, and limitless *doing*; leisure/living time to work, freedom to slavery, and culture to technology. All social space was appropriated, transformed, developed, and sold to the highest bidder, a form of cultural vandalism without parallel in the history of human evolution. The *reductionism* that both preceded and followed such processes of devaluation of *non-productivist* social ties is the recreant author/architect of the grim malaise of our times and the sullen desperation of our lives. The dollar standard was universalized to all activities, on a non-stop "24/7" basis, quantifying life, standardizing culture, and cynically abasing the impulses of human generosity, charity, and giving, with the superimposition of the calculus of amoral greed upon all processes and interactions.

Both science and materialism succeeded admirably in disenchanting the creatively nourishing mysteries of the social world, and in reducing all actions to the simplest norms of self-interest and possessiveness: Hobbesian ideas, with barely any refinement, were to similarly distort theories of the polity and human interaction. Humankind was being force-fed the virulent ideology of separateness, competition, and *estranging* individuation (as with standard Hollywood fare today) with progress being measured precisely in terms of the development of these *asocial* norms. The natural world, in all its physical and metaphysical complexity, was reduced to its tangible, exploitable, *materiality* in a vulgar philosophical trope, despite the profoundest discoveries of both *quantum* and *post-quantum* physics (and the remarkable work of Ilya Prigogene, in another sphere) where "materiality" is not at all a simple matter of tactile bundles of inert mass alone: Nature was but another domain to be "conquered," and harnessed to the manifold urges of the profit motive. In naïve, and idiot *anthropocentrism*, economists would cravenly boast of "our" ability, as with Nobel Laureate Robert Solow, to "do without" nature.

Positivist and reductionist science naturalized the social world and materialized the natural world, stripping both of their fundamental propensities to succor and sustain life-giving processes, as they have for millenia, thereby not only threatening the vital habitat of humans, and other fellow species, but also rendering our imaginations derelict, defunct and forlorn. The sense of awe and wonderment once reserved for the mystery of life and the wonder of nature, is now consigned to the far humbler, if more exploitative, province of the strip mall and the supermarket whose glossy wares deliver by far the only light in the eyes of a jaded, and overworked, populace that is profoundly out of touch with its own creative genius.

Analysis exceeded, if not totally anulled, empathy; and the scientist was reified as precisely the creature who embodied the bloodless, cold, and clinical, caricature of the anointed *expert*, the practitioner of a remote mystery with rotes and rituals beyond the comprehension of ordinary people now reduced to being the *subject-servants*, and feckless victims, of the scientific (and military-industrial) establishment.

Violence, the inevitable concomitant of masculinity and patriarchy generally, though ubiquitous enough in history, now took on a putatively "rational" form. All the liberties of the modernist world were still premised upon *the monopolistic appropriation of the technical means of violence*—now multiplied beyond the scope of human comprehension,—by the apparati of the state; force, far from being replaced by reason in human affairs, as the propaganda of the system still claims on a daily basis, was only institutionalized and made subject to the systemic needs of pattern maintenance requisite to corporate conquests.

The clear and simple marriage of modern science with military technology (by far the largest funded sector of scientific endeavors) was only the visible tip of the iceberg; *violence* was intrinsic to the very modus of the European scientific temper characterized by *misogyny* (as in the medical field where generations of "detached" *male* physicians affected to both comprehend and treat *female* ailments), *misanthropy* (where humans were seen as merely subjects and objects to be studied, analysed, and dispensed with as required by *raisons détat*, as in the myriad deadly human experiments carried out on vulnerable populations by the U.S. government, and its affiliate agencies, suitably exploited in media form by a series such as the *X-Files*), and rabid cultural and racial chauvinism.

Another form of violence, far more subtle but equally deadly, was the general *disposition* toward *nature* and other species. The Cartesian view of animals as akin to unfeeling machines, of necessity, carried terrible consequences, with the abominable treatment of animals, even in the putatively humane slaughterhouses of technically advanced European societies to this day, a special disgrace all in itself given the exaggerated self-image of European civility. Matters were no better even with respect to the inanimate processes of nature—the scientific revolution adopted a disdain for the renewable aspects of nature and a thoroughgoing contempt for its balances, so complete was its arrogant ideology of universal mastery, domination, and conquest. *Looking at it philosophically, the domination over, and despoliation of, non-Europeans, women, and nature, were all cut of the same instrumentalist cloth, wanton domination, rapine and plunder being directed toward each.* And, like a subterranean lake that feeds all rivulets, aggressive anthropocentrism, better understood in this context as *androcentrism*, served as the undergirding, even triumphalist, metaphysic of exploitation.

Even as materialism levelled all *things* (and *non-things*: consider social facts as "*things*," wrote the great Durkheim, in the ultimate spirit of objectivism), stripping human conduct of its humanity, and social actions of their inherent sociability, analysis was reified and placed in overlordship over empathy. Materialism travels under many guises in modernist discourse; in one form, it was simply the *assertion* of the nonexistence of a *First Principle* (i.e., a Creator), an early weapon employed in the power struggle with the Catholic church; in another, it was a *reductionism* of all human motives to material ones ("*in the last instance*" as the hoary Marxian fudge runs), as is favored in many of the social sciences; finally, it is the *presumption* of the ubiquity of greed and "self-interest" in "human natures" (as in the standard economics template). In all three instances, modernism *legislates* (and legitimates) the materialist viewpoint by *fiat*, not by any convincing combination of subtle argument and/or evidence. Suffice it to say that none of these tenets can be taken as self-evident, if only because they are all profoundly "one-sided": *materialism is only one epistemic,* that is, *presumptive, slant on the nature of the ontic universe—reality*, both "natural" and "social," elides such dispositive, univocal, *capture by definition.*

At any rate, the *scientific pose*, the very acme of dehumanization, was to be distal and aloof and apart from the wretched subject-objects that were to be "studied" putatively with Olympian detachment (though in reality informed with far more terrestrial political and ideological motivations), whether human or nonhuman, living or inanimate. Reason, in all its barren distemper when excised from feeling and emotion, was elevated over intuition, instinct, and revelation—in short, of all the routine human traits that allow for interactive perception, understanding, and identification. Introspective inspirations were permitted, as in the select ideological assumptions of economic theorizing, but only when in tune with necessary systemic drives liaising strictly with the requisite axioms of modernist discourse.

Social life, in rank positivist fashion, was objectified, atomized, compartmentalized, and dissected, until the pieces were so ill-formed, and deformed, that even a constitutive ideology could never again remember, let alone resurrect, the whole. In fact social science, astonishingly, was to become *the very means of doing away with society as an ontic entity*, by its being sliced into so many autonomous, and horizontally placed, and separately situated, "*sites*" of social *praxis*. Thereby modernism makes execrable isolates of us all, both ontically and epistemically, the better to order, sort, manipulate, and exploit the competing atoms with little other than the cash or the power nexus to bind them.

Linear views of progress helped to keep Sysiphian individuals climbing the proverbial hill and pacing the wheel endlessly convinced that on the morrow would be the promise of better vistas, regardless of how awful today might seem. Entire societies were thereby convinced of their own lowly and/or laggard nature, and instilled with the paradigmatic necessity to "*develop*" and march along the rocky yellow brick road to even more estrangement, lack of self-worth, and loss of identity. Succumbing to the bait of the modernist cornucopia of glittering commodities, that daily glare at us in full color through the diagonal of the standard cathode-ray tube, the numbing despair of everyday life, *outside the healing pale of self-direction and self-ratification*, was now to be forever routinized across the globe.

Science adopted the pose of sullen impersonality in the name of *objectivity*; indeed, having objectified the natural and social worlds into but so many marketable or appropriable artefacts, the latter feint was easy enough. The impersonality was far from reflecting a mere *affectation* of science at the ideological level:it reflected also the deep and thorough going *depersonalization* of a human society, an odd tendency given the regime's exaggerated fetish of individuality and humanism. Knowledge was not merely *de-personal*; it also had to be *abstract. In fact the more abstract—and general*—that is, *the more "context-free" one's ideas, the greater the scientific plausibility*. Small wonder mainstream economics and psychology are full of the tritest, most truistic propositions that are sufficiently banal, one would think, to "*apply*" anywhere and everywhere; and yet, despite their necessary, and considerable, vacuity, they simply, given the grace of a culturally diverse world and the inherent quirkiness of human behavior, still did not.

Contra the universalist prejudice of David Hume, *humankind is not pretty much the same everywhere, nor indeed anywhere. Social life is concrete*, and social behavior is *contextual*; the "scientific" resort to abstractions only suffices to create a spurious halo of omniscience in the detached observer, but is almost daily contradicted by the stuff of everyday life. Of course, the smart social scientist wisely relegates such bald objections of empirical reality safely to the netherworld of "*anomalies*." The very warp and woof of everyday research in the social sciences relate solidly to its system-maintaining, social control, function: endless studies of deviant behavior, studies of the underclasses, the poor, welfare recipients, peasants, women, and "other" cultures, *reflect clearly who is studying whom and for what*. Once again, sponsored analysis was to be the mortal enemy of empathy.

The feint of *universalism*, much as the pose of *objectivity*, was egregiously specious; the urge to classify, tabulate and record was a reflex of the governing, and growing, need to assess and control. *Contra* the beloved liberal prejudice, to affect *universalism* is precisely to deny the living humanity of peoples whose main commonality is their enduring sets of *differences*. *Culture is the supreme matrix of difference*; and the "universalist" form of modernist materialism by denying the specificity of culture, both debased and debunked it, with a view to deliberately fostering the identity of an *acultural*, social and economic being who could be *standardized* for both marketing and/or other allied purposes of exploitation. *We do not live in one world, but many*; and the globalization we see today is an extension of the corporatist need, modernist in provenance, of homogenizing it, as but a necessary prelude to exploitation and conquest of the resources of the globe. *To be humanist is not to erase difference—which is the quintessential hallmark of intolerance—but to respect it, and make allowances for it*: this is precisely what corporatist modernism denies almost as a First Principle.

Objectivism, a ruling fetish with modernist science, thrives only to the extent that, ontologically, things and non-things can be *objectified* (i.e. considered as "objects") and epistemically, we can be moved to view and review each other and ourselves, and our natural and social environment, as similarly depersonalized, dehumanized and/or *despiritualized*. It is this capacity for sovereign *detachment*—drawn deep from the icy hoard of *instrumental reason*—that the European has developed to the finesse of high art, although the nature of *abstraction* it presupposes, and requires, is a generalized *masculinist* attribute much as it is also the ruling ethos in the province of the cultivated indifference of ruling elites toward their satellite dependencies.

The horrific devices dropped on Japan represent, on the scale of human evolution, *the most calculated acts of barbarism in recorded history*; but they also exemplify the apotheosis of that clinical, abstract, capacity for *detachment* of grimly deliberate and conscious (modernist) human activity from its concrete, and catastrophic, consequence. To objectify, in a human context, is always to invite the certainty of disaster whether this attitude is projected to society or nature. *To dislodge reason from its nest in human empathy is another cardinal, egregious sin of modernism.* To then go on to counterpose it as superior to human affections is to descend a step lower and deeper into the darkest Hades of a dire misanthropy.

Eurocentrism, therefore, is none other than the constellar paradigm of Euro-capitalism, in its rich contusion of allied, conjunctural elements made up of capitalism, patriarchy (i.e., *misogyny*) *misanthropy, racism, colonialism, anthropocentrism, and recharged Christian ideology—or modernism, in a word.* If Europe will always remain the classical, paradigmatic *locus* of modernism, it is because that specific juxtaposition of elements was not, "naturally" so to speak, to be found anyplace else. Of course, hybrid and artificially bred versions of this classical specimen are cropping up today, here and there, in the non-European world, but rarely imbued with the raw dynamism and brute force of their awe-inspiring ancestor-template.

The Crusades were the first momentous step in the Great Modernist journey; within their adventurist fold were bred the early ideologies of colonialism, the unity of white Christendom, and that all too mundane missionary zeal: conquest for the Cross,that later would take on its uniquely modernist, capitalist form.

(26)

The Enlightenment ravished the animate and inanimate world with its fetishism of science, its delusive visions of progress, and its crass fealty to materialism. Worshipping wealth, warmly embracing the chimerical metaphysics of materialism, and passing off its ever devolving stages of moral and social debasement as so many memorable milestones in the magic manifest of progress, the modernist European strode the world with his oversize seven-league boots, reducing all of the grand experiments of human culture, the product of millenia of evolution and change, to the sullen, hollow grid of his own terrestrial (and now, *extra*-terrestrial) ambitions. Eventually, in our time, at the brink of a new millenium, he did achieve a modernist *nirvana* of sorts: the near-total *commodification* of all human values, near universally.

Decade after decade, more and more peoples spoke his tongue, aped his manners, and begged his attentions. In politics, economics, and societal mores, the *Great European Way* was to prevail with a monovalent monotony that is without parallel in the history of the human species. All *isms*, all icons, all idols, genuflected to his triumphal, scrofulous *modus* as greed, amorality, and normlessness swept the world in his terrible wake: *we are all Europeans now, regardless of creed or clime*, capitalism on our minds, patriarchy in our groins. It is the unhappy fate of the planet today to endure this *techno-barbarism*, and play its self-destructive war games to their frightening finish (Incipient *techno-fascism*, the ultimate apotheosis of European capitalism and modernism, a form of corporatist managerial ideology, rules the capitalist roost today, most clearly expressed in the evolving *geist* of U.S. society that celebrates the world as a corporate community transcending all other loyalties. Rejecting both liberal individualism and representative democracy, much as autarchy and socialism, it offers *one system for all* based on the modernist *Troika* of science, materialism, and progress, promoting a form of *corporate internationalism* that supercedes both nationalism and sovereignty. Fetishizing markets and reifiing technology, it offers the ideal of the consumptive life for all, with its governing laws to date as simple as: *consume, obey—be silent*).

Who with the temerity now to oppose his ways? The globalization of his ethos is complete; his networks, military and commercial, span the globe: we are prey to the meretricious gloss of his wares, and the awesome power of his war-machines, and all species now await his pleasure with trepidation. The terrible consequences of the paramountcy of his all but irresistible ways are already visible all about us as the planet reels from the unceasing, accelerating, and multifaceted affronts to its eternal balances; the grim charter of ecocide and the annihilation of the vital bases of human and social existence perennially located within a matrix of civility and hospitability has been granted a *carte blanche* without parallel or precedent in the history of human existence, as we all lurch on, benightedly, from crisis to crisis, with the imminence of some or other form of impending disaster almost coded into our expectations of everyday life.

Never have so many faced the prospect of slow, but certain, extinction from the actions of a few; and never has ordinary human greed, traditionally confined to the venality of the few, and the vanities of a few others, taken on such a systematic, crusading, global form of evangelical faith. The climax of a short but horrific history of modernist annexation and annihilation that stands put to end all human, and planetary, history is upon us now, in this dangerous new millennium of the rule of finance capital and racketeer capitalism, and may no longer be elided. What can be done? How might he, and his ways, be resisted? How can this flagging planet now be exempted from his ruinous sway? These, in a nutshell, are the great, pressing, even vital, questions of our times.

4. On Human Emancipation: The Archaeology of Discontent

(27)

European social ideologies, within which modern (and modernist) *social science* occupies a hallowed and hegemonic space, as evolved in the great ferment of the so-called "Enlightenment," were conceived within the ruinous premises of an A*nthropocentrism* that was undoubtedly *Judeo-Christian* in inspiration (albeit within a significantly *corrupted* version of the latter). The necessary subordination of "*nature*" to "*man*" (this casual *androcentrism* is far more commonplace in the epistemes of the human world than *anthropocentrism*, and needs to be carefully distinguished from the latter) within such an episteme had predictably disastrous consequences for the planet, and its luckless denizens.

Euro-rationalism would bifurcate the human subject herself, as it already had all of Creation in its *nature-culture* antinomy, into a *rational-emotive* divide wherein all impulses stemming from our "*natural*" being were debased, disregarded or otherwise disparaged as being "lesser" attributes shared by such unworthies as women, savages, and animals (the German term, "*naturvolk,*" for instance, admirably captures this general sentiment of revulsion with respect to indigenous peoples). *"Man" was thereby separated from, and elevated above, "nature": similarly, all men from all women—and European men from all other men, women, and cognate species. In effect, the white, European, capitalist male was to be seen as the very embodiment of pure reason, the standard, and template, against which all lesser forms of life, suitably categorized as constituting but the "white man's burden," were to be measured (and, quite "naturally," found wanting).*

Few can scale in the incredible consequences, social, ecological, and political, stemming from the paramountcy of such a simple, if macabre, epistemic assumption. Realists and traditional materialists likewise need to take serious note of the cataclysmic power of (simple) ideas in human society; ideas have profound material consequences regardless of their "rightness" and "wrongness" as judged by external and "independent" ontic standards. At any rate, this untoward presumption, carried over from theological premises, conferred an implicitly subterraneous, but nonetheless prepossessing perspective that *justified*, at the level of deeply held beliefs, real ontic oppressions and depredations as momentous for human history as the conquest of Africa, the domestic subjugation of women, and the destruction of living ecologies everywhere that Europe went. The human (i.e., *male*) propensity to seek high honorific, preternatural *justification for conduct* (whether becoming or unbecoming) is apparently as intense as the more terrestrial desires of avarice, exploitation, and rapine.

At any rate, the unnatural elevation of "reason"—or, more accurately, a *modernist rationality*—above other human characteristics involved, necessarily, the wholesale suppression of motivations, instincts, and propensities that were at least as natural to the human species as reason itself (*emotions explain nothing*, wrote the great Levi-Strauss loftily with the aplomb characteristic of lawgivers: *they* that must be explained). These "*lower*" traits were "naturally" consigned to the *lesser* races, women, and workers (as in the rabidly misanthropic fantasies of Thomas Malthus wherein both the Irish, early colonial victims of English ire, in particular, and workers in general, are singled out for much choice abuse), but *verboten*, in *noblesse oblige* idiom, to the European ruling elite males that were to contentedly believe that they embodied the very soul of an elevated reason even as they were committing, or planning the execution of, abominable atrocities unworthy of the most undeveloped "savage."

The premise of this highly (gagged and) *bounded* rationality was, at another remove, to verily be enshrined as the guiding norm in the study of social motivations, as in the case of *economics*, thereby *prejudging* an entire cosmos of human innovation and practice and almost completely nullifying both the explanatory and predictive value of the aspirant "science." Worse, entire areas of anthropic *conviviality*, from sexuality, to food, to simple enjoyment of life itself, was trivialized and debased as belonging to the unwholesome sphere of "*primitive*," indolent, and slothful biological drives. The European, in the name of reason, was canonizing and consecrating, as in Calvinist ideas of elevated conduct, *the ineffable drabness of a joyless economy* and an eternally competitive, *unhappy* society as the distinctively exemplary ethos of modernism.

Of course, the non-European world initially received all this with a suitable sense of shock, dismay, and disbelief, until prolonged exposure, and much duress, pushed them into succumbing, albeit in varying degrees, to such a perverse inversion of normalcy. Closer to their *species-being*, closer to emotions, passions, and instinctual drives (all of which were to be ridiculed by Europeans as manifest signs of "*underdevelopment*"), they could only marvel at the European capacity for radical self-delusion in these areas. Suspecting something amiss all the while, they still could not desist from marveling at the (misanthropic) spirit of *rational calculation* that the European exhibited in all spheres of social conduct, despite the frequent shocks of painful learning as available in those recurrent, yet unpredictable, acts of treachery, betrayal, and bestiality that their colonial masters could mete out, in violent disregard of the dissembling cloaks of reason and temperance, whenever their self-interest, or *amour propre*, so demanded it.

The inherent *dualism* of the ruling European character here—*reason but a thin cover for an utter lack of ruth*—has never really been transcended, with the United States, in the modern period, setting even newer and lower standards of betrayal of promise, treaty, and contract, while urging all others, upon sufferance, to obey the "*rule of law*." The non-European can only remain bemused by this transparent double-standard; and the astute Chinese may well be pardoned if they never accept, in all due and civilizationally based cynicism and distrust, *any* European pronouncement at face value today. In effect, that reason is ever mediated by self-interest to the point of its wholesale subversion is a story that is not told enough in modernist folklore with its forever expanding and *simpliste* charters of *asocial* freedom, *amoral* peace, and commodified progress, as daily fed to its tractably gullible, and blandly trusting, citizenry.

(28)

What the consequences, one might ask, when all that has been "*naturally*" human: love, passion, and all of humankind's recreational instincts, are banished into exile, privatized within the rapidly eroding limits of the individuated household, and rendered worthy only of regulation, denial, and suppression? The answers lie in the quintessentially modernist divide between state and civil society that the bourgeois-Calvinists were to enshrine as a socially viable model at the dawning of the modern era, or more simply in the schizophrenia that radically divides the *public* from the *private* spheres in the modernist epoch. The role of the male in this new societal model of patriarchy is quite crucial; not only did Calvinist "*Man*" appropriate the public domain for himself, capturing it so to speak and insulating it, until only very recently, from women (and minorities), *qua* "Man" he also reserved the right to move freely between the two spheres, a right not available to *non-males* (and *minorities*, epistemically assimilated to the latter classification). Only *He*, in effect, could be the "head" of the family and the "head" of the political household at the same time.

The harder the lines of this *critical separation*—a variable within the various modernist European tribes themselves—the more pronounced the social division between men and women, exacerbating the various *momenta* of the *natural* divide between them. The appropriation of reason, and its highest *masculine* use—*statecraft*—to the public domain carried the implicit implication of denying its pedagogy within the household now reserved only as a site for reproductive, and consumptive, rites, relations, and rituals. With reason and its applications, including, and especially, *productivity*, being attributed to the *male*, *women*, and their counterparts, stripped of power and authority, could now perform only subordinate, *consumptive*, emotive, functions once their social importance had been suitably downgraded and diminished. Metaphorically, the traditional run of the "*first-world/third-world*" divide is yet another version of this very schizoid ideology of Calvinist patriarchy, with the "third world" largely being placed in the role of the submissive, "*feminine*," subaltern counterpart of its productive, "advanced," first world, masculinist masters.

The ontic/epistemic consequence of such a horrific scheme of ideas is simply the banal, modernist world we all inhabit today, reversing as an article of faith all self-evidently obvious, natural, and historically human, polarities. Stated simply, the hard-driven "*producer*" of capitalist economic mythology (which betrays as mortally unidimensional a bankruptcy of a *real* understanding of the social economy as the dry cosmos of barren reason itself) could hardly last a day if the putatively "*passive*" *consumer* did not exist to provide him regular, and dependable, ontic sustenance, as must be self-evidently, and trivially, obvious to all those not succumbed to the lure of the false weightings of *Euro-ideologies*.

In terms of critical, anthropic, priorities, for example, *the ecology of food production is far more vital to the well-being of the species than the economy of laptops*. And yet, the society committed to laptops ranks immeasurably higher in modernist parlance than the community resolved "*only*" to producing food (much as *women "only" produce life itself*, and have that activity scorned and ridiculed in the grim litany of modernist ideology); worse still, given its implacable *logos*, modernism is likely to render, suicidally, that "*other*" domain, the very fount of its own nourishment, extinct as fast as market, and allied, forces allow!

The debasement of women, of nature, and other cultures, is based on a self-similar, radical, and grotesque misappreciation of real values as opposed to marketized ones. The entire thrust of modernist polity, economy, and culture is not merely to devalue and dominate *femininity*, but to render the *personal/social economy of nurturance* itself historically defunct.

(29)

The general predisposition toward the unavoidable fact of human *mortality* is, inevitably, a key index of the stature and quality of civilization in a human society. Mortality may be assumed to be the underlying cue to the preservational preoccupation of all species in the state of nature; yet the very human capacity to *mediate* direct apprehension of all reality with various epistemic dodges places limits on the nature and extent of this self-realization. The capacity to *sublimate* the more awkward and unpleasant aspects of existence is itself part of a species of protective devices that may also be taken as "*natural*" to the human species being the corrective cost of the free gift of conscious self-realization. To that extent, the *delusive* side to all epistemes needs to be considered as a serious issue in human life, reflecting our so-called "*myth-making*" capacities, which are quite considerable.

Faith is the necessary anodyne making bearable the grim, and finite, limit to human existence vested in us by the anonymous author(s) of creation. It is, thereby, natural and fitting that almost all premodern peoples nursed some abiding belief in an extraterrestrial force, from magic to religion, as expressed in a litany of rites and rituals. *It was the singular contribution of the European to convert this spiritual and religious faith in a supernatural entity into a secular and material religion worshipping far more mundane idols, thereby contributing to the desanctification of reality and its concomitant despiritualization.* It was this that Max Weber understood as the process of *disenchantment* that "*rational*" philosophy set into motion virtually inexpugnably: but of course he was wrong. Neither science, nor rationalism, nor even the philosophy of materialism, entail any such *necessary, or inevitable*, dissolution of the very basis of the emotive life; indeed civilizations have existed, and still exist, possessed of both science and reason, without implying, or necessitating, any form of *spiritual* reductionism.

It was not that the paraphernalia of science, rationalism, and materialism were employed as intrumentalist weapons against religion; *rather that religion itself was corroded, and corrupted, from within, so as to exist only as parody. Protestant thinking is not so much reform as much as a grim, rejectionist parody of Christianity, reflecting the Europeanization—or Modernization—of a deep, and affective, Eastern faith.* The *Great Inversion* of Calvinism made the high points of the religious life, on the basis of a specious ideology, for the first time in human history, entirely subservient to more mundane, and profane, pursuits.

Indeed, the sobrietous hollowness of the typical Protestant church of today set against the backdrop of modernist corruption where, once a week, there is a solicitous exchange of superficial banalities between pastor and congregation, each anxious to get back as soon, and as decorously, as possible to the normal, and far more appealing, business of life, is a singularly *underwhelming* sight to behold. A swat team, or a parade of nuclear weapons, might well inspire more reverence for, and a greater fear of, the Maker, than your typical Protestant Sunday mass. The modernist Caesar, in the guise of Mammon, wants, and demands, far more from his populace, apparently, than any vengeful, despotic, oriental god; but, in contrast, no church could ask for *less* from its listless congregation of the suit-and-tie vassals of Mammon.

The virtual suppression of all the variegated intimations of mortality is modernism's greatest, if highly dubious, success; *Euro-capitalism* has excelled in engendering a *robot-consumer* who, virtually from cradle to grave is unaware of her own patent of transience. The glare of neon, the glitz of the avalanching commodity stream, and the strobe of randomly re-directed pangs of desire have suppressed the very memory of our daily dying. A *desublimated* Eros has banished Thanatos to the designer cemeteries that dress up as flowering wonderlands, the better to disguise their truth as the final, shabby abode of *man*'s (gender specificity intended) reckless, and ultimately unrequited, greeds.

This silencing of the grim, muted, mnemonic echoes of our dire and incomprehensible mortality requires the abundance of the noise cacophonic that twenty-first-century media specialize in producing and reproducing almost without cessation. *The sun is never allowed to set over the proliferating sonic waves of the great soundbytes of modernism.* So ubiquitous is the smothering blanket of noise in modernist life that the only true moments of social embarrassment left are the occasional, unscripted pauses, when we are left face to face with our own inner void, where the life spirit surges up inspiring self-recognition only to be swiftly smothered again by some mechanical artifice.

Endless activity, the breathless pursuit of this and that to the point of radical *neuro-exhaustion*, is the uniquely European, modernist, means of escape from our primordial, genetic fate. Indeed, *the tempo is everything*: the electrifying pace at which everything is produced and delivered in the media universe, the manner in which we are increasingly required to post ourselves over land and sea as if we were merely a set of inert, insentient packages and not psychosomatically alive *beings* with convivial attachments that may not be sundered without serious injury to our emotive lives, are reflective of the need for everyone to be kept "*busy*," moving, and restless.

Everyone is busy; no one can afford not to be—and leisure, reflection, reclamation of the social appropriation of private time, are all understood as subversive of the very spirit of modernism; *as such, the new initiatives in globalization are only the thrust to extend this sweatshop, hothouse, mental frame to all cultures and climes*. The more mindless the pursuit, the more trivial the impulse, the more appropriate it is: *for the stark truth is that if we "take thought," even for an instant, we die*. Worse, in that pregnant pause, we are reminded of our cosmic bio-clocks—so we die in dwelling, for just an instant, on the unwelcome foreknowledge of the inevitable.

And so it is that even the rest and recreation reflexes of the system are consumptive of high-energies and high costs; modernism "organizes" the getaway itself to be so resource/energy-intensive that it makes an early return to the daily treadmill seem by far the cheaper, calmer, alternative. *As such, we only meet ourselves, none too cheered, returning from our spasmodic breaks from routine even before we leave. Modernism does not, will not, let us die real, anthropic deaths* of social rupture and grief primordial: we are supposed, instead, to suddenly and indecorously disappear, as images do on TV screens at a flick of the undertaker's all but invisible switches.

The expected reaction to such a *modus* of social organization can only be the burgeoning of a resistive resolve stemming from our inherent *anthropic* capacity to seek expressive outlets for *spiritual* faith; as such, it is only fitting that the largest modernist entity of our times—the United States—is the site of more registered mini-faiths, from the sublime to the grotesque, than all the religions and cults of the rest of the world taken together.

Effulgent activity, that is, action multiplied by speed and made deafening by amplified sound (as available in the ubiquitous video arcades of modernism), is the real means by which we erase the normal human function of memory, history, and recall of things and non-things past, dissolving it in the abiding sense of a *decentred* fleeting nothingness as we fly through a mall or an airport hoping to leave all unpleasantness behind, from broken hearts to busted bank accounts. Life begins anew not every day, nor with each "new year's resolution," but virtually every instant as we invent ourselves over and over, discarding old, and unserviceable selves, striving for a new identity in the surreal glaze of hallucinatory images that are our visions of ourselves and others. It is no wonder that, within such a state of mind, death itself comes as but another cloak, another mantle, another psychedelic "state" of being—and becoming. It is meant to take us unawares as we are lingering in one or other of the hedonistic stupors that the sensate life, as carefully organized by a corporatist culture, provides us incessantly.

The old churches were quiet, secluded cloisters for reflection; the new temples of modernism are the garishly lit sites for insensate stupefaction. So *non-living* are we, that it is doubtful that the true new millennium denizen, in his/her purple haze of delusion, might even notice that he/she is about to be overtaken by the fell sweep of mortality; nor would the passer-by, in a heady rush herself, take a second look. This is quite apart from the common social practice in human societies of the wanton *sublimation* of sex, death, and eliminatory functions, *and is in fact their desublimation*: to be exhumed and displayed in the public domain, quietly and politely, but only so as to *desensitize* the perceiving world already inured to the starkness of the rupture at stake. Classical Christian anthropocentrism did not just involve placing "man" at the centre of evolution, but also to draw a veil over his obvious "*animalism*"; its latter-day modernist corruption has now rudely torn off that decorous veil. It is all right, like a Bruce Willis or a Schwarzenegger, in latter-day Hobbesian fashion, to be bare brutish in aspect, because, heck, it is "a jungle out there."

(30)

The human being is a mammalian animal, with few traits, if at all, independent of the characteristics of that species. Like some others, the male of the species is a predator vested, bio-chemically, by his Creator with the will to kill and inflict violence in the search for sustenance, space, suzerainty, a mate, and family. The female of this species, biochemically, is driven also, by instinct, to engender offspring and seek the means of sustenance to nurture them. It is this set of invariant impulses, howsoever mediated/mitigated by culture and socialization, that explains, in large part, the story of human history and the never ending real and illusory tension between, and within, the genders.

At least initially, the "social" is simply an *extension* of such primordial mammalian units, *with mother and child being perhaps the basic, enduring unit of the original, and perennial, societal frame*, given the apparent fact that the maternal instinct is more enduring than the paternal one; as such, the "need" for security and safety and hospitability—*toward children*—and hence for some semblance of permanence in social relations, is a reflex merely of biological necessity.

The universal guarantors of civility, and hence civilization, is the set of expectations and requirements surrounding this primordial, feminine, "social" unit. In this important way, "nature" is at the very basis of the construction of human "culture"; in this way biology impinges on society. Despite the offense this does to the various myths of Creation dear to Christian anthropocentrism, and its secular "social science" equivalent, the human is only a self-sublimated version of the mammalian animal (in a grotesque transmogrification, it would appear that *Euro-modernism* almost succeeded in imbuing, that is, *re-engineering*, this warm blooded human mammal with manifestly *reptilian* traits by radically cooling the social temper of affections).

Nonetheless, this sublimation is a social fact; and culture is nothing but a given set of modalities within this social process. The extent to which such acquired cultural traits can suppress the more basic organismic attributes is a matter of empirical reality differing both *within* the various tribes of the human family as much as between *individuals* within those tribes. However, the near invariant fact of *warfare* across the species is standing tribute to the thin veneer of civility that masks, but only slightly, the truculent organism underneath, in particular the virulent, masculine aspect of it.

Most, if not all, of the ills of humankind stem from the genus, and instinctual drives, of masculinity, not merely in its social-ideological form of *patriarchy*, but in its stark, genetic form that is common to all human formations, the decorous myths of Margaret Mead to the contrary notwithstanding. *War is not (merely) a "social" device, as argued in European, modernist, ideologies, but a far more prior, natural artifice* and is the direct, or indirect, efflux of singularly masculine instincts of success, survival, and suppression. Refusal to countenance this simple fact accounts for much of the ills of social policy in the modernist era, based as they are on a wilful, disingenuous, ignorance of the real provenance of much of our behaviors.

Violence is to men, or rather to *masculinity*—which is both of "natural" and social cultivation—as uranium presumably is to nuclear devices: *it is their very essence.* It takes on multiple forms in their *persona*, not at all restricted to its more brutish expressions as in rape, assault, and murder, but also in simpler manifestation of anger, churlishness, impatience, egotism, and irascibility. It is expressed every day, at home and abroad, in a panoply of ways, in modes of speech, body language, knee-jerk reactions, and such. *In all its forms, it is deeply misanthropic, misogynist, and predatory toward all forms of life and constitutes a deeply embedded threat to the very notion of nurturance and empathy upon which the future of this planet may now well depend.* Its most recognizable symbol today, within the extant *culture of death of modernism*, is the new prototypical Hollywood "*hunk*"—as symbolized in its original, menacing, *Rambo* avatar—that is now the biggest cultural export of the United States, globally. In effect, the Great American Propaganda machine is succeeding in educating and inducting the naïve, and the less developed (within this *genre*) of *other* cultures, in the stereotypes of repressive, patriarchical, *desublimation: that is, modernist androcentrism.* The kinder, gentler social forms globally, where they still exist, are succumbing to this violent celebration of this quintessential paradigm of male aggression. The ideological militirizastion of American life, hearkening back to the early adventurist, guns and glory history of colonial America, is the outstanding feat of cultural engineering of the late twentieth century, vested with portentous consequences for the world.

Masculinity abounds also in a critical domain not always understood for its significance for the project of human violence, that is, the suppression of emotions by the intellect: indeed, this is at the very heart (or is it head?) of the internalization of a *structural attitude of violence.* "Pure" reason, that is, *reductionist* reason, is always at the expense of spirit, of feeling, of warmth; it is cold and dry—it objectifies, detaches, and desensitizes us to all but our own interests. European modernism has, thereby, taken the "*natural*" project of masculinity to its cultural apotheosis: the steely resolve of reason unchained from its healing matrix of feelings stands ready to sweep away all that stands in its path—*and this much unites disparates such as Napoleon, Stalin, Hitler, or Reagan.*

This infelicitous "*capacity for abstraction,*" when wedded to Calvinist materialism, has already produced two world conflagrations, in this past century—the "greatest" century of modernism—and nearly started an apocalyptic third one. If the truth be told, however, there is a *Third* World War, an Armageddon, already, and far ahead, on: *it is European modernist cupidity and avarice versus the survival of this planet and all its dependent species.* At any rate to *feel,* to be concrete, to be local, and kindred-based in our affiliations and interests remains the only solicitous alternate to the tyranny of detached, abstract, world-conquering, male-driven modernism. Until recently, women, workers and native peoples the world over unself-consciously exhibited these consilient traits, though they too are now capitulating, but only slowly, to the avalanche of modernist behavioral grids being imposed on them. To stem this ruinous advance of amoral, hedonistic, materialist, masculinist, science and reason, might well be the first order of this grim business of ensuring planetary survival; or rather, more pointedly, the survival of humans on this planet.

The ills of social life (wherein the possibility of War might be adjudged the most critical), thereby, are as much a necessary adjunct of *social forces, as* the latter themselves stem directly from the relatively invariant, knee-jerk, "*natural*" attributes, behaviors, and responses of the male ego. Interestingly, while this glaringly obvious aspect of patriarchy is common to all societies, there is yet a significant difference between modernist European formations and pre-modernist cultures with respect to the nature and form of the sublimatory veils drawn across such prepossessions.

So-called *gynocentric* forms of patriarchy appear to be qualitatively apart from their *androcentric* counterparts; in the former, the "status" of women assumes a marginally elevated role that carries an ideological, and relatively benign, stereotyping centred on their maternity (most matrilineal social formations seem to embody this relatively benign *fertility* based "vision"), whereas the androcentric forms, closer to the modernist variant, debase the female principle, *in toto*, virtually commodifying the very person of the female as in the contemporary slatternly, but typically modernist, contusions of the porn parlor. *It is also useful to note that the pornographic impulse itself is a unique episteme of modernism with no pre-modernist surrogates.*

If *masculinity*, both ontically inherent, and augmented ideologically, is the critical mainspring of the ills of this world, other than the desperation(s) prompted by the higher ordinance of mortality itself, then the only hope for any genuine amelioration of the human condition must stem from the sustained effort to contain its structurally predatory impulses. Like so many scourges, to a limited extent, the disease is itself a part-cure; that is, one great and enduring check to the depredations of masculinity is the similar endowment(s) of other men. However, such internecine warfare neither eliminates the problem (though the cold war certainly brought matters to the brink of all human extinction), nor has it sobered deeprooted, masculinist resolves which are, *au contraire*, in a phase of a resurgent "great leap forward" with modernism unbound at the present conjuncture.

The other, ancillary, mechanisms may be briefly addressed: standing at the apex of such resolves, *sublimation* is an almost "natural" device for taming the male ego, and indeed may be the most plausible (given its "natural" roots) reformatory instrument, though it apparently requires the fortuitous intervention of a rousingly charismatic nature, a possibility that these perilous times may yet provide. In point of fact, *religious* charisma has often intervened in human history to subdue the wilder passions, at least for a duration. Ideological education, of a more secular nature, can go a small distance but is unlikely to be forthcoming, in the present instance, given the capture of power structures by the *male principle* even where and when women constitute, as they increasingly do, the (office of) *nominal* governors.

Indeed the current age, led by the ever barbarous United States, has not only led a popular culture offensive of *desublimation* for decades now—as part of a planned cultural *counterrevolution* against the "*decadence*" of the sixties era of mass protest—but also has increasingly, by means of policy, enforced the induction of women into male norms of performance, attitude, and behaviors Given its influence on the rest of the world that lives now in its hapless ontic shadow, it is safe to assume that such norms, unless unchecked, will soon spread worldwide. Patriarchy inadvertently, and by force, protected half the human race from *modernist* corruptions; now it is hastening the induction of women into those very misanthropic mores.

One beguiling side issue may now be referred to. If women, apparently, can be so easily and ideologically stripped of their *affective femininity*—at least at the level of the self-conscious mind—is something similar not also possible in *reverse*, with masculinity being robbed of its essence, similarly, by policy means? Regrettably, the answer is a simple no: *to convert virtue into vice is a simple matter, given the lure of temptation, but vice versa (!) is possibly going against the grain*. Also, purely mental conditioning that goes against nature's implants is unlikely to prevail, except temporarily, as a transient phase: in that regard, even the current *masculinization* of women is also only a passing aberration not likely to rise to the level of *mutation*. So-called civilization is, sad to say, for all its vaunted importance in human history, barely skin deep; and the bestiality of masculinity is not only easily aroused but darkly stalks virtually all dimensions of everyday life with its ugly presence; only the dissembling contours of modernist ideology, itself the apogee of masculinity, makes us all but inured to its virulence and ubiquity.

The radical feminist dream of a world without men is, thereby, quite implausible despite its potential appeal; and the token *de-linking* from men, if not male institutions, that some women are able to achieve *micro*-cosmically within human society—another possible "solution"—is as yet the preserve of the few, often bought at the expense of the many. The financial independence of some European women in the nerve-centres of European society, which gives them the possibility of a measure of emancipation from male relationships, is not independent of the servitude of their less fortunate sisters in the periphery of the modernist world, and may even be contingent upon it. Despite the *qualitative* importance of such experience for the women involved in such experiments, in numerical terms it lacks serious proportionality in relation to the depth of the problem; and it is entirely possible that the tolerance—or indifference—of modernism toward such *ghettoized* cloisters of women is simply because their numbers are, still, so few. Any escalation in this regard, and the possibility of preemptive policy strikes against them becomes a very real and credible check to this emergent *modus* of freedom.

Nor is genetic engineering, despite the fanfare about the Human Genome Project, a credible salve, though the dream of a *lobotomic* rearrangement of the male psyche is, admittedly, an attractive flight of fancy; but, as must be obvious, technologies of this kind belong only to fantasies of a robotic, *techno-fascist* nirvana. Species instincts can be, within limits, tamed and sublimated but not eradicated without risking wholesale extermination of the original template itself by dint of the engineering, deliberately or fortuitously, of mutant forms. In effect, there *is* immanent purpose to the universe—*nature does have a "plan"*—the thwarting of which can only produce that which we do not, and cannot, know.

The problem, as posed, may appear inherently insuperable whilst approached in conventional terms; the "trick," however, is to dispense with the conventional "materialist" logics that we normally employ in such discourses The possibility that has stared humanity in the face for *aeons* is the possibility of *spiritual transcendence*, not of the "masses" at large, which is absurd, but of a *critical mass* within them which *is far more sustainable. Being herd animals, as given by our* hominid natures, the rest can usually be expected to follow where the few lead; indeed that has been (for all the offense this realization offers to the run of humanist ideologies) and still is, the way of human society. This is neither to be lamented nor celebrated: it is just an ontic truth which is as obvious as daylight—it is the few that everywhere not only sit astride the commanding heights of the social-scape but also point the way, to the many who dumbly follow, to greener or gaudier pastures as the case may be. However, short of such charismatically inspired spiritual transformations—which do occur in history—there is yet hope for the idea of a *convivial* society, if in another, more promising, domain.

The possibility of redemption appears realizable only because various *premodernist* social formations exhibit its reality in various approximations. *The political economy of care and consideration is not in need of either discovery or invention: it is the very founding principle of kindred-based tribal formations.* The fact that it coexists with patriarchical, masculinist, even violent, institutional artefacts is a statement not of the rank failure of such living experiments but in fact of their lack of *full closure* within the matrix of the principles they espouse. At the very least they hold out an abject, but instructive, lesson to the votaries of the *Hobbesian-modernist* society as to the real possibilities of a *non-competitive*, relatively pacific, social environs of *human* design.

Civilizations, a term that should, *a priori*, exclude *all* modernist societies in principle, managed, across millennia, to subdue the murderous impulses of men, imprisoning them—howsoever fragile the cage—within the healing bonds of *affective* ties, such that even their predations had limited success and scope. It is true that, placed on a continuum, such forms range widely in terms of levels of pacifism and cooperation; significant, though, that any and all modernist formation(s) would be at the wrong and extreme end in that regard—for it is *Euro-capitalist* modernism that has departed the farthest from the blessed ideals of the anthropic Eden ironically cloaked in the dissembling guise of the pharisaical slogans of liberty, self-interest, and progress. *The Modernist has been the most war-like of all human tribes; and the United States, where modernism is state religion, is today the most war-like of all modernist formations.*

The secret of the civility of tribal formations is quite easily revealed: it stems from their embrace of the "*feminine*" (of course, in a social sense, it is *separatist* male ideology that has bestowed the "*feminine*" adjective on the set of values that patriarchy shuns; this does not obviate the fact of a "*natural*" basis for nurturance pre-given "naturally" to women as child-bearers) values of care and cooperation, itself the foundation of kinship based institutions where the tribe is merely a larger, more extended, family than the foundational, base unit. At the heart of this formation is the hearth and home, with the *mother–child* relation as the "real" foundation of the latter. As pointed out, the possibility of civility in a human group arises "*naturally*" from the need for a modicum of peace and stability to allow for procreation and child-rearing, given the gestation period of humans and the prolonged infancy, hence vulnerability, of the human child.

In this vital way, it is nature that makes the social not merely possible but necessary. Clear and obvious, also, *that women stand at the epicentre of this civility and hence are the real trustees, the very founding members of civilization; as child bearers, and embodied with nurturance as an instinct, they are also the ever perpetual founts of human conviviality*. Aeons before the so-called "*welfare state*" entered the calendar/lexicon of modernism (by dint of the struggles of the *sans cullote*) women nurtured the anthropic family, through thick and thin, with their *gratis*, and incessant, labors: and they do so still.

This is merely a bald statement of fact and does not pretend to address the issues that go to the heart of the feminist revolt against the "*madonna*" style stereotyping of the nurturing roles of women within some modes of patriarchy. Epistemic freedom allows humans—that is the meaning of the much vaunted "*free will*" of philosophy—to often strike out beyond the constraints of ontic bounds, though the latter can, and do, often impose themselves, oft-times ruthlessly, on our self-assumed "freedoms." Or so it would appear (*the fact that women were "condemned" to nurturance, within patriarchy, as many feminists would argue—despite the real, anthropic basis to this felicity—does not disparage nurturance itself as a pleasing human value*: the point is not to belittle care and consideration, which ennobles all, nor to tear women forcibly away from such activities under the false modus of "liberation," *but rather, perhaps, to draw the male himself into the varied hospitalities of the paradigm of nurturance*).

(31)

But what are these ontic bounds, anyway? *The real cannot be subsumed under the apparent, or even the obvious, since the latter is a reflex only of our limited, and limiting, anthropic senses*; it is traditional European physics, under the spell of a vulgar materialism that sees nature as inert, "dead" (when we as *humans-within-nature* defy that inertness and lifelessness, *ipso facto*, by our very existence), flat, and monotonic. *After Prigogene, we should not doubt that matter is "intelligent"; after Bohm, that we live in a "participant" reality, wherein there is an "Implicate" order of which the observed universe is only a silhouette; after Schrodinger and Heisenberg, we should know that matter is also elusive and escapes easy detection and/or determinate self-measurement. And, after post-Quantum physics, that we live, not merely in a self-aware universe, but in a self-fulfilling universe, all of which should gainsay the pretensions of the Positivism of modernist science with its strict canons of an intransitive separation between observer and observed, and simple inductions from a frozen reality of "facts." Contra* Einstein, "god" not only plays dice—but a myriad other games of which we know very little.

True that, with the development of Quantum physics in this century, and a somewhat deeper understanding of the multi-textured nature of the universe, much of the traditional *naivete* of classical physics, at least in the area of cosmology, has waned in comparatively recent times; yet, given mainstream orientations, matter still remains defined (at any given time) in traditionally reductionist, "material" terms whereas it is, in reality, as abstruse, and fundamentally undecipherable, as life itself.

All we can claim to know is that "reality," like a layered onion, may only be peeled in endless regress, not "revealed" once and for all, with each layer (or "state") only showing us the pathetic bounds of our own sensate ignorance (which should gainsay the recent, rather vain, Stephen Hawking vision of achieving "closure" in the discipline within a few years, as boastfully uttered by this canonical modernist physicist decades ago; curiously, his "big bang theory," upon which he based his rash ebullience, is now already being discredited in line with the discovery of endlessly repeated cycles of creation and destruction, in line *again with the prognostications of Vedic physics: sic transit gloria mundi). Reality, like truth, is an unfolding, not a frieze to be "captured" by the all-seeing eye in one flash of anthropic vanity* (finite in so many ways, we yet seek, but only in the modernist vein, complete knowledge of infinity).

All we anthropic beings know, if only vaguely, and within the pre-given anthropic limits of our highly fallible senses, about the "apparent" universe ("natural," "societal") is that there is "determinism" (*macro order*) and also "free will" (*sub-atomic disorder/unpredictability*), randomness (*arbitrariness, chance*), and some unknown/unknowable "*other order*" principle/force that immanently endows us/others with life/consciousness much as it endows the universe with its specific character. The first three attributes, logically comprehensible/testable, are enough to constitute a mundane, secular view of the ontic; the last requires an additional intuition far from unknown to our species and as such (given the ubiquity in human society of super-ordinary "faith") is possibly intrinsically vested in our instinctual apparati. If admissible, then the cosmic chariot runs, at least, on four distinct wheels; at any rate, "admissible" or not, *a complete cosmology of the anthropically perceived universe cannot, perforce, omit any of these hypothetical attributes. Modernist science ordained the first trait, disdained the second until very recently, can make nothing of the third, and disallows/debunks the last, purely ex definitione.*

Ancient Vedic philosophy gleaned much about such matters, but only in terms of subtle and elliptical general principles, which modern physics is only now approximating, about the multi-textured complexity, and the playful and delusive nature, of the manifest universe. Given this apprehension, *the traditional, modernist, distinction between ontology and epistemology begins to fade; it appears to be an "interactive" universe where the viewer and the viewed are apart only in a shared delusion.* If so, the ontic limit is an unknowable one; and it may well be that epistemic delusions can "*create*" an *explicate* reality quite indistinguishable from any other *implicate* one that may, hypothetically, be presumed to "lie beyond."

Certainly, the little we know from clinical studies of *parapsychology* and *extra*-sensory perception tell us, if nothing else, at least how scant is our knowledge about the properties of the reality we live in and under. Far from standing atop the very apex of human knowledge today, as with triumphalist European delusions of scientific grandeur, we appear to be only at the brink of the very dawn of consciousness of the larger universe both within and without us. Close to four hundred years of modernist, materialist, positivist, reductionist, and "*scientistic*" vandalism—insisting on a mechanical, unconscious universe of a "dead" nature—has all but destroyed the higher forms of knowledge, nay wisdom, bequeathed us by our forebears that yet might light the way to self-knowledge and redemption, *if only we pay heed.*

The fact that we can measure, decipher and gauge the world around us (not necessarily *qualitatively* better than the ancients: the Indians and Chinese calculated the value of *pie*, hundreds of years ago, without electronics, more accurately than the versions extant in the high schools of the colonial British Empire but six decades or so ago) with fine tuned instrumentation does not in itself confer the bounty of understanding *why things are as they are. Modern, mainstream, Physics is spectacularly, and astoundingly, dumb on the issue of the fundamental nature of who we are and why anything exists.* It is in context of this default that we need to excavate the traditional garners of learning buried deep in the archives of civilizations banished into the netherland of obsolescence by wave upon wave of *Euro-modern* vandalism. Time now to resuscitate the dead, and those condemned to such epistemic death, all over again: the shamans, the *rishis*, the medicine-men, the ancient raconteurs of the multi-faceted story of humankind, exhuming at long last the long buried imaginations of our universally glorious ancestry.

The European penchant for disembodied, abstract reason, devoid of feeling and empathy, as the *sole* means of acquiring knowledge (the latter sought only to be pressed into the service of accumulation) has seriously retarded our understanding, and appreciation, of both things and non-things; yet there have always been alternates and complements to reason such as instinct, intuition, intimation, and revelation (the fantastic, yet wholly intuitive, contributions of *Srinivasa Ramanujam* to modern mathematics being but only the revelatory, and educational, tip of the iceberg in this regard). The fact that we do not know how such means and methodologies "*work*" only suggests that modernists have not yet *cared to know* (the *enterprise* of modernist knowledge is only savvy about the *real* game: of *control* over knowledge, its subjects and objects): but they do—and we need to resume the interrupted task of inquiry into their specificity, for they are *human* properties and attributes, much like reason and the senses.

It is a *magical* universe, and an apparently shy one, which, like a sensitive person, quails and shrivels up under unkind scrutiny; and if it resists comprehension, it might well be because the motives of the modernist are often so unnatural. Nature might well be averse to be "mastered" or "exploited" as in classical Baconian terminology: rather, it is perhaps to be coexisted with in complementary empathy and reciprocity. W*e are nature and nature is us*—to understand "it," is to understand ourselves. Worse than the proverbial fly on the cartwheel that imagines it makes the wheel go around, we have assumed, under the grip of the modernist spell, the fantastic fiction of "*mastery*" over the cart itself, much as the winding road it traverses. Nature, as far as we know predates us; and it will, given the way we are going, *sooner rather than later, postdate us as well.*

The ontic limit is a limiting notion, because reality is itself *open-ended* and the idea of limits in a limitless universe is itself anomalous. We have yet to learn of the secrets, the enigma, of the abounding universe, leastways if the modernist sciences are our frame of reference. It is revelatory in itself that nature, to the modernist prober, has revealed herself, like a coquetting courtesan of male imagery, or a scheming diplomat, only in rarefied *micro*-bits, and that too with great, big temporal gaps in between: think, for example, of the time span separating Newton from Einstein, a time span by no means deterministically "necessary" given the available means of knowledge.

It would appear, given such distal apprehensions, *that "nature" has never been in a rush to expedite our epistemic reach in the modernist period*; and yet, as yet unscalable examples such as the impeccable insights and acumen of ancient Vedic wisdom suggest that there might have been a time when such revealment(s) was far more forthcoming and profound. Perhaps, in the eternal scheme of things, there were natural secrets, such as those pertaining to thermonuclear reactions, that humankind was never intended to know, though such knowledge has been wrested by force in the modernist era. If we are the progeny of nature itself, would it, one wonders, wish us to seek, let alone find, the means of our own, now perhaps inescapable, *auto-destruction*? The question can only abide our slow, and costly, ascent to wisdom.

Modernist science, wedded to greed and arrogance, themselves the correlates of masculinity unbound, violently rent the veils of nature pushing knowledge on to annihilatory and misanthropic paths; given that, as opposed to the benign wisdom of ancient civilizations that preserved not threatened human and other habitats, it may well be that the discovery of nuclear reactions will be *the* critical modernist discovery that will terminate the possibility of any/all other discoveries. In effect, it might just be humankind's *last revelation*, prior to the apocalypse of its own making. *In that sense, the nuclear age is most likely the last age of modernism after which humankind has need to reinvent itself*; who can doubt that this will involve a wholesale rejection of the Great European Way as has characterized societal evolution of the last four hundred years? It is also likely that the rabid masculinist path taken by human civilizations will then, finally, be at an end, hoisted ingloriously on its own petard.

The cosmic dance of fiery molecular orbs, both big and small, is but a species of play, pantomime, dream and delusion; the tactile reality we inhabit, however precariously, is but an aliquot part of that larger universe of imponderables. Modernist materialism effectively prevented, by means of its overriding *idée fixee*, any excavations of the *extra-material* realms that we are all dimly, at one level or other, conscious of (indeed *consciousness itself is but a state of matter*); in this regard, modernism has all but subverted the exciting project of a real *gnosis*. Yet it is entirely conceivable that the answers we seek, as sentient beings in an only *apparently insensate* universe, lie in that deceptively distal, non-terrestrial, extraterrestrial, and "implicate" domain.

It must be clear then that the consummation of a whole epoch of modernist accumulation of banalities, initiated by Europe, which have almost extinguished the very possibility of civilization, may well be nigh; the trades, tools, and technologies of modernism, enhancing the inherent destructiveness of masculinity, have virtually guaranteed that outcome. We have been indecorously stripped of our birthright to a congenial planet given the all-ravaging *momenta* of modernism. Fortunately, however, contrary to Cartesian mechanics, the planet is neither dull nor inert, but *lives*; and just might be fighting back, *through us*, to preserve itself.

Stated differently: *we are the planet*—and the stage may indeed be well set now for that classic, even epic, struggle for evolutionary survival: *mother nature versus the modernist vandals*, and the outcome can hardly be in doubt. The various scourges of our time, such as AIDS and BSE, both latent and manifest, might verily now be the harbingers of the arrival of the proverbial equestrians of the apocalypse.

(32)

The oppressed cultures of the non-modernist world are now the secure bases of the *Great Rejection* that is gathering steam even as the votaries of neoliberalist globalization ply their meretricious wares with gathering arrogance and insistence. The cultural dimension of the so-called peripheral world has been all but ignored in materialist analyses that focus blindly on *per capita* output and income; but this is the fatal flaw, if you will, of the original colonizing impulse of modernism. The conquering Anglo-Saxon, *the first today among the European* (tribes of) *Unequals*, for example, saw little that was worthwhile, other than that which could be plundered and confiscated, in the social-scape of, say, a civilization such as India that was, then, crushingly humbled *twice*: *once*, materially and militarily, and a *second* time, far more decisively, *ideationally*, by being reduced and stripped, in external evaluation, to the barest "economic" indices as calculated by the perverse accountants of modernism: and all appeared to be but barbarism and decadence in that leprous, frosty vision.

Providentially, given the fortuitous fact that one does not suppress what one deems beneath notice, these mainsprings of indigenous cultural constellations not only survived the colonial era, unscathed, but *thrived*; and it is their, and similar *others*', self-governing renascence that now set the final, impassable limits to modernist depredations.

The modernist elites of our time, east and west, are scurrying fast today to consolidate their gains—the privatization of social wealth and the forced integration of the world economies under the current suzerainty of predatory *finance*—within a transcontinental web of modernist trade, credit and commerce. But their success, dizzy and vast as it is at the current conjuncture, is doomed to be shortlived: and globalization will be, without any qualification, sort of the last huzzah of the modernist conceit. Indeed, unnoticed by all but a few, the structural opposition to the *Euro-modernists*, their *Nemesis* so to speak, almost from the very inception of that ignoble devolution in human affairs, has always been constituted by the near-invisible activities of women, workers and indigenous peoples, a nether-world within a vibrant, and parallel, *moral economy*. It is they who, for various rationales, ontic and epistemic, are the *qualitatively* inherent opposition to the rational realm of capital and all its allied hangers-on.

The opposition that comes from these social forces is primarily in behavior, motivation and attitude; unlike the conquering waves of modernism, these forces are predominantly *nonrationalist, non-accumulationist, and nonabstract*—and given these traits, and only in so far as these traits allow, they are, in consequence, also *nonviolent*. They are also, and always have been, the real *producers*, not the *appropriators*; the guardians of social wealth, not its pillagers; the custodians of the simplest norms of morality and culture, not their ravagers. *It is their self-sustaining, self-provisioning, activities, especially when self-directed, that will offer to us the faintest semblance of hope for planetary survival* (as the modernist marauders sweep and scour the world bare like a swarm of locusts) after the holocaust of modernist globalization has wreaked its predictable havoc. *In their sparse and simple economies of care, we shall discover the opulence of life; in their facile technologies, the promise of a benign, give-and-take approach to our natural heritage; in their humble felicities of social life, the secrets of a convivial human existence.*

The ways of women, workers and the original, primal cultures of this planet—both within and without the corrupting vistas of modernism—are, and always have been, *homologous (quite symmetrically, the very language of the Modernist betrays the same isothermic pose of contempt toward all of them; nature could also be included here as a fourth victim, similarly ill-treated)*: located, indeed rooted, in the humble *praxis of the concrete*, in the search for simple norms of subsistence and *coexistence* based on real anthropic *needs*, far from the madding logics of greed and accumulation. They have been also, for aeons, the carriers and standard bearers of what modernist elites affectingly, call *folk culture*, which is only a highbrow, supercilious term of alternating romance and/or opprobrium for the multifaceted, and ever evolving, tapestry of their *self-securing* activities within the charter of, as the poet Gray had it, "the short and simple annals of the poor."

It is in this domain of non-acquisitive life processes that the seeds of civility and uncoerced reciprocities are sown; it is within the matrix of these social behaviors that the possibility of civilization is engendered howsoever unconsciously; and it is in these highly localized, indeed parochial, interactions that the genius of self-directed human productivity, leashed always to the ordinary norms of ecological responsibility, first flourished.

The raw grace of human contentment unbesmirched by the crippling flaunt of greed, and the disabling fanfare of power, may still be found—but only in such hinterlands of the now fast waning, elementary forms of the anthropic life. *Women are the progenitors of both productivity and civilization; simple peasant labor the basis of the grandeur of empires, and tribal cultures the origins of convivial innovations. Their implicit, complementary, unity is the unity of the story of the propagation, and preservation, of humanity.*

Nothing in their lot may be, or needs be, *idealized*; nature, anthropic instinct, and the masculinist impulse conspire, even within *their* world, then as now, to corrode their otherwise quite essentialist pacifism. This is not, nor could it be, a world devoid of cruelty, passion, struggle, and intolerance; but their universe is one that securely confines these unedifying attributes to limited and limiting domains, as far as possible within the orbit of our ontic attributes, powers, and capabilities. The world, the planet, and its various ecologies are, so to speak, safe in their hands, indeed safer than they themselves are in the random lotteries of the natural life, or, worse, within the *exterminist* logics of modernism.

The planet could easily contain, sustain, and survive, their petty, humble, and exoteric ambitions. Their contributions to continued human existence far exceed any of the dubious bequests of modernism on any scale; and they are the ones that still stand between us and the yawning abyss of perdition. Howsoever bedazzled by the glitter of modernist temptations, and bedevilled by the ever more menacing modernist snares, they remain the still living laboratory wherefrom the lost arts of life might yet be retrieved *tout a court* when modernism has completed its agenda of subverting the very basis of life on earth and, in process, suborns itself—and we are not far off at all from that illimitable climacteric.

(33)

The modernist utopian drive can go no further than shallowly cranked out, and crassly materialist, pipe dreams of a grossly misconceived *plenitude*; the traditional Marxian and capitalist emancipatory visions, are thereby only the two equally ugly faces of the Janus of modernism. The *neoliberal* agenda of free trade and laissez-faire *au courant* today reveal its travesties quite clearly as this age of modernist globalization proceeds apace to a necessary self destruction; as such, the capitalist dream of yesterday of a *capitalized planet* is about to be realized, in the present period, with its grim reality of ecological catastrophe and social devastation.

Accordingly, capitalism invites no need for yet further critique; it is glaringly transparent in its own misanthropic worthlessness. The hoary Marxian slogans of yesteryear might yet entice a few misguided souls still clinging dearly to the crudity of what is ultimately only a mere rule of scrip: "*from each according to ability, and to each as per his/her needs*"; only the slightest reflection can reveal the grotesque reductionism, mechanism, and materialism, of such a pedestrian, modernist, dream that, regrettably, yet inspired, until very recently, millions of the misguided to court a predictable, if tragic, annihilation. The "masses" might be presumed to wish to live a somewhat more colorful life of light, love, and laughter than contained in those arid, stolid, scientistic tropes of nineteenth century *distributive utilitarianism*.

The convivial community can hardly inscribe such crudely materialist rules of "*allocation*" upon its own being without becoming in itself a *machine*; the modernist conceit of appropriate "process" here conceals only its overriding, substantive bankruptcy of imagination. *The modernist constitution, the unsanguinary fruit of the erstswhile parlor game pastime of our modernist forebears* (arrant armchair drivellers for the most part like Rousseau and Mill), *in any of its present forms, has always been a straitjacket within which to imprison the human spirit*; rules written for and by some (and the few) cannot become the permanent patrimony of others (usually the many) who never consented to such an irremovable charter of inheritances. We might yet learn to distrust and disdain such cavalier "law-givers."

The convivial society has no hard and fast rules that might not be transgressed and any such procedural rigidity can only invite self-destruction; indeed it is in the open-ended *free play* of argument and counterargument, in the flux of device, artifice and erasure, that a social frame ensures a *liberative mobility* to all relationships. It does not, in the abstract, crave the masculinist fiats of "justice" or "order," and yet would allow an elastic space to any and all such notions. Rules that stand hard and tall above society are mere abstractions at best and rigid oppressions at worst; *it is in contextually derived norms, that are always subject to change and unchange, as the spirit is moved, that human conviviality, the condition for the free play of human creativity, is best expressed.* Since contexts change, so do the norms appropriate to their expression: as such, *lex scripta* is not necessarily better than *lex non scripta*.

The modernist ideologue, inspirited by the abstract drives of *Euro-rationalism*, has neither the subtlety nor the patience to comprehend these niceties. Enough for him to proclaim overarching constitutions and insist on a subject populace's absolute obedience: and therein lies revealed the inherent masculinist affinity for the punitive exercise of power(s). America's city police, by far the most brutish even within the ungentle plane of modernism, are dyed in that rabid image and point to the abruptly tyrannical limits to real liberty in that deeply unholy land of wilful self-delusion. The "land of the free and the home of the brave" is none other than (at least in its major cities) the land of uniformed, gun-toting cowards, licensed by a ruthless state, and a terrified, cowed populace (especially if of *minority* origins, or belonging to the "*other*" as defined in this work) seeking a huddled safety behind closed, even quickly locked, doors: the average Masai, on the range, is freer and prouder than any New Yorker could ever hope to be (even on a Saturday night) despite all the latter's swagger and tough talk.

At any rate, the specification here is not of some futuristic "*ideal*" society as a sort of a recipe for *social engineering*, but only of its near-firm, real basis in the received heritage of traditional "simple" cultures that have embodied its basic truths for millennia. Only under the vagrant spell of European mythologies could humankind have neglected these rich garners of human innovation which are a frothing brew of a slew of creative ideas. To make the key point here: *the matrix of tribal society has within itself the seminal basis for convivialism*, not as an "*ideal*" condition to be necessarily "*realized*" in some teleological sense, but as a real abiding entity within the flawed, anthropic problematic of our given natural habitat that is our lot on this planet.

There are no ideals to be realized: to appreciate this reality one has to yield up the legacy of the vague belief in the alleged all total "perfectibility" of humans, within a linear time frame, that has marked the triumphalist European visions of "liberation." *Human nature is neither good, nor bad, nor indifferent*, though capable of an ever fluid transition through all those modes; yet it is not "human nature" (odd oxymoron!) that is at issue but the *paradigm of masculinity* which remains, in all climes, potentially predatory and menacing. *The secret of emancipation is to find social and cultural ways and means to imprison and "tame," this set of virulent impulses, within the "feminine" web of relationships of care and consideration.*

A cursory glance at, say, traditional Tibetan culture (a grimly endangered entity) would reveal the genius of our ancestors who sought and found such elaborately conceived expedients for the *social pacification of masculinity*. The point is not to "*idealize*" such communities, nor at the other remove to dwell unduly on their many "weaknesses" as construed from an *external* (*and, usually, quite warped*) vantage point; rather, to learn from those who preserved this planet intact for us and appreciate their gift of an abiding cache of social and philosophical empathy, that resides at the very epicenter of societal life, that makes it so very different from our misbegotten ideologies of conflict, competition, and desolation: *it is, I submit, still not too late*.

It is true that, as a purely historical matter, the many martial *empires of* both east and west were to banish such manner of cultural experiments to the periphery of the more mainstream cultures of patriarchy; but the fact remains that modernist European world mastery has made such an outcome historically definite, certain, and inevitable by its relentless "search and destroy" missions as have continued now for some three hundred years. To state the point differently, there is precious little to "choose" between the historically given patriarchies/empires of east and west; yet it is also clear that the modernist predators were far more relentless, and more to the point, *successful*, in their *exterminist* drives than their more "lazy," sybaritic, cousinages whether in pre-modern Europe, Asia, or Africa, who stopped far short of overrunning the very basis of the possibility of civilization. *Tribal* India, for example, survived all of Moghul imperial rule virtually unscathed; and yet, under but a few decades of British and current Indian *modernist* rule, it faces a near-certain, even accelerated, annihilation. In short, capitalism and socialism corrode and rend the social fabric of care more efficiently and totally than all the barbarian empires of the past taken together: it is not just that modernism alienates this or that societal feliciity—*modernism, in effect, is alienation.*

To repeat: *there are no ideals to be realized in the abstract* (even were such abstractions to be embraced as *ideals*, we are as hominids unable to transcend the pivotal attributes of our anthropic condition, as the futility of *all* modernist "utopian" attempts in recent history indicates), in the classical *genre* of European/modernist posing of utopian discussions about the "ideal" state or society; *au contraire*, real societal forms, evolved through millennia, still exist today that themselves are revelatory of the vital clues to a congenial survival of the species which are not so much, therefore, to be "theorized"—as *learned from.*

There is an immanent basis for the utopian yearning, that constitutes in itself the mnemonics of that prepossession. The ontic basis for that "intuition" exists securely in the genus of the kinship based social form usually overrun either by "empire" or the modernist "civil society." The relational secret of tribal society is the kinship link that is emotive and affective and feathered over with a tight web of reciprocities, and the essence of the extended kindred form is the familial unit; and at the heart of that familial unit is the engendering role of the feminine principle.

Indeed, there is no social formation, tribal or otherwise, which does not ultimately rest, in an ontic sense on the manifest fruits of this principle (though modernism goes farthest in attempting to suppress the very memory of it). As noted, for this reason, *it is women who have held alit, and aloft, for aeons, the vital torch of our very anthropic existence, not merely civilization* in some "exalted" sense.

The fundamentally misguided nature of European, modernist, conceptions of utopia may now be understood: *all of them, Smith to Marx, and beyond, were predicated upon a materialist causation/consummation as though plenitude, whether obtained through free trade or socialism, were both the necessary and sufficient basis for human contentment* (i.e., they presupposed an inherently acquisitive, *masculinist–modernist* view of utopia). Indeed, truth is, that it is *neither*; the social is not a precarious balance of critical interests (as in the vulgar "*social contract*" view), but a precious balance of vital *affections. It is not affluence that breeds contentment, as the modernist pharisees have it, but a sense of contentment that engenders a state of affluence*, by reining in an explosion of superfluous *wants.*

Of all the peoples of this planet, it is the modernist European who first lost sight of this elementary insight of the convivial life; and almost all the quandaries and quagmires of European social life to this day stem solely from this original, and quite horrific, dereliction. *Marx was categorically wrong*; it is not "labor" that is the essence of our *species-being* (so much again was mere anthropocentrism seeking a careful separation of "us" from "animals") but the search for the *warmth* of a kindred-based felicity as given by our hominid roots: *we are not "laboring" but "heat-seeking" mammals, possessing/craving not a love of labor, but labors of love.*

Given this larger understanding, it is not difficult to see why there are so few *female* utopians; women already *experience*, and still try to retain, despite vile male depredations into their terrain, the emancipatory social form within their activities of care and consideration as accompanies childbirth and child-rearing. Unlike men, who know it not, they have no need to write books on it, nor spout poetry: *women live the utopian dream concretely, not dream about it abstractly.* The social relations of conviviality have no need to be invented or discovered, least of all by *male* imaginations: they exist and flourish all about us in the *social/ moral economy of affections* that women engage in on a daily basis, except when modernism corrupts that *satisficing* state and imposes its alien, repressive grids under the dissembling charade of upliftment and progress. *The rediscovery of utopia is really the rediscovery, by alienated and alienating Man—of the Paradigm of Femininity, of the centrality of women within it, and of its distinctively benign and felicitous sets of traits, norms, and behaviors.*

(34)

Modernist ideology succeeded supernally in seriously deforming our understanding and expectations of the social *genus* and its various cultural modalities. Situating the *organon* of anthropic society within the false *modus* of the *contractual* form, a scalpel-wielding "sociology" split up an organically integral entity essentially spontaneously derived from our "natural" impulses into so many disparate structures and sectors to be "studied" as though great dividends existed (other than the vital procurement of vital "control" information for ruling strata) as the end product of such investigations. The sheer *mechanism* of this methodology is breathtaking, closely related as it is to the Cartesian world view (wherein the only "certainty" is the individuated consciousness of the atomized subject). The social, not being viewed as a *complexus*, was to be swiftly fragmented: "economy" was distinguished from "kinship," and "religion," and "magic," and "politics," and so on, *as though the ontic unity of the societal organism was but a mere patchwork assemblage/collage of such discrete sub-systems.*

In all of these unnatural dissections, any influence, or understanding, of *nature*, and of our essential *species-being*, was carefully abstracted out so we could delicately leave our "*animality*" behind, so as to rise in *androcentric* splendor as the self-generating Titans of the Universe, *provided, of course, "we" were white, male, rich, and conservative.* In true Cartesian dialectics, all was first atomized, and then "reconstructed," like an inert frame in Legoland, on the basis of the most tawdry of modernist delusions.

Anthropic *needs*, originating primarily in our *natural* being, no matter how mediated by cultural norms, were to be all but absent in this radical surgery, and instead we spoke in the highly abstract language of the *social* determinants of wealth, power, and societal interaction. The "involute" structure of roles prevailing in simpler social formations was readily disparaged as revealing a "*primitive*" lack of complexity together with a similar, despicable dearth with regard to the adornments of bourgeois attributes; thereby, the otiose *ideology of separation* and separateness, in the individualist Calvinist mould, was quite inherently, and all but unconsciously, enshrined and canonized as the guiding lodestone of inquiry. In such tendentious investigations we found what we sought, quite readily—but in the hollow manner of epistemic *invention* rather than ontic discovery.

Weber was only partially wrong when he suggested that the world had been *disenchanted* by modernist *analysis*, to the extent that the latter suggests a critical *demystification; instead, the fact is that the social world was essentially re-mystified on the basis of a uniquely modernist set of illusions.* As the vital follow-through to such vanguard ideational constructs, policy intervention based on the former saw to it, in Europe first and—by imperial extension—the world afterward, that the social domain would be *practically reengineered* to such serviceable, if invidious, specifications.

The Neoliberalist *juggernaut* of present times, standing at the apex of the modernist *corporatist* impulse, under the stewardship of the United States, where a *video culture, a casino economy, and a technofascist polity* define the contours of this newest, imminent, latter day *avatar* of modernism, is the awful culmination of that four hundred year old endeavor to refashion the globe on exclusionary modernist lines. It may only be karmically fitting, no matter how tragic, if that moment of the all-total triumph of this inveterate philosophy of greed also signifies the possible extinction of such manner of artificial society, in all its global manifestations, together with all its vanities, affectations, and superfluities.

Economic and political forms, to use *Eurocentric* terms, have flourished in a thousand, multi-variegated ways until the modernist put paid to this opulent diversity by imposing his hollow grids of "capitalism-socialism" (i.e., tweedledum and tweedledee) on the economic life, and the banal binary of "democracy–dictatorship" in the political domain. This elaborate reengineering was only possible once coherent social formations that bore the shared values of a common evolution—as say in tribal Africa before the European colonial onslaught—had first been ravaged and desecrated beyond recognition. Out of the wasteland of colonial devastation, a "modernist" frame was slowly and painfully crafted in the periphery such that a "*new*," alien, societal form bearing no connection with either its own heritage or culture now stood lumbering, uncertain of itself, and ever looking to Western inspiration to keep itself upright.

This is the sorry plight of most Asian and African dependent formations today, now permanently debauched of their history, and disarticulated from their own indigenous genius, but also cut off from even such marginal capital flows as existed in the period of the Cold War. Military power, economic pressure, and political chicanery have kept such *paper-machet* systems functioning erratically until recently: but we stand now at the threshold of an era where their collapse can only be imminent. Cultural roots are, of necessity, everywhere, sunk deep; and though the branches may be bare with all customary foliage plucked clean by the vandals of modernism, the tree itself may yet flourish—for it is far from dead, despite the manifest desecration. This rather late resurgence reflects only the inherent *inertia* of cultural modes that may slumber on in a stupor for long periods of time, and put on strange cloaks, but always assert themselves eventually given the right provocation.

The challenge of modernism in this era of its final consummation and denouement cannot but ignite such a universal revival. And, whether we fancy it or not, the prodromes of such a *revolt of the oppressed*, in cultural terms, are present today in the gathering storm of Islam, and religions worldwide in general (as already manifest in similar, and significant, stirrings in India, China, Korea, and Japan), whose ultimate momentum and trajectory remain both unknown and unchartable.

Religion, wrote Sir Namier, is a sixteenth century word for nationalism; it may well be the twenty-first century term for cultural revival and revolt. Other than the impressive rise of feminist, and tribal, awareness, apart from the world-wide efflorescence of NGO's articulating their causes, it is the surest sign that modernism has been unable, for all its deluge of propaganda, to achieve the necessary epistemic closure to make its conquests irreversible. In effect, and highly instructionally, the strongest rejectionist movement of our times takes its inspiration from *premodernist* sources; and it is only a matter of time before it is emulated across the globe by similarly inclined forces. Their time is, arguably, nigh.

While it is certain that modernism is doomed to a self-ordained extinction, it is not at all certain whether the forces that it galvanized into a mass movement through its own egregious misdeeds, motley groups as they are, will, of one mind, recall the promise of human conviviality buried under the invidious modernist avalanche for centuries. *Human history, regrettably perhaps, is not an anthropic passion play with a designedly happy ending*; however, it is arguable that the planet would still, indeed, be far safer in their hands—and that is no trivial statement of their potential for a very meaningful achievement. By corralling the forces of societal destruction and moral decay, and stemming the rot so to speak, these inevitable revolts of the *sans-cullotte* will have bought us all much needed time, and space, to glance at our many wounds and reflect on their provenance.

The rollback of European ideologies, through resistance rather than revolution in keeping with their propensities, and the ascent of premodernist cultures to dignity will be worthy momenta in the march to the plural self-realization of the human species. Only such species of cultural change will ensure the necessary diversity, and complementarity, upon which all planetary balances, for millennia, have been built. No longer will the majority of humankind be required to march to one tune, indeed to a siren song, put out by a distant piper who has not their, or even his own, best interests at heart. No longer will a vulgar philosophy of greed, the defining hallmark of modernism, threaten the vital *lebensraum and lebenszeit*, of the weak, the vulnerable, and the voiceless.

The manifold amenities of modernism are not provided out of any sensibility of *civility* and its placement in human society; indeed the very fact that civility itself is not a readily available amenity in the modernist frame—but a day in New York, or any other modernist metropole, should set one at ease about that—should confirm the truth of that proposition.

Stated simply, all of modernism is given over to the dominant logics, or *pathologies* rather, of *accumulation*; and any lingering residuals of grace that might still anchronistically exist are hungrily being scavenged now as *neoliberalist* storms proceed to annex every inch of unregulated social space. This is not to say that such civilities are extinct, or even extinguishable—that element of a human society can never entirely be suppressed for some of the ontic reasons stated earlier—but that they are allowed rein only *after* the more primary tasks of successful *greed management* have first been performed effectively. *Christmas is allowed in, so to speak, but only at the end of the year, after more important business has been securely conducted* (and then, too, only after it is converted into yet another avenue for further, even more frenzied, *business*).

(35)

Marx understood the annexation of *work*, or rather its product, as a distinguishing feature of class society. He also understood, leastways in his earlier writings, *self-directed* work as an important means of the fulfilment of human creativity. However, he did err in *two* important ways; restricted to the modernist frame, he confined discussion of labor to the (materialist) value (surplus) creating kind ; and, based on that, his vision of the "*allocation*" of labor (socialism) was again, for all the appealing tropes inevitably,given modernist prepossessions, a *productivist* one. He was far from unaware of tribal formations (indeed so-called *primitive communism* was his *original* inspiration in these directions) where productivism was either unknown, or where all of social labor was not destined to either create or maximize a surplus for the few or the many. Yet their obviously "*satisficing*" behavior was of little use to him: *he was both a materialist and a productivist despite all the rhetoric of human needs* that interlaced his passionate words. In effect, the self-creative, self-redemptive, side of human labor was lost—buried—in his *programmatic* works in favor of the idyll of "raising the level of the productive forces," within a collectivist frame. Little wonder, then, that the socialist dream—and reality—(wherein, one might say, allegorically, the *Reality Principle* almost wholly eclipsed the *Pleasure Principle*), within the modernist theatre, was such close kin to the capitalist one (from the vantage point of the oppressed) and why today, as the joke goes, capitalism appears now to be the highest, even more desirable!, stage of "socialism."

If the fall of modernism carries today with it the declension of the Marxian utopia, it can hardly come as a surprise; Marx was unable and/or unwilling to move beyond his Enlightenment based "*progressivist*" dream of *scientific—materialist* emancipation; in effect, he visualized affluence in the *Euro-modernist* mein of constituting a blinding surfeit of commodities. He might have learnt from the Buddhist, or the Bushmen: *that limiting the domain of labors to the relatively simpler perimeter of human needs, regardless of the level of "productive forces," is a more painless and more pacific way of generating a real opulence*—the enabling haven of leisure, play, and free time. *He might have understood, contra modernist conceits, that humankind is more blessed in a state of "being" than "becoming."*

The real "economic problem"—not its vulgar textbook perversion—is a question of striking a balance between human needs, social vanities/conventions, and natural resources. In general, nature has been far from niggardly (which is why the human species is still around) and women, workers, native peoples and tribal cultures have usually been content with what is disparaged by progressivists as mere "*subsistence.*" The Gandhian can live within her means and seek, and find, pacific and benign ways of securing the vital werewithal, in both social and natural space, to both survive and flourish; the modernist can only thrive at the expense of ravaging the planet and all that lives on it. Two different ways; two different epistemes; two different motivations; two different approaches to life and living; and anyone who can fail to see which is the sure and sane way to planetary and societal survival, and the possibility of the continued coexistence of nature and human culture, is but a dupe of the slash-and-burn ideologies of modernism.

If modernism fundamentally misconstrues, or rather *misdirects*, the economic energies of humans, it equally fails to comprehend the real, *existential* basis of politics. It is easy, and banal, enough to see politics as having to do with *power*, and its exercise, and the usual means for the acquisition of a more favorable resource allocation. But modernist politics fudges on the question of its *source*; power and politics are not a "*human*" propensity shared by all—it is uniquely a *male prepossession. Politics is the preeminent area for the expression of masculinist urges*; power, in effect, is a man's game, played with masculinist traits, skills, tools, and aptitudes.

The fact that women and children and the sans-cullotte have historically borne the brunt of this violent struggle for male preeminence as "collateral" victims is one of the enduring tragedies of the human condition. It is not, as Hobbes had it, that the life of *humans* is nasty, brutish and short in some apocryphal "*state of nature*"; it is that *male despotism*, and its ever-ready lust for warfare, makes that unenviable condition the expected lot for all others in real, anthropic, actually existing *society. Only a man could have planned a nuclear device; only a man could have detonated it upon the human species.*

The "state," therefore, is but an association of racketeers—ever but a camp of armed men—and predators whose offer to "*protect*" lesser men, women, and children (largely from their own predations), *originally dispossessed by the self-same force*, is made good only with a heavy, and permanent, extraction of ransom, revenue, and obedience. *In that sense a state (in its modernist guise) is always illegitimate*, no matter what the "theory" of legality that serves as its fig-leaf, because it is located in the problematic of the predominance of masculinist predations against the rest of society—which is quite capable of independent self-organization on peaceable mores of coexistence without recourse to either guns or goons.

The modernist state, much like the empires it descends/devolves from, has gone the distance—and far beyond—in legitimizing, even encouraging, the stockpiling of arabesquely lethal arms and weaponry under the pretense of assuring the "*security*" of the society it commands (whilst actually *imperiling* that very attribute owing to the self-same build-up). Few such awful paraphernalia of mass destruction were ever found necessary in simple tribal formations to keep the peace which rely instead on the consilience of custom, and shared cultural mores, for the most part. Indeed, the unwilling last resort to violence, in such formations, could be seen as a good measure of the *organic solidarity*, and the sheer *civility*, undergirding the matrix of its social expectations.

(36)

It might be useful, at this point, to specify and sum up the principal theses of this work, in general terms, as they pertain to what might be understood as the critical *Organa of Anthropic Existence* that defy received modernist "*social theory*" in all its speculative moments. Given their somewhat novel nature it may also be fruitful to delineate them, albeit schematically, in terms of numerous *Theses*, as follows:

I: Contra modernist misformulations in this region, in its most fundamental sense, *Politics, en generale*, is simply the *relations between men*; more specifically, it refers to the modalities of *masculinity* as expressed in the "*public*" domain whose very illimitable extension is an index *of the atrophy of the "domestic economy of affections*," that is, *convivial* relations. *II: Economics*, on the other hand, refers to the *momenta* of the *material life*, and takes *two general* forms: *one*, the efforts invested in extracting a conventional subsistence which is originally a "*feminine*," *non-modernist*, activity involving various reciprocities with/within natural and communitarian resources; and the *other*, which is the uniquely male-driven search for command over a "*surplus*," potential or actual, involving asymmetrical, and adversarial, relations between disparate cadres of men, in overlordship over "*Other*" men and women, other species, and nature: it is this latter thrust (by no means restricted to modernism) that merges concordantly with the masculinist "*politics*" described above. *III:* The *Social* is, fundamentally, the matrix of *familial relations* centred around the modalities of child rearing, and child care, and is, therefore, again a uniquely *feminine* site of *praxis*. The ordinary, "natural" human state is one of *tribalism*—the *anthropic* version of mammalian *herds*—which is a simple extension of the familial principle. In essence, humans exist as both *pack* and *herd* animals (modernism breaks the tribal tie by inventing the novel domain of "*civil society*"—*not an anthropic society at all*—which is the ultimate home of the arid *masculinist* paradigm, shorn of all affective affinities). *IV: Culture* is a hierarchical set of values, tastes, and preferences whose tone, form, and content are set by the historically specific *gender balance* of ideologies and practices—*masculinist* and *feminine*—extant in a given ecosystem at a given moment of evolution. *V*: And *Civilization* is the *extent* to (and *intensity* with) which essentially *feminine hospitalities*, as conceived within the *familial* moment (as defined above) are extended, in evolution, with, by, and through the consent of the ruling patriarchs who are the final arbiters of power, in a given culture, to the full range of human activities and possibilities.

Viewed in this light, the vital importance of the all but "*invisible*" *gender struggle* for the evolution of human society is placed in high relief in contrast to the far better known "*class struggle*" notion of Marx; whilst both these very different kinds of tensions have their historical place, the sheer *priority* of evolving (or *devolving*) gender equations to the general tone and tenor of the evolution of society and culture should be quite obvious. Indeed, it might safely be said that gender struggles have indisputable *primacy* because they obtain quite "*naturally*" and *universally*, whereas even by Marxian admission class struggles occupy only a distinct, and limited, set space in the social history of society. Finally, the gender tension encapsulates the vital role of *women* and their eternally anthropic "*paradigm of femininity*" critical to the continued possibility of the *hospitability* of life on earth both for hominids and, indeed, all forms of life.

In this frame, we can now situate the *Great Modernist Elision*, and all that it entailed, and implied, more generally, as follows. It becomes clear that the European enlightenment, in the modernist wake, sanctified the domain of the material interests, supplanting the hoary paradigm of primal affections that ruled the world for millennia. Given that unsavory legacy, and the reactions that could be expected given our own *species-being*, it is little wonder that we stand today on the brink of several extinctions, the most significant of which is the very legacy of that "*modus*" of Enlightenment, which, for all its meretricious show of high Ideals, was the ultimate exemplar of misanthropy, misogyny, and materialism unbound. For almost four hundred Years, this *policy driven* paradigm of *Modernism*, ran amok, conquering Europe first, its Colonies next, and then the World, at large, afterwards.

Far from the expectations of the naïve, this unbounded rationality of material interests did not harbinger an era of the pacification of human existence, but indeed savagely disbanded societal forms, debunked harmonies, and destroyed ecological felicities, making this the most unstable and dangerous of all eras. Self-interest, unbridled by communitarian sentiments, contrary to the wretched fables of Smithiana, real and apocryphal, is *not* what binds us but what divides us, creating the Hobbesian, adversarial, universe we now cheerlessly inhabit. *Euro-Capitalism*, one variant of modernism, carefully and forcibly fashioned such an inhospitable world for us deceiving us into accepting it as *natural*, indeed as a "higher" form of social existence.

The *real* societal history of humankind, in contrast, has always rested on other, distinctly different, preceptual *metafoundations*, taking *two* general forms, existing either apart or in combination. The *family*, as *modus* one (immanent in the *Tribal* Form), has always been the eternal *social economy of affections*, nurtured by the feminine principle and bonded by the activities of women, despite (and within) the oppressive grids of a grim, and unedifying, patriarchy. The *State* (typified in *Empires*) as the other archetype, was the equally perennial abode of the *masculine principle*, that is, *patriarchy*, populated by *men*, and their rank ambitions in the areas of power and domination.

The so-called *Civil Society*, in Europe, arose, at least conceptually, as a *median formation*, hypothetically purged largely of *both* these ancient drives, ensconcing itself instead in the banal sphere of the *political economy of* (self-serving) *Interests*, that is *greed*. Not a society at all, except as pure aberration, the eager propagandists of civil society nonetheless touted this novel version of the social as *univeralized egoism* as "*progressivist*" despite its provenance in the entirely negatively conceived notion of a *balance of Interests*, a misanthropic, masculinist, Hobbesian view that still dominates all Modernist formations today, and informs all of its institutions. It is this vacuous, and *meaning-free* social form that is the real provenance of all the *angst* and *alienation* as has informed European life since.

Political economy, as the dismal self-reflection of this arid formation, was but the privileged crown jewel of the hegemonic ideology of this very civil society. Modernism, the more encompassing *Matrix Credo of Civil Society*, was itself erected on the *Base Metaphysical Triad* of: (a) a near blind faith in *science*, (b) an eschatological, if self-serving and triumphalist belief in *progress*, and (c) a philosophy of rampant *materialism*. The emergent *Capitalist* social formation, taken as a whole, was but the undergirding *structural dual* of Modernism.

As this so-called civil society expanded, the interests necessarily gained at the expense of the affections, men at the expense of women, expropriators at the expense of toilers, the material life at the expense of the social and the natural, the European at the expense of the Non-European, the modernist at the expense of the traditionalist, *Gessellscahft* at the expense of *Gemeinschaft*, becoming at the expense of being, monism at the expense of pluralism, effulgence at the expense of repose, the abstract at the expense of the concrete, and appropriative drives at the expense of caring and civility.

In effect, Modernism, at its very inception, swiftly demolishes both the ontic and epistemic foundations of civilization. Contrary to the hallucinations of the Enlightenment, however, real, *Anthropic* society is not a *balance of interests* but a *balance of affections*. It is held together by the seamless affinities of sentiment, not by a presumptive "*division of labors*." Thus, even a communitarian intent, when conceived within an oppressive paradigm of materialism, like *Euro-Socialism*, devastates, surely and swiftly, in consequence of its metaphysical foundations, both social and ecological felicities. As such, both European capitalism and socialism, the *Tweedledum* and *Tweedledee* of modernist discourse, their separate and often lofty ideals notwithstanding, have succeeded only in bringing this fragile world to the very brink of disasters, known and unknown. *In sum, modernism destroys, and absolute modernism destroys absolutely.*

The human prospect is bleak therefore, owing to this modernist *Agenda* and its implacable masculinist vision of uninterrupted accumulation based on science, materialism, and violence (against women, workers, native peoples, tribal formations, dissenting minorities, and nature) and will not brighten until we re-embrace those simple, perennial, convivialities, unmediated by the corporatist logics of *State* and *Market*. Importantly, no modernist *politics* can find a cure for this malaise, left wing or right wing. Modernism can only be overcome by rejecting it altogether, not by internal reforms.

There are many strata, groups, and peoples only *marginally* incorporated into the Modernist fold, either for cultural, anthropic, or structural reasons; these are, in the main, women, workers, tribals, native peoples, and various cultural, and other, minorities. They might be thought of as constituting a perennial *Moral Economy* subsisting uneasily in the interstices of civil society, lodged within the great inclusive *paradigm of femininity*, wherein rest the ever affective values of care, consideration, and consilience upon which eternally leech the founding relations of family, kinship, and tribe: all our notions of society, culture, and civilization are simply extensions of this vital paradigm of the *Sympathy of Life*. It is within them that the *seeds of modernist dissolution* have always been nurtured: it is amongst them that the *Great Rejection* will commence, as indeed it already has. Therefore, women, workers, tribals, and minorities outside the sway of modernist formations, constitute the still standing, and ultimately indomitable *Ontology of Cultural Revolt* within whose matrix of nurturance we may yet discover the means with which to save this world from materialist depredations. *They are the everpresent and abiding Other within and without the modernist fold* (as such, conceptualizations, such as Said's, placing the site of the Other, cartographically, in the *non*-European world is an error).

In effect, it is the philosophy of *materialism unbound* that is at war today with the many matrices of nurturance extant in anthropic society: the *mammals* are at war with the *reptiles*, the primal *passions* with the material *interests*, the predations of masculinity with the regenerative modalities of femininity, *abstract* idealisms with *concrete*, experienced, *co-respectivity*. Modernism will be overthrown and materialism decisively rejected, for being both unnatural and asocial in the near, and contingent, future.

The European Enlightenment was conceived within the movement of a great philosophical revolution, though itself of unrecognized *non-European provenance*, highly local to Europe; it will be overcome by an even more mammoth but universal and inexpugnable *cultural involution*. The great historical irony is that the very *subaltern* peoples, practices, and affections, that an *Arch-triumphalist Euro-Modernism* hoped to leave behind forever, are now awake and ready to engulf, in a moral/ethical crusade, the thermonuclear, *technofascist* regimes of rational greed. Humankind's indelible *tribal* (i.e., *familial*) nature, which modernism ignores and derides, will reassert itself, and the primal passions, simmering beneath, will once again tether the vampire obsessions of its calculating cupidity. Contrary to our anthropocentric delusions of grandeur, we just might yet be restored to our true *species-being*, that is, to our larger *trans-anthropic mammalian family*. The (vainglorious) *great European divide* between nature and culture, but one of the host of perverse, adversarial, *dualisms* inaugurated with the Enlightenment, will then, and thereby, cease to exist.

Contrary to the dualist, anthropocentric, delusions of the Enlightenment we are, in essence, but a sub-species of *Hominids*, self-glorifying mammals, vested with indelible species characteristics that we ignore only at peril. *The human herd is a tribal formation corralled into nations and states by the cupidity and cunning of modernist predators.* This "*human essence*"—our species being—is not primarily "*social*" but is truly *Trans-Human*, belonging to the larger *species-nature* of hominids. It cannot be "realized" in the vacuity of modernist constructions, in either civil or political society. *In effect, modernism is alienation, from our primal state, writ large.*

Anthropic Civilization (as opposed to *anthropic society*), where it becomes possible at all, an extension only of our *trans-anthropic* roots, is forever built quite simply on the foundation of the universal anthropic, communal ethic of *conviviality*: *Euro-Modernism*, in violent rejection of that essentialist paradigm of the *sympathy of life*, in fatal conceit, disdained that pedestrian truth: and now faces certain extinction. As but a trivial sideshow to this great historical spectacle, *political economy*, the last epideictic parapet atop the great Berlin Wall of modernism—*separating humankind from its own essence*—will succumb to the sweep of this species-driven, trans-anthropic, transcendental ethics.

The material life will be restored to its true proportion, as a necessary, but mundane, complement/adjunct of living, minus the stultifying reification it suffers at modernist hands. No further need thereafter for an abstract "*economics*," the certain index only of our loss of control over the material conditions of our own existence: only transparent, expositive, *communitarian choices*, with respect to pecuniary *means* and preferred *ends*, inspired by prevailing norms and respectful of larger cultural covenants. The various productivist and/or consumptivist paradigms of modernism which demand the ever extortionist sacrifices of involuntary human Labors, to propitiate its incontinent, satyr-like, lust for gain, will yield to the more gentler, lambent, irrefragable persuasions of *being*, not *becoming* or *doing*; with *living*—and the extension of the quantity and quality of *lebenzeit*, living time—as the only, and possibly ultimate, "meaning of life."

It is only in these myriad latticed *Matrices of Conviviality*, that nurture our deeply communitarian natures, that we might yet find the diacritical potential for transcendence of the divisive *dualities*—the bane of binarism!—that dog and deform the desperate drudgery of everyday life within modernism. As such, the project of Utopia, a mere *Cri de Coeur* at a real paradise lost, is not one of construction, or invention, but rather the simpler one of *reclamation*. However, the very real danger to all life forms today, even in the very face of this still unfolding evolutionary redemption, is the fact that, in its valedictory last agonies, modernism may well destroy, not merely the baseline normative scaffolding of civilization, but much of human habitat as we know it, even as this planet, *a living thing in its own right*, fights back to restore lost felicities, defiled boundaries, and fractured balances.

The radical divide that this set of ideas involves with received knowledge of human societies compels repetition: the historical "models" of societal forms are few indeed—*tribal societies, imperial formations, and modernist entities ("civil societies").* Within these templates, *tribal society* is one where kinship rules through affective ties thereby fitted "naturally" within the paradigm of femininity, *despite the prison of patriarchy. Civil society* is the great modernist innovation, free of affective relations, subsisting on a routinized "structural violence" and embodying masculinist drives of *avarice and greed*; *empires* are the pinnacle of the *paradigm of masculinity* rent by masculinist power-and-greed drives, either singly or conjointly. *The tribal form is the "natural," anthropic societal form carrying the added bonum of the restraining power of affective ties that sets "natural" limits on the predations of masculinity: civil society is an airless wasteland where the anthropic spirit asphyxiates and dies an unnatural death; and empires are insecure male despotisms incapable, thereby, of subsisting within the bounds of anthropic civility for long. Importantly, all of social science errs in its lapidary, and quite willfully modernist, non-cognition of our "natural," anthropic "humanity."*

Finally, men and women are radically different subspecies of the human family, with respect to traits, behaviors, propensities, and instincts: and they may not be assimilated, except tendentiously, into aggregative speculations about "people" or "society" or "humanity." Such aggregations not only blame the victims for male-driven (take the term "human aggression," for example) *proclivities but also compound injury with insult by allotting misplaced credit to the victimizers for the unsung contributions of women* (as regards the real causal factors defining terms such as "*humanism*" or "*civilization*"). *Once again, it is high time we understood who we are as a species, much as our own real placement in the universal, natural, scheme of things.* Women don't hold up "half the sky" as the fulsome adage of Mao runs: but hold up virtually *all* that is worthwhile in anthropic existence.

(37)

At any rate, *so long as masculinity abounds*, no state in current, or any other times, is ever going to "*wither away*"—which was more or less a modernist fantasy ideal shared by thinkers as far apart as Marx and Cobden; as such, the task of any reconstruction in this area would have to begin with enchaining the mechanisms of state solidly within the clamping matrix of affective, personal relations, as tribal societies were able to do quite effectively. Kinship, another "*natural*" device, no matter how mediated by social ideology, within limits, is yet capable, thereby, of moderating the violent urges of masculinism. *Kinship is the closest that a man comes to, in terms of the values of nurturance, to a certain modicum of convivial pacifism.*

The problematic, by now should become clear. Modernism, by dint of ruthless conquest, succeeded in building the "*loveless*"—and hence lightless—civil "society" of privatized, hedonistic, individuals driven only by *universal egoism* and the gloss of consumptive—and destructive—desire. The traditional forces of opposition to this relentless crusade of greed are still with us today as they were at the very outset of the unleashment of modernist barbarism: *workers, women, and native/tribal cultures*—despite the fact that many of their struggles for *autonomy* have suffered grievously at modernist hands. The *Marxians* "led" workers into even greater miseries than they had experienced under traditional capitalism; the *feminists* who aspire to "lead" women are still struggling to find a unified, coherent voice, and the indigenous peoples are heroically offering resistance to modernist logics to preserve their critically eroded ways of life.

The first two struggles, leastways as revealed in the ideas/manifestos of the leadership rather than the bodies they claim to represent, suffer a critical, indeed mortal, weakness in sharing much of the very *ideology* of the oppressor that they hope to replace: *only the last is still relatively free from such contamination.* Hope for this world will arise when *all* of these forces finally free themselves from the debilitating hegemony, and the treacherous snares, of modernism. Neither women/workers nor tribals/natives have any real need to "lead" or be "led": to be simply "*left alone*," to pursue their own self-directed ends, would be their true manifest.

It is easy now to decipher the tortuous script of modernization or "*Westernization*," as it was to be visited upon a hapless world, and as it used to be called in the bolder days of imperium. It meant, in effect, that peoples still ensconced in the enveloping sanity of a moral and ethical social universe were required to shed that shielding, nurturing, *nonutilitarian* cloak, step by step, to embrace the many vanities of a privatized and individualized, *asocial* self-interest such that society became, for the first time in human history, a mere means to a vacuous drive for self-fulfillment rather than the vital medium of living, and an *end-in-itself.*

A *regimen* of use values was compelled thereby to succumb to a regime of *exchange value*; worth had to give way to wealth; and the pacific drone of subsistence to the passionate, clamorous, drive for accumulation, need based activities now genuflecting to greed-directed enterprise. *The paramountcy of culture was to be eroded in favor of the* predominance of *commodities; the riches of emotion to the drudgery of material reason.* The powerful, socially felt and respected, *extrinsic* restraint of "*shame*," as underpins traditional formations, succumbed to the purely personally carried, internally conceptualized, voluntarist, modernist burden of "*guilt*": *thereby blunting the critical edge of social constraints on amoral actions, and creating, as with the United States, a "shameless" society replete, paradoxically, with shameful behaviors.* What a fall the human species took in embracing these alienations! The modernist appetite knew but only how to feed greedily on such gross meat.

The elementary first steps, in the *Great Reclamation*, would take the form of rejecting the patrimony of modernist *science*, its deleterious philosophy of *materialism*, and its tyrannical ideology of *progress*. Left to themselves, women, workers, and indigenous peoples pursue self-sustaining paths that are quite independent of these false epistemes; however, their accelerated socialization in the mores of modernism—mainly under economic and/or political duress—does present a serious challenge to the ancient *political economy of affections* that yet survives if but as an endangered *sub-culture*, though it vitally undergirds the preservational aspects of all societal frames. Workers and women have always been the *real producers*; and neoliberal modernism, in its current pitch of pirating/patenting the discoveries of native peoples everywhere, represents the most sophisticated attempt to date to appropriate the knowledge, fruits, and the habitats of their spontaneous, self-sustaining labors.

The project of saving the planet, or more aptly, the human hominid species, from the terrible implications of this dreadful misanthropic construction is to somehow check, retard, and ultimately reverse, the suicidal progression toward the certain annihilation of life on earth before it is too late. While the task might appear formidable, and daunting, it is far from hopeless since modernism is capable of a fair amount of *self-destruction* just given its own restless propensities. The *desideratum* is merely a certain preparedness—and awareness—on the part of the long-suffering victims to step in when the time comes to resurrect the possibility of human civilization and the continuity of planetary life, *en generale*.

On this, one can have little doubt: sheer survival will, in an ontic sense, demand from these social agencies the will to resist the modernist holocaust, without the necessity of any great, intercalated, epistemic revolution to precede it. And it is inherent in the nature of the oppressed to reclaim their rights when pushed to the limits of their endurance; contrary to elite pretensions of a liberal latitude toward the *sans-cullotte*, it is modernism that has enjoyed, thus far, if only as an ill-deserving beneficiary of this ragged trousered philanthropy, *the languid tolerance of the wretched of the earth*. That generously extended rope, stretched out for centuries, is now set fair to be pulled.

(38)

We need to reject the partisan mythology of an alien "*state of nature*" preceding our ascent into civility as modernist writers of the enlightenment sketched matters in the early modernist centuries if only to paint lavish, self congratulatory, portraits of the achievements of European *society*: *for society itself is a "natural" artefact* despite the investment of our varied "cultural" genius constituting its staggering *diversity* (indeed, the hidden hint in all of the modernist "*state of nature*" analogies is the false premise that *premodernism* is a nasty free-for-all of brutish forces; nothing could be further from the truth: brutishness, that is, callousness is as modernist as Dachau, Stalin's Gulags, and the infamous English "*workhouse*" of late Tudor times).

The human, as but another mammal, is an animal, and belongs in the same domain as all of living matter: above all, mammals are *heat* (i.e., *warmth*) *seeking* animals. The "point of life" is, for us individuated modernists, a matter of choice; and if modernism were simply one metaphysical choice among many, on free offer, one might have no quarrel with it. But modernism, unlike, say, Bantu philosophy, is brutishly hegemonic and brooks no dissent from its strictures, even from nonmembers. Even then, one might yet have endured it by the customary human standbys of stealth, evasion and exile; but the modernist temper, not content with engulfing all of cultural diversity, takes one fateful step further—*it threatens, in imminent form, the survival of all life*, including its own, by its inveterate, and insatiate, appetite for incessant, unbounded and interminable gain. It is in that last regard that it invites, all but unconsciously, the spontaneous, and universal resistance of a living planet *in its entirety*. A finite planet simply cannot survive infinite greed.

Culture is a heirarchically ordered system of values; and although similarities abound, no two cultures are exactly alike. Through adoption and adaption, cultures evolve over time, passing on a reasonably coherent set of values to its members that helps to codify, order, and regulate the preconditions of life. As such *cultures may never be judged—fruitfully or relevantly, that is—from the outside*; they do not exist, in the first instance, to flatter any particular norm or principle, as given from *without*. Significanlty, *although incommensurable, they are not incomprehensible*: human empathy is entirely capable, but only given such an intent, of comprehending, howsoever imperfectly, the immanent logics of cultural behavior. Given the plurality of cultures, and their *incommensurability*, does it not then follow that the critique of modernism offered here is gratuitous?

So it would appear, at first blush; but such an impression is erroneous. *The rationale for mutual tolerance, it might be allowed, is mutual survival*; but where modernism invokes, and invites, countervailing moves is in the threat it poses to the very foundational habitat that nurtures all of us, including itself. It is in this vital regard that modernism sets itself up as the planetary *nemesis par excellence*; but we do not live, despite the fantasy of mainstream physics, in a passive or inert universe—and it would be anomalous indeed if the dire challenge of modernism to our continued existence, were not to be met, effectively and decisively, in the final climax of that ultimate struggle between modernist practices and the possibility of life on earth.

Human society has lumbered on, ever regulated by the inexhaustible claims of masculinity until the oppression(s) inherent in the latter condition have now become cataclysmic for human survival. The resurrection of civility after the modernist holocaust might well necessitate reformulation of all of social life on the *feminine principle of conservation* (rather than the archetypically *masculinist* one of *conquest*). In this, as has been noted, no spectacularly idealist, and heroic, deviation from preexisting norms is called for; the innumerable tribal, kindred forms of society littering the planet have, quite "*unconsciously*," evolved on the basis of such preservative norms of *consilience* despite the customary male domination of all institutions.

History, or rather anthropology, has shown the extant possibility and feasibility of such formations; so there is nothing remotely "*utopian*" about them. And, if it were possible in our past, it remains open to emulation in the future—for *crisis, given the masculinist mindset, is the dependable midwife of change and adaptation*: it will be, in effect, the "natural" route to follow, but regrettably perhaps only after the consummating annihiliations of the coming "*armageddon*."

(39)

Alienation and *angst* have been the specific modernist contributions to the ensemble of human misery (tiny little Denmark has stood at the economic apex of modernist, capitalist formations for decades, and yet also has the highest suicide rate in Europe: Kierkegaarde might have known the answer to that modernist puzzle though modernist philosophy is unable to fathom it) exacerbating the despair of the many, unavoidable, insecurities of both natural and social existence. Philosophical emptiness, the so-called "*postmodernist*" condition, is the ultimate metaphysical basis for insanity, *anomie*, and that uniquely modernist form of chronic dissatisfaction and hopelessness which may not be allayed or pacified (it is doubtful, for instance, whether nonmodernist societies have even the *word* "boredom" in their lexicons, let alone any apprehension of that modernist condition itself).

The commodification of gratification, the mechanization of desire, and the privatization of societal life, are the grim alloys with which the human spirit has been robotized, desensitized, and divested of its vital emotive currency, such that communal feeling and convivial relations, the precious lifeblood of a living social form, have suffered systematic, structural and even ineluctable erosion. If modernism was built upon the bright hope of material accumulations, the *postmodernist* condition today has succumbed to the inherent hopelessness of such arid, banal, motivations.

Even Adam Smith, the Scottish materialist/moral philosopher, was well aware of the lack of an immediate, or intimate, connection between wealth and happiness, taking it to be, nonetheless, a fairly widespread mass delusion. Yet, despite this insight, he helped in his own way to perpetuate the dominant illusion of the European epoch, *that* (*a la* Mandeville) *private vices can, magically, produce public benefits*. That pedestrian philosophy of *primitive accumulation* has now conquered the imaginations of the world, both European and non-European, through the pervasive mediation of the modernist enterprise, now scrofulously grown to *transnational* dimensions: thus do bad ideas drive out good ones, in an epistemic twist of *Gresham's Law*. The birthright of civilization has now been auctioned off for a sorry mess of pottage as nation after nation succumbs to its logics of advancement; and we rush headlong, willy nilly, into a swift but certain extinction.

Being is now sacrificed to *becoming*, and the latter to owning and consuming, even as the planet shudders unable to withstand the pillage of its resources, and the destruction of its fragile balances. The modernist has set sail on a dark voyage of perpetual enrichment, from which no one will ever return, for there will be little left to return to. *Economics without ethics, liberty without restraint, freedom without responsibility, growth without conservation, order without justice, and wealth without equity, such are the mainsails of the neoliberal shallop*, as we all jump aboard, recklessly and without reflection, for the game is afoot and there is no place on board for the losers who will now add up in the millions.

With the recent eclipse of *intra-modernist* struggles—the so-called quintessentially modernist Cold War that threatened the planet for half a century—the *capitalist* variant of the European modernist *juggernaut* has returned to its temporarily, and partially, interrupted quest for global empire; indeed, the vulnerable amongst the non-European periphery face far more irresistible threats to their autonomy today than even in the era of classical colonialism, much as women, workers, and minorities are up today against a radical erosion of their fragile securities within European formations given the Great Reversal and the roll-back of previous, hard-won autonomies. Under cover of putatively *multilateral* institutions, the European is now consecrating a new world order of absolute obeisance on the part of the global family of man to *his* dictates, rules, fiats, and decrees. No one *monoculture* has ever dominated over, and desecrated, other cultures and societies as the *Euro-modernist*, in the corporate mold of global privatization, plunder and monopolization of scarce resources, is able to in these portentous times.

Yet, even as non-modernist *elites* capitulate to political pressure and the temptation of riches, the masses of the disenfranchised will learn, *as a natural expedient of survival*, to *resist*: their storm is yet to break, and dark clouds and tempests are nigh. *No one can draft the manifest of their struggle, for it is a spontaneous one. No one can direct or lead such struggles, for they are localized in a myriad contexts. And no one can control or coordinate the outcomes, for they are plural, carrying the signature of various, but specific ways of life.*

The rules of *formal* rationality that have enchained the planet will succumb to the resistance of a concrete, *substantive rationality*, that is, the hoary banalities of civility, survival, subsistence, autonomy, and cultural freedom. These form the silent, but conscious, *credo* of the anti-modernist revival and reclamation. It is happening; it is here. Since the much publicized "Battle of Seattle," where anti-globalizers paralyzed, if only for a few days, the Grand Circus of the meetings of the World Economic Forum, the shadow government of corporatist world policy, even the rulers of the world are aware now of the clearly drawn lines of struggle as never before.

The *deconstructionists*, for all their *avant garde* posturing and often vacuous rhetoric, are not wrong in their central insight: *words are important in a human society*—indeed as important as *deeds*, if not more, given that language is an important avenue for cultural expression aside from being a near permanent repository of cultural values. However, in many senses *words are deeds, expressed otherwise*. The traditional *deed-worshipper*, as say with Marxians or Anglo-Saxon empiricism, is a vulgar materialist imputing arbitrarily high value to *practices* and denigrating the power of linguistic, and other cultural, *conventions*. Few deeds, it might be supposed, that were not inspired by prior words; but, in effect, *words and deeds are duals* and may not be prioritized—each implies the other. Modernism was a series of constructions, linguistic, cultural, and political; and its *deconstruction* will take place, and is taking place, broadly along similar lines. *The modernist center will not, can not, hold.*

(40)

The lapidary errors of received European visions of emancipation—capitalist or socialist—may now be simply expressed: in the corrupt, modernist vein, *they elided the issue of the human, hominid essence, constituting it, not in the mellow sphere of simple harmonies, but in the hard tundra of human cupidity and avarice.* Stated more accurately, they wrote their scripts of amelioration in the *masculinist* vein—the early modernist elites being *men* for the most part, anyway—thereby side-stepping the garner of possibilities immanent in the generous bounty of feminine grace. In that dark world of masculine machinations, amelioration could only take the familiar form of material greed (i.e., an enhancement of material values), usually requited by means of a generous amount of blood-letting. Interestingly, all *varieties of Euro-modernist politics call for blood,* whether the "struggle" is ostensibly for the "*free market*" or for "*socialism*": it was seemingly almost imperative that people had to die in securely large numbers for the enterprise to merit the badge of seriousness.

The actions and passions of politicians as unlike each other as Napoleon, Hitler, Stalin, and Reagan, to that extent, are yet all dyed in the same blood, so to speak, of their fellow humans. Significantly, *there is no, and never has been, European version of, say, Gandhian politics* (the imperially minded Churchill, true to his churlish character, summed up the modernist reaction in a famous animadversion libeling Gandhi as little more than a "*half naked fakir*"—though Gandhi had enough *moral raiment* to clothe the entire British Isles several times over; more drearily, the fact that the now securely Europeanized, consumerist elites of rapidly modernizing India are likely to similarly disparage this prince of amity is a grim reflection of the degree of integration of non-Europeans in the ideology of their oppressors).

Modernism entered the world purveying wildly improbable, and tendentious, ideals of human rights and equality as part of its revolutionary euphoria and as the necessary rhetoric required to topple the *ancien regime,* as expressed in both the French and American Revolutions. In neither case was either the "equality" or the promise of equal rights for all achieved as proclaimed. As might appear obvious, rights are not a matter of revolutionary declarations, in societies as artificially constructed as modernist ones, but of the grim empirics of real and relative access to material and political resources (which were always blocked off as far as women, minorities and workers were concerned). Besides, the very ideal of *equality, as some sort of a societal goal, is itself a wholly modernist chimera.* To be the alienated, separatist, individualized, "*equal*" of some other (in some reductionist "economic" or "political" sense) that is similarly constrained confers neither joy nor satisfaction by virtue of the equalness; the right to *equal alienation* and unrequited misery may hardly be deemed an uplifting boon. Perhaps the only "equality" we come close to possessing in common lies but in our *capacity for suffering* our shared anthropic lot.

As the familial metaphor makes clear, inequality is not in itself unnatural or perverse: it is all a matter of the nature of its existence and constitution within the overall matrix of social relations; the *family*, for example, is an unequal entity within which, nonetheless, caring, warmth, and affective reciprocities prevail. *In fact, the formal, strident and aggressive "declarations" of rights—as with modernist societies—is the loud and transparent index of the breakdown of mutuality in human conduct.* within a family, for example, no such "declaration" is needed: "rights" are implicit because of the *inherent, unstated, implicit presumption of care* that underlies the entire set of constituent relations.

Modernism first destroys the *nexus* of caring and then artificially "announces" a pious schemata of "*human rights*" (that are honored, usually, in the breach) as its hollow ersatz; it is this "*mechanical*" approach to *the basic reciprocity of human obligations* that is presumed by the anthropic nature of the social that vitiates the modernist social endeavor, no matter how well-intentioned. The aggressive ideology of rights is both necessitated by, and is a cover for, the fact that modernist *civil society—the ultimate materialist wasteland*—is rent by irreconcilable conflicts and irresoluble contradictions of interests. Far from being symptomatic of "*progress*," as is commonly believed, the statutory declarations of human rights as they stem from the American and French Revolutions in modern history, aside from their dissimulating nature as ideology, are also the emblematic badge of the very palpable *destruction* of a preexisting civility, honor, and *co-respective* behaviors.

Democracy, similarly, is a flawed modernist entity, where the entirely conceivable eventuality of tyranny by a majority (or, elite capture of the dominant institutions) is considered acceptable; at any rate, compared to the patient, consensual nature of *premodernist convenance*, democracy may be viewed, thereby, only as a rather dismal means of achieving a shaky accord, more an insecure and impermanent *détente* really, itself the result of a divisive, *adversarial* contest. Given the latter-day parameters of European plutocracies masquerading as democracies, it may be seen as achieving, far more certainly, and on a daily basis, cynicism, corruption, impotence, and apathy. Voter turnouts, and general perceptions of politics, in modernist mass societies can only confirm the reality of the latter (metaphorically, if modernism seeks but an uneasy "détente," a temporary truce, between hostile groups of men, premodernism constructs the basis for a permanent "*entente cordiale*" for the group as a whole).

Men are not, in any sense, emancipators: but they do *affect* that politic language of amelioration given the restless ebullience of the male ego that is constantly seeking new arenas of battle in the feud for supremacy. *There is not much difference between the little man fighting for justice and the Big Men arrayed against him* (it is in the "fighting" that they are both united) except that they are, on either side of the divide, *Men*, and likely to be equally ruthless. Besides, in time, with monotonic regularity, "little" men, once having triumphed, turn quite swiftly into "Big" men. *Male power produces its familiar dual, male fear of power and powerlessness*: and so the *circulation of elites* (i.e., of *men*) goes on in an eternal cycle, with misery the lot of those caught in between.

Thus far, a cursory glance at European (or other) history should reveal the indubitable fact that all revolutionaries betray the "*ideals*" of the revolution as a matter of course, and all too swiftly. *It is not merely that power corrupts, as Lord Acton memorably phrased it, but that power itself—and the very seeking of it—is the very determinate index of Male corruption.* And yet, our credulity is purchased daily by the incessant rhetoric of "*just*" struggles and just wars and just revolutions (or counter-revolutions); let there be no doubt—few men sign on enthusiastically for *bloodless* wars (their inherent violence sees no heroic capability in such struggles), deriving a special satisfaction in risking death for the sake of "conquest" (expressed in eternal, if in mordantly trite form by Sir Hilary who, in that very mind-set, "conquered" Mount Everest merely "because it is there," albeit on the backs of his teams of Nepalese sherpa-servants); it is not the lemming, perhaps, but the male ego that has a determinately suicidal bent.

Add to male violence *male sexuality* (a closely linked and related attribute), and it is easy to see how the United States, the high society of modernism, displays its steely street reality of rabid masculinity in all its contemporary public cultural and political imagery, blending different variants of a raw, exploitative, *reductionist, genital* sexuality (a breed apart from a *polymorphous sensuality* that is more feminine in its sensitivity) with rank *violence*. It is this potent combination—that spells a near-certain cultural disaster for the oppressed of this planet—that Hollywood has made its staple export in the past fifty years to the point where *Americana* is inconceivable without these two hellish elements of that all-potent witch's brew. *Repressive desublimation*, the real and intended consequence of such productions, accounts for much of the explosive, tinder-box, discontent that stalks American life.

The corporate domination of the world today threatens to engulf the world with such malignant, commodified forms of misanthropic, misogynist desublimations. The "Rambo" trope, in both image and reality, threatens both women and "other" cultures worldwide. *Let there be no doubt: the world is more unsafe today, owing to such modes of modernist anti-culture, for women, workers and native peoples than it ever has been* (the recent reports of the U.S. anthropologist-assisted Nazi style clinical testing of live subjects amongst the hapless Yanomani Indians of the Amazon, if true, is a grim reminder that *Euro-modernism* is as genocidal in its impulse today, in the late modern period, as ever in its fateful history). *Techno-fascism, to put it succinctly, is the highest, meaning most baneful, stage of modernism.*

(41)

The nuclear essence of the human emancipatory impulse, and its ultimate resting place, is the matrix of social relations that is best expressed in the conventional notion of the "*family*." There is no societal formation on the planet that does not, in some mode or other, possess such *a base unit of social/natural* life, no matter how the actual "*familial*" instinct/impulse is expressed, defined, or legally recognized, as an institutional artefact (i.e., regardless of the empirical diversity in the constitution/composition of a "*family*"). It is the cradle and the womb of the hominid endeavor in this world, though men, *qua* men, obsessed with their abstract power drives in the *extra*-familial domain, habitually lose sight of its structural importance to their own well-being.

The fox has a lair, the bear its cave—and the human, its familial nest. This is where life usually begins and often ends. This is where the *human animal, created "half to rise and half to fall"* as Pope had it, finds refuge and sanctuary in any and all modes of production and in any and all cultures. This is where warmth and conviviality and *corespective* behaviors are both learnt and practised; this is where civilization is both born and nurtured. Masculine drives for appropriation of the means of wealth and power, directly proportionate to the strength and intensity of those drives, lead to the dire neglect of the *affective vortex of familial relations* in favor of the eventual construction of the abstract, alien, extra-familial, conflictual, "*public*" domain (i.e., to the familiar modalities of *civil society*) that is necessarily cold, and harsh, and inescapably "*Hobbesian*."

However, given his ineluctable mammalian genus, Man is not, for all the wealth and power garnered, ever wholly gratified in that desolate domain (the myth of Midas is a telling myth in that respect) and seeks *instinctively*, even in that arid zone of acquisition and mastery, the cheer of conviviality and the security of the familial bond. Even within the distrustful, adversarial, public sphere of modernism, spontaneous eruptions of societal emotions, mass celebrations, and exultations (as with riots and revolutions) take on that *primal kindred* aspect where, however briefly, the emotive spark is relit and recaptured with a special kind of mutual joy which is at the heart of the natural bond of *communality*, revealing a mammalian herd instinct to *huddle* in foetal contact and feel a blessed contentment therein (*recognition of our innate "tribal" nature would go a long way toward debunking the delusionary, and disingenuous, dreams of modernist discourse*).

All the utopian drives of the Enlightenment at the dawn of the construction of European modernity stem from this urgent, unquenchable thirst to relive and re-experience what was being lost by the very inception of the universe of modernity and its solvent, corrosive effects on all traditional close-knit social bonds. Community, family and social life were being *modernized*, that is, made more *alien*, perhaps from the fifteenth and sixteenth century onwards; organic social links were being supplanted by the market and the cash nexus; exchange value was penetrating the hoary preserves of use values. Human life, accordingly, given the taxing constrictions of a regime of material advancement, was being rendered barren and *joyless*; *from More to Marx, the utopian impulse was a long, extended, but yet intense, cry of pain*, the instinctual mourning at the ineffable loss of the very essence of the social (and this long drawn *primal scream* could not but strike a chord in the hearts of the oppressed) in the novel creation of the aberrations of civil society.

The European modernist elites, captains of commerce and masters of the polity, all canny with rationalist calculation of net returns, looked at a peasant economy and saw only penury there, not the genial currents of *comity* that enshrined, enveloped, and enlightened the lives of its humble denizens; in the tendentious struggle to "liberate" the latter from their putative servitude (in effect, to subordinate them to another, more profitable form of labor regulation), they succeeded only in raising their misery on par with their own.

Their dreams of Utopia, stemming unconsciously from the hurt of this original and radical dispossession—*the rupture of organic ties of solidarity from anthropic society*—took the peculiarly *masculinist* form of seeking materialist solace in an externalist, alienated, *public vision, attempting not to abolish the public domain, itself vital to the modernist drive, but to somehow make it more harmonious and convivial.* This was, as we must be aware now, a foredoomed effort to square the circle. In fact, their cardinal errors in this arena were *two*: *first*, to retain the very dissipative, and schizoid, *public* domain/divide of "*state*" and "*civil society*" within their dreams of the promised land that were the original provenance of alienation to begin with, in varying degrees; and *second*, in believing that a surfeit, or a cornucopia, of *goods* would somehow soften, and ameliorate, the ills of the human condition all by itself.

In effect, masculinist materialism—*and acquisitive materialism is the quintessentially definitive masculine philosophy*—could not fathom its own fatal delusions, nor could it comprehend that the ultimate consummation of the utopian drive lay in the far simpler, and more readily available, demesne of what they instinctively disparaged as *domestic* felicities fit only for the likes of women, children, and savages. They failed to glean a far simpler truth; that *the pacification of human existence is a matter of affections, given and received; not merchandise, bought, sold*, or "*allocated*."

Armed only with supernal ignorance, they "*left home*," materially and symbolically, aggressively seeking Utopia, and could not find it anywhere either for themselves or for anyone else, precisely because they had left the very object of the search irrecoverably behind in that very first, uninspired, step. Metaphorically, European humankind, dizzy in its day dreams of modernity, was forsaking *its matrix home of tribality, familiality, and consilience (i.e. the epistemic "third world" that lives within us all)*, but not understanding the meaning of that loss, of that estrangement, of that momentous dispossession. The native American, and the Australian Aboriginals, on the other hand, had no need to scribe phantasmagoric Utopias, or other such imaginary blueprints for salvation; *they had never abandoned their communal roots of fulfillment, in the first place*, seeking *abstract* salvations, and that too in the name of the false, and treacherous gods of Mammon.

The secret of the long drawn European struggles for emancipation is now forever unveiled: *the kernel of the utopian impulse consists in attempting to recreate the sanctuary of a paradise lost (i.e. the affective, familial habitat of "home") even amidst, and during, the perilous descent to the bare, cold, harshness of civil society; worse, on the misconceived basis of the delusive abstractions inherent in the modernist way*. To think that affective, anthropic solidarity of a tribal kind could ever be achieved within the dispiriting alienations of civil society was the fatal conceit of the entire lineage of modernist utopians as characterized Europe in its classical, late modern period.

Indeed, the chronic dissatisfaction of sensitive people, even amongst the modernists, as the age of industry advanced, could only have stemmed from their distal, anthropic *memory* of a better world being gradually abandoned; the proverbial "*garden of eden*" was not a myth—it referred precisely to the *relations of consilience* as they obtain *immanently*, not just in some archaic prehistory, within the domain of the familial no matter how rent with conflict, rivalry, or competitiveness (even when conflicts, indeed blood feuds, emerge in tribal society, they generally pose no annihilatory threat either to the tribe or the larger ecosystem: they are, instead, one way or other, "contained," eventually, by societal sanction).

Marx was categorically, even disastrously, wrong; it was the very "*primitive communism*" that his progressivist modernism disdained that held the permanent keys to the *joyful* society: *want what we may, all we need is love.* And, at the very heart of those blissful, riant conciliations, in apostolic patience, stood the silent grace of femininity, since times immemorial, forever pointing the indefectible way to a sylvan concomitance of human affections and gratuities. The bane of modernism is this: that, forever seeking the *el dorado* of an imagined peace and contentment, in all the wrong sites, it systematically destroys the only abode that made the memory of those felicities possible in the first place. Not an *iron cage*, as Weber had it, but the even more ineluctable clamp of the Plathian *bell-jar* that is the lethal gift of modernism to the human condition—an ineffable epistemic tragedy, since the possibility of utopia is *ontically immanent*, and perennially available to all, and at virtually no cost, within the freely available *moral economy of affections* (not a *material economy* of collectivized labors as erstwhile socialism turned out to be). As such, utopian consummations are a matter of recovery and *rediscovery*, rather than invention and innovation.

(42)

The extraordinary diversities of cultural innovation obscure, within their glittering *manifest of difference*, the one important commonality within the *human mammalian family*, its desideratum of *autonomy*, even when blissfully chained within the confluent mores of custom, convention, and convenance. Given its nature, it can only have educed from the very real instinctual drive toward *self-preservation* (which is not at all the equivalent of the modernist episteme of an untamable "*self-interest*" parodied by *Smithiana* and its apologists) that appears vested in all species. *The ceaseless, if silent, and unpredictable dissonance of the dynamics of personal autonomy in the daily face of communitarian restraints might well explain and account for the phenomenon of continuous change in human societies* (as apart from the more infrequent *discontinuous* modes of radical change that modernist historians have dwelt on) despite (and sometimes also owing to) the persistence of the conserving restraints of cultural mandates. In this way we are always changing, if within similarly altering boundaries.

Even given the binding intercalations of cultural idioms, the human animal, by the pre-given variability of chance and design strikes out, modestly, in marginally *different* directions—thereby serving the accretion of new *ideas*, which, upon finding the right reception, become embedded in (slowly) altered *practices. The fabled constancy of change rests but upon this simple species attribute.* When this ever modest need for *autonomy* encounters a superordinating force, an *axiology of resistance* develops, once again "naturally" as an instinctual matter, its *modus* a function only of the individual personality concerned. Marx was preoccupied with the mechanics of *aggregative*, even catastrophic, *macro* class conflict, but there are many other, less dramatic, sub-modalities of conflict that are by no means irrelevant; *in fact, tensions between the specificities of individual self-definitions within and against the more routinized patterns of societal intercourse are the more constant source of creative tensions within all societies, class divided or not.*

Importantly, *exploitation*, in the Marxian sense, can go virtually unnoticed (aside from requiring a primer in political economy to comprehend it), but *oppressions* are nearly always immediately felt and "understood": little wonder that, even within modernism, *it is oppressions that are mightily resisted* whereas only the most educatedly "class-conscious" can rise to the level of understanding and acting upon the dry, and veiled, facts of surplus value transfer(s). *By treating oppressions as "secondary," not least within "socialist" societies, Marxians defined themselves ruinously outside racial, ethnic, tribal, and gender, that is, cultural, movements* (quite interestingly, and instructively, in this regard most of the unrest in the West Asian region today, associated with Islam, *is less aimed at capitalism as it is at the larger vortex of modernism; indeed culture is the vital domain of politics today*).

The *dialectic of change* within premodernist formations has little to do, however, with the institutionalized restlessness of modernist society which is premised on conflict, adversarial politics, and the refractory veto of force. *Consensual societies turn to the employ of force reluctantly, and only as a desperate expedient when all other means of reconciliation have failed to be persuasive.* There are, in the historical docket of societal modes, one might note, at least *two* contrasting precepts of justice (the latter-day Rawlsian set of ideas on the subject—*justice, tautologically understood as "fairness"*—that have dominated discourse are fatally flawed for their casual adoption of *civil society* as the template, and within it of the *individual* as the policy unit; in effect, the Rawlsian imagination is constricted/confined by his own *modernist* presumptions): that of *justice as vengeance* which is quintessentially *masculinist*, and *justice as reconciliation*, which is its *convivial* alternate. Modernism melds its basic idiom of masculinity—*justice-as-vengeance*—with the capitalist notion of *justice-as-restitution*, the latter pertaining to property matters, while applying the former to *criminal*, as opposed to *civil*, issues of violence against the person.

In *premodernism, reconciliation is the dominant norm of accord*, with restitution a subordinate and complementary idea. Rather than simply invoking and inflicting the ever abiding *wrath of masculinity* on the offender, the resolve is to heal the *breach of relations* caused by the offense as swiftly as possible. Modernist justice in its abstractness, impersonality, adversarialism, and lack of caring, deepens and blackens the void within the social soul for which no reparation is possible. As such, every day, modernism becomes an *angrier* society compounding the misery of humans buffeted by forces over which they have no real measure of control.

Additionally, in this regard, the key modernist elision lies in extracting, and then excising, the idea of justice from its traditional sanctuary in *morality* so as to make it the negotiable artefact of *legality*; legality is the dessicated modernist substitute for morality and spells, wherever it is imposed as a modernist artifice, the atrophy of moral sanctions open henceforth now to the bargaining, bazaar-like, *modus* of a contractual social form. The difference should be clear: morality is categorical, organic, and immanently indisputable; the law is mutable, negotiable, debasable, and subject to arbitrary and politic interpretation. The degree of advancement of modernist legalisms, thereby, is a true index of the degree of decay of moral and ethical sanctions. Social relations are critically imperiled, as in the United States, when the law is, tragically, *virtually the only sanction preventing asocial actions and behavior* (a "Statue of Liberty" may be acceptable as a grand flourish: but where, one might ask, is the corresponding "Statue of Responsibility"?).

The U.S. constitution, blissfully ignorant of the philosophical import of the phrase, and dizzy with its own revolutionary rhetoric, virtually *demands* from its hapless citizenry the mandatory "*pursuit of happiness.*" Sadly, millions remain forever trapped in the doldrums of an ever unrequited pursuit, whilst "happiness" itself, in typical modernist devolvement, has colloquially come to be defined in the banal lexicons of the objective greed(s) of the uncharismatic New England Carpetbagger. *Happiness is a hyperbolic figure of speech; contentment, on the other hand, is an observable and attainable emotion/state connected as it is with the satisfaction of far simpler human needs.* Little in the ideology and institutions of modernism speaks to the *idylls of contentment*, nor is modernism structurally equipped to recognize the primacy of human *needs*: it is a formation driven by a restlessly expansive vision of endlessly accommodating itself to a plethora of exploding *wants. But needs are as real as wants are delusive* (needs are, in principle, satiable: but the limits to wants, if such exist, are set only by the avaricious imagination).

In so denying the very existence of *species human needs*, modernism denies our anthropic state, and withdraws from popular consciousness, as a permanent excision, the very possibility of ease and tranquility; in offering the phony lure (elusive fleece!) of a *commodified* "happiness" while expropriating all the means of a *real* contentment, both material and ideational, modernism guarantees but the permanent persistence of a chronic *discontent*—of each, with herself, and with all.

(43)

Truth is, ultimately only a *value*, and as such takes on an import that is pendent on the nature of a docket of other values. *Not all values are created equal in any cultural setting*, and thereby, regardless of the apocrypha of liberal humanist rhetoric, *truth cannot be, in any universalist sense, taken to be a prepossessing, or super-ordaining value, in or by itself.* For one thing, in the societal world, the epistemic and the ontic are both ever in flux, despite the gravitational pull of our basic, anthropic natures. There are, also, obviously, in a situational sense, in any frame, *competing* values, which are equally "*humanist*"—if not indeed more so: such as justice, kindness, pity, mercy, peace, and so on. It might well be, therefore, that *the value of a given value depends on context*—that is, depending on the specificities of the real human situation involved. But values, additionally, are also related to, and are therefore *relative* to, *culturally specified hierarchies*; in sum, human values are a complexus of interpersonal, *anthropic, and intra-communal resources*, and may not be *abstracted* in the manner of shades of idealist philosophy such as rationalism (this is not to take a "materialist" view, but a *concretist* one) that lay down the epistemic "rule" to be followed, in this domain, in speciously "*universal*," and "timeless" terms.

This poses a problem—a conundrum—for this discourse as conducted thus far: the critique of modernism cannot be *absolutist*—it can, but only by forsaking *relevance*. In effect, to be "real" it must necessarily reflect some anthropic perspective within which modernist drives are to be seen as inherently ill-founded, or else it would appear that any casually articulated perspective on modernism is as good as the point of view it privileges. However, due reflection will suggest that the dilemma is chimerical; as pointed out, it is arguable that the *minimum condition for discourse between any contending opinions is the presumption of continuity of both the debate and the debators* (this is not a *rationality* postulate; it is really an *existence* axiom) *at least until such time that the debate is "settled"*.

Modernism poses a demonstrably imminent *ontic* threat to the existence of the very platform which is being debated, that is, *the planet we inhabit*, and as such sins against the otherwise generous accommodations of *relativism*. In effect, even the votaries of modernism are unlikely to survive the modernist destruction of human and nonhuman habitats; only in that important sense, *this critique of modernism is both concrete and real as much as it is, as a contextual matter, absolutist and universal*, despite its unique, and ontically specific, vantage point. While an example of how the particular and the general sometimes fuse (another sign of its "truth-value"), it is also an illustration of the requirements of concrete *truth* being, in this case, conveniently, in accord with the mandates of a concrete *justice. Epistemic dreams founder usually on ontic reefs: time and again have unenlightened revolutionaries taken us but out of one frying pan into another fire.* It is time now to base the emancipatory (i.e., the *convivial*) impulse on our real anthropic natures rather than on fantasy: as such, the need for emancipation may also consist in being set free of the very tribe of modernist emancipators.

The cardinal lesson for anthropic amelioration is as simple as it is ineluctable: *the instincts are not programmable, but behaviors are*—and tribal formations have optimized that insight by the wisdom embedded in their construction of *human* (i.e., in particular, the *masculine set of traits/impulses*) personality safely within the matrix of *kinship* (i.e., nurturance). Given our anthropic natures, this "solution" is unlikely to be improved upon.

(44)

Individuals, ensnared and enslaved, *within modernism*, have choices that cultures, *in the aggregate* (oddly enough, even in the presumably *inanimate* domain, there is more *micro* freedom than *macro* freedom: that is, individual atoms can behave *randomly* whereas aggregations behave in more *orderly* fashion. *In society and in nature, aggregate behavior is subject to laws and order, individual behavior is, usually, more erratic and unpredictable*) don't; so there is, also, a purely voluntarist exit available to any and all to choose to escape the modernist wasteland by simply relinquishing its ideas, ideals, norms, and practices.

The fact that such deviance will come at a price is obvious enough, but the benefits—so to speak—if in a nonmaterialist frame are legion. To step off the accelerating treadmill of ceaseless labor, and ceaseless wanting, and ceaseless accumulation is to rediscover the amities of life and the *joys of being*, as opposed to the *dispossessingly possessivist state of endless becoming*.

Most of us "opt," usually unconsciously, for a life of predictable drudgery, living and performing to *external* specifications, foreign to our instincts and alien to our felt needs, so as to carve out lives whose worth is measured by the meretricious criteria that are set by the few remotely situated pacemakers to whom much is given without the necessity of extravagant labors. The modernist chains have fallen upon us, so to speak unawares, in our deepest slumbers.

Most of us surrender, as part of this Faustian pact, the vital *autonomies* that are so much the defining feature of our species, losing our inner sense of self-worth, normal evaluative propensities, and even common sense judgment, yielding it all up to the "experts" who think for us, choose for us, and act as our surrogate selves, directors and supervisors. The modernist individual is the most pathetically vulnerable being ever designed—permanently insecure and uncertain about his or her "success" within its institutional structures, leading a shadowy, isolate, lorn existence cheered only by the occasional symptomatic relief of *consumptive* and (vanishingly) *relational* gratifications.

Yet it need not be so. It is, *despite the ravages of Man*, a resplendent universe that can easily be made anthropically nourishing and entertaining, once we reclaim our personal autonomies and thereby reestablish contact between our divided selves forced to keep the "personal" and the "public" spheres not merely apart but in apparent conflict and contradiction. Empathy and goodwill are easily capable of resurrection, and have a tendency to replicate themselves provided we step out of our privatized "*rational-material*" spheres of material containment. It takes, nonetheless, a species of courage to step out of that protective shell which is, really, a coffin and a cloister shading us from the healing light that pervades this universe.

The social is our natural state, a truth that Eurocentrism has hidden from view in all its intellectual contortions: to contain it is to limit our own development and thwart the possibility of fulfilment of our own personalities. *We are tribal animals (much of the "social" that is otherwise impenetrable becomes clarified instantly when we comprehend this fact!!) and unconsciously and instinctively create tribal bondings wherever and whenever possible; and we can, thereby, quite easily rebond with our fellow-beings, not in any abstract "humanist" sense, that gracious sounding term which has gratuitously concealed its own glaring vacuity of meaning, with the unknown and unknowable many: but concretely, with the few who inhabit our real, recognizable, and intimate, domains of care and consideration, rebuilding our lives outside of the cash-nexus and competitive market relations, well before the eclipse of modernism as a hegemonic force.*

All the social pathologies of modernism, from suicide to serial killings, are but the grisly *stigmata* arising from loss of contact and connection with each other, the greater the pity when that redemptive *relinking* is never more than a heartbeat away. *Children, prior to being rudely socialized out of their joys by enforced discipline and schooling, live in that state of primal exultation that is available to all, regardless of a society's economic mode or political form.* We need, therefore (and easily could, given the will) *to "de-school" ourselves as swiftly as possible.*

For the sensitized (whose time is come), the way out is clear enough. Although this will eventuate anyway as an implacable societal tidal wave given the immanent human dialectic of action and reaction, it would be helpful, as a matter of personal *volition*, to rid ourselves (ahead of any aggregated modes of social salvation) of any and all modernist delusions which, in practice, involves the summary excision of any and all modernist ideologies (wily, perilous snares!) of progress, growth, and global amelioration emanating from liberals, conservatives, radicals, and others. Modernist politics, economics, culture, *all* need to be—and will be—expunged, consigned to the trashcans that will eventually envelope and entomb the execrable modernist/masculinist yearnings for *imperium*.

The *Great European Enlightenment*—itself the product of the even *Greater Colonial Encounter*—was the epistemic source of modernism; so, to *break* with its hegemonic ideologies would be a voluntarist first cut approach to deliverance. *The negative dialectics of modernism demand only creative resistance, in ideas and practices—not revolution*: the latter is always a masculine power drive ever doomed to bloody self-immolation.

Epistemic freedom is no mean achievement, and should not be disparaged; actions follow ideational emancipation, and the latter itself is an important, oftentimes vital, "*action*," in and of itself. From commodity fetishism to the barren dialectic of formal democracy, false and vapid *Euro-modernist* ideas of an impersonal, acquisitive, self-absorbed existence have ravaged the global landscape concealing their craven hollowness behind the glare of publicity and the blare of propaganda. Modernism is as bare of any real, genuine satisfaction as a night in Vegas: and, like that abject and gaudy desert vanity, needs be left behind, sooner than later, to recapture our *species-being* dispensations of sanity and wholeness. Women have pointed the way, silently, in their manifold nurturings, for millennia, to that not unattainable, cost-free haven of a luminous contentment—and no fabricated "vision" of utopia could deliver more. The never-ending "free lunch" has always been their *gratis* contribution to civilization.

The "nation state" and "civil society" are aberrant, "unnatural," social forms unique to European modernism: it is within their malignant constrictions, imposed on all by dint of *imperium*, that the human spirit has now been securely entombed with a predictable docket of alienations being the inevitable consequence. Given their provenance in Modernist agendas, such entities cannot outlive, or endure, the dissipation of their policy underpinnings. *As such, what we are witnessing today, in incipient form, worldwide, is the return to more primal identities as seems to befit our anthropic state: real communities, as apart from artificially contrived "nation-states," are built upon more enduring identities forged by shared language, ethnicity, and culture* (attributes seriously miscalculated/misunderstood by socialist policy czars trying to build "nations" upon the enthusiasm, merely, of a shared "class consciousness") Even within modernist civil societies, such locations, and loyalties, routinely castigated as retrograde and "primitive" (Marcel Mauss and Durkheim were early modernists in this vein), spring up spontaneously defying the secular myths of abstract citizenship decisively. *The modernist plan to standardize us all within the extant modernist world*, by *fiat*, so as to serve the ends of capital accumulation, fails, in that sense, almost daily, and is likely to be an even more spectacular failure in the current drive to extend its profanities to the world as a whole under the title of "globalization."

The long night of modernism has been a dazzling dream of acquisitive pageantry for the few, purchased at the dire cost of the wholesale destruction of a myriad human, social, and ecological decencies. It is now time to wake—and view the abounding degradation in the sobering illumination of enlightening day, prior to turning our backs on it, *delinking* our lives from it, forever. *Predatory masculine drives, the reflux of our species-being, may not be expunged, but they can be contained; anthropic* culture, the empyrean efflux of the human imagination, and the perennially seminal pond of human resolve, *once connected*, can still rise, like a hydra-headed dragon of determinate endeavor to extirpate the modernist clutch of vices. Indeed, to the extent that we are such stuff as dreams, and the stars, are made of, *that much is simply our birth-right.*

Religiosity—itself little other than our original, innate, anthropic, spiritual sense of reverence for all life—will find within its deeply moral passions the final, and fitting, answer to the decrepit debauchery of the aberrant philosophy of materialism. In that sense, Marx was, again, infelicitous: *religion is not always an opiate—more often than not, it is the amphetamine of the "masses."* At any rate, in so succumbing, ironically, to the very force that it humbled in all triumph but three centuries ago, the wheel of modernist history would then have come full circle: nature, it might be contemplated, cannot but be expected to repair, but in its scale of time not ours, all of our pathetically conceived "*human*" ravages. Masculinity has had a long, miasmic, allodial, and inexpressibly catastrophic innings; time now for a uniquely feminine, cathartic, even inexpugnable absolution. Until benighted by the straitjacket of modernism, ours has been, within anthropic limits, a dazzling, effulgent universe of an opulent diversity: it can, and will, and must—be so again.

Epilogue

The European might, verily, have been the last to come to civilization, were it not that the advent/onset of modernism put a definitive end to that eventuality. Over a century ago, Wilde joked, but only half in humor, that America, Europe's irrepressible foster child and prodigal genius, had streaked straight from barbarism to decadence, bypassing that incidental felicity entirely. And yet It is doing far worse than that today: forcibly taking existing civilizations, thin residuals as they are of the originals, rollicking *backwards, nolens volens*, into *both* decadence and barbarism, in its own recklessly feral image.

The rationale for the *Great Regression* of our times must be clear now: the theory and practice of *Modernism* swiftly puts paid to the very possibility of civilization wherever it is introduced, regardless of creed or clime. *War, and the will and the means to wage it, were the only unmistakably clear European source of decisive "superiority" over all others* since the inception of the modernist era: today, it is that very set of skills and motivations that threatens to overcome our ability now to live hospitably, and co-respectively, on this planet.

The fact that Modernism gratifies innumerable human vanities abundantly, for the many if not all, should not have us hesitate to shake off its coils, because at its epicentre is an egregious *moral vacuum*, a veritable black hole, that is simply beyond normal, anthropic comprehension; and it will, if left unchecked, lead us all, helter skelter, into a very earthly perdition in the near, and none too distal, future. Indeed, we are part of the way there already.

Its inherited ideology is a perilous snare, and a beguiling trap. *Our received ideas about ourselves, our placement in the universe, and the universe itself are all critically wrong, misleading, delusive, mechanistic, and misanthropic.* The goals and motivations it ordains for us, in any and all domains, are both self-destructive and mortally corrosive of our bondings with each other and with our environs.

And yet we can, given our anthropic roots, without too Herculean an effort, rise above its scrofulous and baneful cajolements. We can connect once again with ourselves, with each other, and this munificent universe, that incessantly calls upon us through its unvaryingly permanent and awesome *presence*, to reflect upon ourselves, our lives, and the seemingly inscrutable mysteries of that unscalably empyrean convocation of fiery, spinning orbs, one of which we call, leastways in our more mindful moments, *home*.

We have, to our great impoverishment, benighted by the sway of *Euro-modernism* and its insistence on *permanent* struggle, competition, and conflict as the means to steadily increase the annual dividend at any and all cost, lost sight of the great, anthropic, universal harmonics of the essential, planetary and extra-planetary, lustrating, *sympathy of life* that connects us all.

It beckons us now (to refrain, perhaps, from further trespass?), through a myriad, luculent signs of ever deepening debility and decay, that are as ubiquitous as they are unmistakable : AIDS, BSE, Ozone Layer Depletions, Global Warming, Planetary Climactic involutions, Nuclear Fall-outs, Air and Water Pollution, Defoliation and Deforestations, Melting of the Polar Caps, Species Extinction, War, random Violence, and ubiquitous Terrorism. In this *Age of Universal Insecurity*, there is, and can be, no other reprise for our species: *we must* (as the poet Auden had it, in the not dissimilar environs of a uniquely *modernist*, global war, not so very long ago), if but within the anthropic bounds delineated in this work, in both epistemic and ontic metaphor, *love one another—or die.*

Works Alluded To

Acton, J. *Selected Writings*, Indianapolis: Liberty Classics, 1985.

Asad, T. (ed.), *Anthropology and the Colonial Encounter*, London: Ithaca Press, 1975.

Auden, W. H. *Collected Poems*, New York: Vintage International, Vintage Books, 1991.

Bacon, F. *The New Atlantis*, 1624–26. From *Ideal Commonwealths*, P. F. Collier & Son, New York: (c) 1901 The Colonial Press.

Beattie, J. *Other Cultures*, New York: Free Press of Glencoe, 1964.

Becker, G. *The Economic Approach to Human Behavior*, Chicago: University of Chicago Press, 1976.

Bentham, J. *An Introduction to the Principles of Morals and Legislation*, London: E. Wilson, 1823. Originally published 1779. Edited and corrected by the author.

Bernal, Martin. *Black Athena: The Afro-Asiatic Roots of Classical Civilisation*, 1987, 1991. *Vols 1 & 2*. New Jersey: Rutgers University Press.

Bhaskar, Roy. *Scientific Realism and Human Emancipation*, Verso: London, 1987.

Blaut, J. M. *The Coloniser's Model of the World*, New York: Guilford, 1993.

Boas, F. *Race, Language and Culture*, New York: The Macmillan Company, 1940.

Bohm, D. *Wholeness and the Implicate Order*, London, Boston: Routledge & Kegan Paul, 1980.

Bowler, Peter J. *The Invention of Progress*, Oxford: Basil Blackwell, 1989.

Calvin, J. *An Abridgement of the Institution of Christian Religion*, 1585, Thomas Vautrollier: Edinburgh, 1585. 8o. p. 398. Translated out of Latin by Christopher Fetherstone.

Carlyle, T. *Past and Present*, London, Glasgow and New York: George Routledge and Sons, 1888. Originally published 1843.

Cassirer, Ernst, joint ed. *The Renaissance Philosophy of Man: Selections in Translation.* Edited by Ernst Cassier, Paul Oskar Kristeller [and] John Herman Randall, Jr. Chicago: University of Chicago Press, 1948.viii.

Chakrabarty, D. *Provincialising Europe*, Princeton: Princeton University Press, 2000.

Chomsky, Noam. *Profit over People; Neoliberalism and Global Order*, New York: Seven Stories Press, 1999.

Cobden, R. *Speeches on Questions of Public Policy*, London: T. F. Unwin, 1908, third edition. Originally published 1870.

Comte, A. *The Positive Philosophy*, New York: AMS Press, 1974.
Condorcet, Marie-Jean. *Sketch for a Historical Picture of the Progress of the Human Mind*, 1794, New York: Noonday Press, 1955.
Darwin, C. *The Origin of the Species*, London: J. Murray, 1859.
Descartes, René. *The Meditations, and Selections from the Principles, of René Descartes (1596–1650)* Tr. From the original texts by John Veitch. With a preface, copies of original title pages, a bibliography, and an essay on Descartes' philosophy, by L. Levy-Bruhl. Chicago, Open court, 1901.
Dew, T. R. *Digest of the Laws, Customs, Manners and Institutions of the Ancient and Modern Nations*, 1853, New York: D. Appleton, 1884.
Dobb, Maurice. *Studies in the Development of Capitalism*, London: G. Routledge & Sons Ltd., 1946.
Durkheim, Emile. *The Division of Labor in Society*, 1893, New York: The Macmillan Company, 1933.
Durkheim, Emile and Mauss, Marcel. *Primitive Classification*, Chicago: University of Chicago Press, 1963.
Einstein, Albert. *Collected Writings (1901–1956)*, New York: Readex Microprint Corp., 1960. Microprint copy.
Feyerabend, P. *Science in a Free Society*, London: Verso, 1982.
Frazer, J. *The Golden Bough*, Garden City, N.Y.: Doubleday, 1978.
Freud, S. *Civilisation and Its Discontents*, New York: W. W. Norton, 1961.
Galileo, G. *Dialogue Concerning the Two Chief Systems of the World—Ptolemaic and Copernican*, 1632, New York: Modern Library, 2001.
Gibbon, E. *The Decline and Fall of the Roman Empire*, 1776–88, London: A. Strahan, T. Cadell, in the Strand, 1790.
Goswami, Amit. *The Self-Aware Universe*, New York: Putnam, 1993.
Greenberg, J. H. *Languages of Africa*, Bloomington: Indiana University Press, 1963.
Hall, J. A. and Mann, M. (eds). *Europe and the Rise of Capitalism*, Oxford; Basil Blackwell, 1988.
Hall, John A. *Powers and Liberties*, Oxford: Basil Blackwell, 1985.
Harding, Sandra. *The Racial Economy of Science*, Bloomington: Indiana University Press, 1993.
Hawking, Stephen. *A Brief History of Time*, Toronto, New York: Bantam Books, 1988.
Hegel, Georg Wilhelm Friedrich. *The Philosophy of History* by Georg Wilhelm Friedrich Hegel; with prefaces by Charles Hegel and the translator, J. Sibree. Rev. ed. New York: Colonial Press, c1900.xvi.
Heisenberg, W. *Physics and Beyond*, New York: Harper & Row, 1971, first edition. Translated from the German by Arnold J. Pomerans.
Herodotus. *Histories*, London: Penguin, 1996.
Hobbes. *Leviathan, 1651*, Oxford: Clarendon Press, 1909. Reprinted from the 1651 edition.
Hume, D. *A Treatise of Human Nature*, 1739, Edinburgh, New York: Nelson, 1951.

Johnson, Samuel. *Samuel Johnson, President of King's College; His Career and Writings,* New York: Columbia University Press, 1929.

Jones, E. L. *The European Miracle,* Cambridge: Cambridge University Press, 1981.

Joseph, G. G. *The Crest of the Peacock,* Harmondsworth: Penguin Books, 1991.

Kanigel, Robert. *The Man who Knew Infinity,* New York: Maxwell Macmillan International, 1991.

Kanth, R. *Breaking with the Enlightenment,* London: Ashgate, 1997.

Kant, Immanuel. [Grundlegung zur Metaphysik der Sitten. English] *Foundations of the Metaphysics of Morals and, What is Enlightment,* translated, with an introduction by Lewis White Beck. 2nd ed., rev. New York: Macmillan; London: Collier Macmillan, c1990.

Kautilya. *Arthashastra,* Mysore: Sri Raghuveer Print Press, 1956.

Kierkegaarde, S. *The Sickness Unto Death,* Princeton: Princeton University Press, 1941.

Kipling, Rudyard. "*The White Man's Burden,*" *McClure's Magazine* February, 12 1899.

Landes, D. *The Rise of Capitalism,* Collier-Macmillan, 1966.

Landry, D. and Maclean, G. (eds). *The Spivak Reader,* New York: Routledge, 1996.

Levi-Strauss, C. *Totemism,* Boston: Beacon Press, 1963.

Levi-Strauss, Claude. *The Savage Mind,* London: Weidenfeld & Nicolson, 1966.

Locke, J. *Concerning Civil Government, Second Essay, 1690,* Chicago: Encyclopædia Britannica, 1955.

Lubbock, J. *The Origin of Civilisation and the Primitive Condition of Man,* Chicago: University of Chicago Press, 1978.

Luther, Martin. *Christian Liberty,* Philadelphia: Muhlenberg Press, 1943.

Machiavelli, N. *The Prince,* London: Printed for R. Clavel, Cha. Harper, Jonathan Robinson, Job. Amery, A. and J. Churchil, MDCXCIV, 1694.

Maine, H. *Ancient Law,* London: Dent, New York: Dutton, 1972.

Malthus, T. R. *First Essay on Population,* London: Macmillan & Co. Ltd., 1926.

Mandeville, *The Fable of the Bees,* London: J. Tonson, 1729.

Mann, M. *The Sources of Social Power,* New York: Cambridge University Press, 1986.

Marsilius of Padua. *Defenser Pacis,* New York: Columbia University Press, 2001.

Marx, K. *On Colonialism,* New York: International Publishers, 1972.

Marx, K. *Pre-Capitalist Economic Formations,* New York: International Publishers, 1964.

Marx, K. "*The British Rule in India,*" *New-York Daily Tribune,* June 25, 1853.

McCrade, A. S. *The Political Thought of William of Ockham,* London, New York: Cambridge University Press, 1974.

Mead, Margaret. *Coming of Age in Samoa,* New York: Morrow, 1961.

Merchant, Carolyn. *The Death of Nature,* Harper: San Francisco, 1990.

Michels, R. *Political Parties,* Glencoe, Ill.: Free Press, 1949.

Mill, J. S. *On Liberty,* London: Longman, Roberts & Green, 1869. Originally published 1859.

More, Thomas, Sir. *Utopia* originally printed in Latin, 1516. Tr. into English by Ralph Robinson. His 2d and rev. ed., 1556; preceded by the title and epistle of his 1st Edition. Edited by Edward Arber, London: A. Constable, 1906.
Morgan, Lewis. *Ancient Society*, Chicago: Charles H. Kerr & Company, 1877.
Mosca, G. *The Ruling Class*, New York and London: McGraw-Hill, 1939.
Namier, L. *1848: The Revolution of the Intellectuals*, London: G. Cumberlege , 1944.
Newton, I. *Philosophiae Naturalis Principia Mathematica* , London: Jussu Societatis Regiœ ac Typis Josephi Streater; prostat apud plures Bibliopolas, 1687.
Nietzsche, F. *Thus Spake Zarathsutra*, New York: Penguin, 1978.
Paracelsus. *Medicina diastatica, or, Sympatheticall mumie [microform]: containing many mysterious and hidden secrets in philosophy and physick, by the [brace] construction, extraction, transplantation and application [brace] of microcosmical & spiritual mumie: teaching the magneticall cure of diseases at distance, &c./abstracted from the works of Dr. Theophr. Paracelsus by the labour and industry of Andrea Tentzelius ...; translated out of the Latine by Ferdinando Parkhurst* ... London: Printed by T. Newcomb for T. Heath, and are to be sold at his shop ... .
Pascal, Blaise. *The Pensées*, translated with an introd. by J. M. Cohen, Baltimore: Penguin Books [1961].
Plath, Sylvia. *The Bell Jar*, New York: Harper & Row, 1971.
Pope, A. *Essay on Man*, 1732–34. New York: Dover Publications, 1994.
Prigogene, I. *Order Out of Chaos*, Toronto, New York: Bantam Books, 1984.
Ramanujan Aiyangar, Srinivasa. Collected Papers. Edited by G. H. Hardy, P. V. Seshu Aiyar and B. M. Wilson, New York: Chelsea Pub. Co. [c1962].
Rawls, J. *A Theory of Justice*, Cambridge, Mass.: Belknap Press of Harvard University Press, 1971.
Ricardo, D. *Principles of Political Economy and Taxation*, Georgetown, D.C.: Joseph Milligan, 1819.
Rousseau, J. J. *The Social Contract*, New York: Hafner Pub. Co., 1947.
Roy, R. M. *Vedic Physics: Scientific Origin of Hinduism*, Toronto: Golden Egg Publishing, 1999.
Ruskin, J. *Unto This Last*, London: Smith, Elder, 1862. (Essays from the *Cornhill Magazine* 1860.)
Sahlins, Marshall. *Stone Age Economics*, Chicago: Aldine-Atherton, 1972.
Said, Edward. *Orientalism*, New York: Random House, 1979.
Salomon, A. *The Tyranny of Progress*, New York: Noonday Press, 1955.
Saraswati, P. *The Metaphysics of Physics; The Background of Modern Cosmological Conception in Vedic and Tantric Symbolism*, Madras: Ganesh, 1964.
Sarma, K. V. *A History of the Kerala School of Hindu Astronomy*, Hoshiarpur, 1972 [note, this is for the MADHAVA reference in the work].
Schlegel, F. *Philosophy of History*, New York: D. Appleton & co., 1841.
Schopenhauer, A. *The World as Will and Representation*, Indian Hills, Col: Falcon's Wing Press, 1958. Translated from the German by E. F. J. Payne.
Schrodinger, E. *My View of the World*, Cambridge: Cambridge, University Press, 1964. Translated from the German by Cecily Hastings.

Schumpeter, J. *Capitalism, Socialism and Democracy*, New York: Harper, 1942.
Shakespeare, W, *Othello*, 1622, Oxford: Clarendon Press, 1975.
Shakespeare, W. *The Taming of the Shrew*, Cambridge, U.K.: The University Press, 1928.
Shiva, Vandana, *Staying Alive*, New Delhi: Kali for Women, 1986.
Sidharth, B. G. *The Celestial Key to the Vedas*, Rochester, Vermont: Inner Traditions, 1999.
Smith, A. *The Theory of Moral Sentiments*, Boston: Wells and Lilly, 1817.
Smith, Grafton Elliot. *The Diffusion of Culture*, 1933, Port Washington, N.Y.: Kennikat Press, 1971.
Sombart, W. *The Jews and Modern Capitalism*, London: T. F. Unwin, 1913.
Southey, R. *Sir Thomas More; or, Colloquies on the Progress and Prospects of Society*. 2 vols. 8vo. London: 1829.
Spencer, H. *Essays, Scientific, Political and Speculative*, London: Williams & Norgate, 1868.
Turgot, Anne Robert Jacques. *Reflections on the Formation and Distribution of Wealth*, London: Printed by E. Spragg, For J. Good, Bookseller, No. 159, New Bond Street; John Anderson, No. 62, Holborn Hill; and W. Richardson, Royal Exchange. 1793. Translated from the French. First published 1774.
Tylor, E. B. *Primitive Culture*, 1871, New York: Harper, 1958.
Voltaire, F. M. A. *The Philosophical Dictionary*, New York: Knopf, 1924.
Wallerstein, I. *The Modern World System*, 3 vols. New York: Academic Press (1974–78).
Weber, M. *The Religion of India*, New York: Free Press, 1967.
Weber, Max. *The Protestant Ethic and the Spirit of Capitalism*, New York: Scribner's, 1958.
Wilde, Oscar. *The Writings of Oscar Wilde*. Uniform edition. London: A. R. Keller & co., inc., 1907.
Williams, Eric. *Capitalism and Slavery*, Chapel Hill: University of North Carolina Press, 1944.
Wittfogel, K. *Oriental Despotism*, New Haven: Yale University Press, 1957.
Wittgenstein, L. *Philosophical Investigations*, Oxford: Blackwell, 1953.
Wolf, E. *Europe and the Peoples Without History*, Berkeley and Los Angeles: University of California Press, 1982.
Young, R. *White Mythologies: Writing History and the West*, London, New York: Routledge, 1990.

Index

This work renders an uncompromising verdict on the scourge of our millennium: i.e. modernism, itself the artifact of certain Late Eurocentric propensities. It argues that, whilst modernism is possessed of some virtues and benignities, they are purchased at far too high a cost—indeed, a cost that neither the species nor the planet can, on any scale, find affordable. More urgently, the author holds that modernism imperils the existence of all species and the mother of all hospitalities, viz., the planet itself. Given the imminence and the gravity of this threat, as portrayed in the work, he further suggests that no other posture is at all, in the highest sense, ecologically responsible. We must, stated simply, he claims, break with the manifold paradigms of the European Enlightenment or find ourselves, soon enough, as mutant beings occupying an alien habitat.

This book goes far beyond the usual genre of critique by actually offering salves and antidotes to the enduring malaise of our times. It also offers a new paradigm for the human sciences locating it firmly in the species being of our hominid natures thereby annulling the spurious distinctions between "nature-culture," et al. drawn by the European Enlightenment. In particular, the book points to the "paradigm of femininity" as the potential agent of a very real, and realizable (and realized) emancipation from the delusive "utopias" of European, masculinist paternity. Finally, the book entreats us to re-evaluate our real placement in an evolving, self-fulfilling universe.

RAJANI KANNEPALLI KANTH was trained originally in Social Anthropology at the Delhi School of Economics in New Delhi. He subsequently taught Political Sociology, as Associate Fellow, at the Jawaharlal Nehru University in New Delhi, before moving to New York to attend Columbia University and the New School for Social Research, taking up the formal study of Political Economy. After a stint as Economic Advisor to the United Nations, in New York, and Consultancy with the U.N. Centre for Transnational Corporations, he returned to the Academy, holding affiliations, in various capacities, with Columbia University, the State University of New York, the University of Utah, University of Aarhus (Denmark), University of Texas, Austin, the University of New South Wales (Australia), the University of Technology, Sydney, the University of Bielefeld, Germany, the National University of Singapore, Tufts University, Oxford University, Harvard University, and Duke University.

His various published works include *Political Economy and Laissez-Faire* (1986), *Explorations in Political Economy* (1991), *Capitalism and Social Theory* (1992), *Paradigms in Economic Development* (1994), *Breaking with the Enlightenment* (1997), and *Against Economics* (1997).

www.ingramcontent.com/pod-product-compliance
Lightning Source LLC
LaVergne TN
LVHW010319220926
848484LV00004BB/803
9781403967374